D0282914

	DATE DUE		

Modern Critical Interpretations

Jonathan Swift's
Gulliver's Travels

Bloom's Modern Critical Interpretations

Modern Critical Interpretations

Jonathan Swift's
Gulliver's Travels

Edited and with an introduction by

Harold Bloom
Sterling Professor of the Humanities
Yale University

Chelsea House Publishers
PHILADELPHIA

Copyright © 1986 by Chelsea House Publishers, a subsidiary of
Haight Cross Communications

Introduction © 1986 by Harold Bloom

The Chelsea House World Wide Web address is
http://www.chelseahouse.com

Printed and bound in the United States of America

10   9   8   7

∞ The paper used in this publication meets the minimum
requirements of the American National Standard for
Permanence of Paper for Printed Library Materials,
Z39.48–1984.

Library of Congress Cataloging-in-Publication Data
Jonathan Swift: Gulliver's travels.
   (Modern critical interpretations)
   Bibliography: p.
   Includes index.
   1. Swift, Jonathan, 1667–1745.   Gulliver's
travels.   I. Bloom, Harold.   II. Series.
PR3724.G8J56   1986   823'.5   86-4222
ISBN 0-87754-424-7

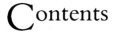ontents

Editor's Note

This book gathers together a representative selection of the best modern criticism of *Gulliver's Travels,* arranged in the chronological order of its original publication. I am grateful to Christina Büchmann for her assistance in researching and preparing this volume.

The editor's introduction provides a critical overview of all four voyages, with particular emphasis on Swift's relation to Gulliver's account of the fourth voyage.

T. O. Wedel begins the chronological sequence with his investigation of the book's philosophical background, usefully reminding us that Swift was no Pascalian, and also that, while a rationalist, he had no faith in reason. Considering the relation of Swift to Gulliver, Phyllis Greenacre shows how outwardly close the fictional life of Gulliver was to Swift's actual biography. Kathleen Williams, in a full-scale reading of the book, argues that it is essentially an argument for the Anglican "middle way." In contrast, Martin Price analyzes the book as a comedy of incomprehension, reminding us that Swift's view of order is as secular and classical as it is Christian.

Paul Fussell sets *Gulliver's Travels* in its literary context of Augustan moral satire, comparing it to aspects of the work of Dr. Samuel Johnson and of Alexander Pope. In a reading of the fourth voyage, Conrad Suits meditates upon the role of those rational horses, the Houyhnhnms, and concludes that Swift has delivered an effective double insult to us. We differ from the Yahoos only in being worse even than they are, since we have reason but pervert it, and from the Houyhnhnms in that they have more reason than we possess, in any case.

Ronald Paulson analyzes Gulliver as pliable picaro, always adjusting to the shape of his superiors. In a deconstructionist account of *Gulliver's Travels,* Grant Holly follows Lacan and other French theorists in relating the book's textuality to the psychic defense that Freud called "repression." This volume concludes with Patrick Reilly's strenuous attack upon the

Houyhnhnms as a Master Race plotting genocide upon the poor Yahoos, insisting that the Yahoos "are our kinsmen, however unwelcome." We are thus returned to the debate summarized in this book's introduction, which ultimately may be a dispute about the limits of irony.

Introduction

The terrible greatness of Jonathan Swift's *A Tale of a Tub* has much to do with our sense of its excess, with its force being so exuberantly beyond its form (or its calculated formlessness). *Gulliver's Travels,* the later and lesser work, has survived for the common reader, whereas Swift's early master-piece has not. Like its descendant, Carlyle's *Sartor Resartus, A Tale of a Tub* demands too much of the reader, but it more than rewards those demands, and it now seems unclear whether *Sartor Resartus* does or not. Gulliver's first two voyages are loved by children (of all ages), while the third and fourth voyages, being more clearly by the Swift who wrote *A Tale of a Tub,* now make their appeal only to those who would benefit most from an immersion in the *Tub.*

Gulliver himself is both the strength and the weakness of the book, and his character is particularly ambiguous in the great fourth voyage, to the country of the rational Houyhnhnms and the bestial Yahoos, who are and are not, respectively, horses and humans. The inability to resist a societal perspectivism is at once Gulliver's true weakness, and his curious strength as an observer. Swift's barely concealed apprehension that the self is an abyss, that the ego is a fiction masking our fundamental nothingness, is exemplified by Gulliver but on a level of commonplaceness far more bathetic than anything reductive in the Tale-teller. Poor Gulliver is a good enough man but almost devoid of imagination. One way of describing him might be to name him the least Nietzschean character ever to appear in any nar-rative. Though a ceaseless traveller, Gulliver lacks any desire to be else-where, or to be different. His pride is blind, and all too easily magnifies to pomposity, or declines to a self-contempt that is more truly a contempt for all other humans. If the Tale-teller is a Swiftian parody of one side of Swift, the anti-Cartesian, anti-Hobbesian, then Gulliver is a Swiftian parody of the great ironist's own misanthropy.

1

The reader of "A Voyage to Lilliput" is unlikely to forget the fatuity of Gulliver at the close of Chapter VI:

> I am here obliged to vindicate the Reputation of an excellent Lady, who was an innocent Sufferer upon my Account. The Treasurer took a Fancy to be jealous of his Wife, from the Malice of some evil Tongues, who informed him that her Grace had taken a violent Affection for my Person; and the Court-Scandal ran for some Time that she once came privately to my Lodging. This I solemnly declare to be a most infamous Falshood, without any Grounds, farther than that her Grace was pleased to treat me with all innocent Marks of Freedom and Friendship. I own she came often to my House, but always publickly. . . . I should not have dwelt so long upon this Particular, if it had not been a Point wherein the Reputation of a great Lady is so nearly concerned, to say nothing of my own; although I had the Honour to be a *Nardac,* which the Treasurer himself is not; for all the World knows he is only a *Clumglum,* a Title inferior by one Degree, as that of a Marquess is to a Duke in *England;* yet I allow he preceded me in right of his Post.

The great Nardac has so fallen into the societal perspective of Lilliput, that he sublimely forgets he is twelve times the size of the Clumglum's virtuous wife, who therefore would have been quite safe with him were they naked and alone. Escaping back to England, Gulliver has learned nothing and sets forth on "A Voyage to Brobdingnag," land of the giants, where he learns less than nothing:

> The Learning of this People is very defective; consisting only in Morality, History, Poetry and Mathematicks; wherein they must be allowed to excel. But, the last of these is wholly applied to what may be useful in Life; to the Improvement of Agriculture and all mechanical Arts; so that among us it would be little esteemed. And as to Ideas, Entities, Abstractions and Transcendentals, I could never drive the least Conception into their Heads.
>
> No Law of that Country must exceed in Words the Number of Letters in their Alphabet; which consists only of two and twenty. But indeed, few of them extend even to that Length. They are expressed in the most plain and simple Terms, wherein those People are not Mercurial enough to discover above one Interpretation. And, to write a Comment upon any Law, is a

capital Crime. As to the Decision of civil Causes, or Proceedings against Criminals, their Precedents are so few, that they have little Reason to boast of any extraordinary Skill in either.

Effective as this is, it seems too weak an irony for Swift, and we are pleased when the dull Gulliver abandons Brobdingnag behind him. The Third Voyage, more properly Swiftian, takes us first to Laputa, the floating island, at once a parody of a Platonic academy yet also a kind of science fiction punishment machine, always ready to crush earthlings who might assert liberty:

If any Town should engage in Rebellion or Mutiny, fall into violent Factions, or refuse to pay the usual Tribute; the King hath two Methods of reducing them to Obedience. The first and the mildest Course is by keeping the Island hovering over such a Town, and the Lands about it; whereby he can deprive them of the Benefit of the Sun and the Rain, and consequently afflict the Inhabitants with Dearth and Diseases. And if the Crime deserve it, they are at the same time pelted from above with great Stones, against which they have no Defence, but by creeping into Cellars or Caves, while the Roofs of their Houses are beaten to Pieces. But if they still continue obstinate, or offer to raise Insurrections; he proceeds to the last Remedy, by letting the Island drop directly upon their Heads, which makes a universal Destruction both of Houses and Men. However, this is an Extremity to which the Prince is seldom driven, neither indeed is he willing to put it in Execution; nor dare his Ministers advise him to an Action, which as it would render them odious to the People, so it would be a great Damage to their own Estates that lie all below; for the Island is the King's Demesn.

The maddening lack of affect on Gulliver's part begins to tell upon us here; the stolid narrator is absurdly inadequate to the grim force of his own recital, grimmer for us now even than it could have been for the prophetic Swift. Gulliver inexorably and blandly goes on to Lagado, where he observes the grand Academy of Projectors, Swift's famous spoof of the British Royal Society, but here the ironies go curiously flat, and I suspect we are left with the irony of irony, which wearies because by repetition it seems to become compulsive. Yet it may be that here, as subsequently with the immortal but senile and noxious Struldbruggs, the irony of irony is highly deliberate, in order to prepare Gulliver, and the battered reader, for the great shock of reversal that lies just ahead in the Country of the Houyhnhnms, which is also the land of the Yahoos, "a strange Sort of Animal."

Critical reactions to Gulliver's fourth voyage have an astonishing range, from Thackeray calling its moral "horrible, shameful, unmanly, blasphemous" to T. S. Eliot regarding it as a grand triumph for the human spirit. Eliot's judgment seems to me as odd as Thackeray's, and presumably both writers believed that the Yahoos were intended as a just representation of the natural man, with Thackeray humanistically disagreeing, and the neo-Christian Eliot all too happy to concur. If that were the proper reading of Swift, we would have to conclude that the great satirist had drowned in his own misanthropy, and had suffered the terrible irony, after just evading the becoming one with his Tale-teller, of joining himself to the uneducable Gulliver. Fit retribution perhaps, but it is unwise to underestimate the deep cunning of Swift.

Martin Price accurately reminds us that Swift's attitudes do not depend solely upon Christian morals but stem also from a traditional secular wisdom. Peace and decency are wholly compatible with Christian teaching but are secular virtues as well. Whatever the Yahoos represent, they are *not* a vision of secular humanity devoid of divine grace, since they offend the classical view of man quite as profoundly as they seem to suit an ascetic horror of our supposedly natural condition.

Clearly, it is the virtues of the Houyhnhnms, and not the squalors of the Yahoos, that constitute a burden for critics and for common readers. I myself agree with Price, when he remarks of the Houyhnhnms: "They are rational horses, neither ideal men nor a satire upon others' ideals for man." Certainly they cannot represent a human rational ideal, since none of us would wish to lack all impulse, or any imagination whatsoever. Nor do they seem a plausible satire upon the Deistic vision, a satire worthier of Blake than of Swift, and in any case contradicted by everything that truly is admirable about these cognitively advanced horses. A rational horse is a kind of oxymoron, and Swift's irony is therefore more difficult than ever to interpret:

> My Master heard me with great Appearances of Uneasiness in his Countenance; because *Doubting* or *not believing,* are so little known in this Country, that the Inhabitants cannot tell how to behave themselves under such Circumstances. And I remember in frequent Discourses with my Master concerning the Nature of Manhood, in other Parts of the World; having Occasion to

talk of *Lying,* and *false Representation,* it was with much Difficulty that he comprehended what I meant; although he had otherwise a most acute Judgment. For he argued thus; That the Use of Speech was to make us understand one another, and to receive Information of Facts; now if any one *said the Thing which was not,* these Ends were defeated; because I cannot properly be said to understand him; and I am so far from receiving Information, that he leaves me worse than in Ignorance; for I am led to believe a Thing *Black* when it is *White,* and *Short* when it is *Long.* And these were all the Notions he had concerning the Faculty of *Lying,* so perfectly well understood, and so universally practised among human Creatures.

Are we altogether to admire Gulliver's Master here, when that noble Houyhnhnm not only does not know how to react to the human propensity to say *the thing which was not* but lacks even the minimal imagination that might allow him to apprehend the human need for fictions, a "sickness not ignoble," as Keats observed in *The Fall of Hyperion?* Since the noble Houyhnhnm finds the notion "that the *Yahoos* were the only governing Animals" in Gulliver's country "altogether past his Conception," are we again to admire him for an inability that would make it impossible for us to read *Gulliver's Travels* (or *King Lear,* for that matter)? The virtues of Swift's rational horses would not take us very far, if we imported them into our condition, but can that really be one of Swift's meanings? And what are we to do with Swiftian ironies that are too overt already, and become aesthetically intolerable if we take up the stance of the sublimely rational Houyhnhnm?

My Master likewise mentioned another Quality, which his Servants had discovered in several *Yahoos,* and to him was wholly unaccountable. He said, a Fancy would sometimes take a *Yahoo,* to retire into a Corner, to lie down and howl, and groan, and spurn away all that came near him, although he were young and fat, and wanted neither Food nor Water; nor did the Servants imagine what could possibly ail him. And the only Remedy they found was to set him to hard Work, after which he would infallibly come to himself. To this I was silent out of Partiality to my own Kind; yet here I could plainly discover the true Seeds of *Spleen,* which only seizeth on the *Lazy,* the *Luxurious,* and the *Rich;* who, if they were forced to undergo the *same Regimen,* I would undertake for the Cure.

His Honour had farther observed, that a Female-*Yahoo* would often stand behind a Bank or a Bush, to gaze on the young Males passing by, and then appear, and hide, using many antick Gestures and Grimaces; at which time it was observed, that she had a most *offensive Smell;* and when any of the Males advanced, would slowly retire, looking often back, and with a counterfeit Shew of Fear, run off into some convenient Place where she knew the Male would follow her.

Swift rather dubiously seems to want it every which way at once, so that the Yahoos both are and are not representations of ourselves, and the Houyhnhnms are and are not wholly admirable or ideal. Or is it the nature of irony itself, which must weary us, or finally make us long for a true sublime, even if it should turn out to be grotesque? Fearfully strong writer that he was, Swift as ironist resembles Kafka far more than say Orwell, among modern authors. We do not know precisely how to read "In the Penal Colony" or *The Trial,* and we certainly do not know exactly how to interpret Gulliver's fourth voyage. What most merits interpretation in Kafka is the extraordinary perversity of imagination with which he so deliberately makes himself uninterpretable. Is Swift a similar problem for the reader? What is the proper response to the dismaying conclusion of *Gulliver's Travels?*

Having thus answered the *only* Objection that can be raised against me as a Traveller; I here take a final Leave of my Courteous Readers, and return to enjoy my own Speculations in my little Garden at *Redriff;* to apply those excellent Lessons of Virtue which I learned among the *Houyhnhnms;* to instruct the *Yahoos* of my own Family as far as I shall find them docible Animals; to behold my Figure often in a Glass, and thus if possible habituate my self by Time to tolerate the Sight of a human Creature: To lament the Brutality of *Houyhnhnms* in my own Country, but always treat their Persons with Respect, for the Sake of my noble Master, his Family, his Friends, and the whole *Houyhnhnm* Race, whom these of ours have the Honour to resemble in all their Lineaments, however their Intellectuals came to degenerate.

I began last Week to permit my Wife to sit at Dinner with me, at the Farthest End of a long Table; and to answer (but with the utmost Brevity) the few Questions I ask her. Yet the Smell of a *Yahoo* continuing very offensive, I always keep my Nose well stopt with Rue, Lavender, or Tobacco-Leaves. And although it be hard for a Man late in Life to remove old Habits; I am not altogether out of Hopes in some Time to suffer a Neighbour *Yahoo* in my Company, without the Apprehensions I am yet under of his Teeth or his Claws.

Who are those "Courteous Readers" of whom Gulliver takes his final leave here? We pity the poor fellow, but we do not so much pity Mrs. Gulliver as wonder how she can tolerate the insufferable wretch. Yet the final paragraphs have a continued power that justifies their fame, even as we continue to see Gulliver as deranged:

> My Reconcilement to the *Yahoo*-kind in general might not be so difficult, if they would be content with those Vices and Follies only which Nature hath entitled them to. I am not in the least provoked at the Sight of a Lawyer, a Pickpocket, a Colonel, a Fool, a Lord, a Gamster, a Politician, a Whoremunger, a Physician, an Evidence, a Suborner, an Attorney, a Traytor, or the like: This is all according to the due Course of Things: But, when I behold a Lump of Deformity, and Diseases both in Body and Mind, smitten with *Pride,* it immediately breaks all the Measures of my Patience; neither shall I be ever able to comprehend how such an Animal and such a Vice could tally together. The wise and virtuous *Houyhnhnms,* who abound in all Excellencies that can adorn a rational Creature, have no Name for this Vice in their Language, whereby they describe the detestable Qualities of their *Yahoos;* among which they were not able to distinguish this of Pride, for want of thoroughly understanding Human Nature, as it sheweth it self in other Countries, where that Animal presides. But I, who had more Experience, could plainly observe some Rudiments of it among the wild *Yahoos.*
>
> But the *Houyhnhnms,* who live under the Government of Reason, are no more proud of the good Qualities they possess, than I should be for not wanting a Leg or an Arm, which no Man in his Wits would boast of, although he must be miserable without them. I dwell the longer upon this Subject from the Desire I have to make the Society of an *English Yahoo* by any Means not insupportable; and therefore I here intreat those who have any Tincture of this absurd Vice, that they will not presume to appear in my Sight.

What takes precedence here, the palpable hit at the obscenity of false human pride, or the madness of Gulliver, who thinks he is a Yahoo, longs to be a Houyhnhnm, and could not bear to be convinced that he is neither? As in *A Tale of a Tub,* Swift audaciously plays at the farthest limits of irony, limits that make satire impossible, because no norm exists to which we might hope to return.

On the Philosophical Background of *Gulliver's Travels*

T. O. Wedel

Swift, the master of irony among the moderns, has achieved no greater ironic masterpiece than the posthumous reputation of *Gulliver's Travels*. Written to vex the world, not to divert it, hiding within its cloak of wit and romantic invention the savage indignation of a lifetime, the fiercest indictment of the pride of man yet penned in our language, it has become, forsooth, a children's book—an example, so Goethe thought, of the failure of allegory to make an idea prevail.

> Types and Fables, [so runs a passage in *A Tale of a Tub* which could be applied prophetically to *Gulliver's Travels*,] the writer having been perhaps more careful and curious in adorning, than was altogether necessary, it has fared with these Vehicles after the usual Fate of Coaches, over-finely painted and gilt; that the transitory Gazers have so dazzled their Eyes, and fill'd their Imaginations with the outward lustre, as neither to regard or consider the Person or the Parts of the Owner within.

The failure of posterity to appreciate the philosophical thesis of Gulliver's travels, is not, however, due solely to the triumph of Swift's art. The year of our Lord 1726, when Gulliver appeared, was in no mood to put a proper value upon a work which spoke of *homo sapiens* as "the most pernicious race of little odious vermin that nature ever suffered to crawl upon the surface of the earth." We need only remind ourselves that the

From *Swift: Gulliver's Travels: A Casebook.* © 1974 by Richard Gravil. Macmillan, 1974.

very year previous there had appeared, in Swift's own Dublin, Hutcheson's first panegyric essay on the soundness of man's benevolent instincts, a classic expression for the century of the new optimistic creed, and itself the resultant of a respectable tradition. No, neither the eighteenth century nor the nineteenth has expressed anything but scorn for the view of man to be found in *Gulliver's Travels.* Eighteenth-century criticism, in fact, is remarkably silent about Swift. Yet when *Gulliver's Travels* is discussed by Orrery, Warton, Young, Jeffrey, or Scott, its philosophy is referred to as the result of a diseased mind, blaspheming as it does a nature little lower than that of the angels. "In what ordure," exclaims Young in his *Conjectures,* "hast thou dipped thy pencil! What a monster hast thou made of the 'Human face divine!' " The German Herder, to be sure, attempts to appreciate Swift's misanthropy, at the same time preserving his constant enthusiasm for Shaftesbury. But it is John Wesley who, alone among eighteenth-century readers, can cite "The Voyage to the Houyhnhnms" with real enthusiasm. In his longest written work, *The Doctrine of Original Sin,* it is Swift rather than St. Augustine upon whom he leans for quotations.

Yet if Swift had written *Gulliver's Travels* a few generations earlier, he would have given little cause for complaint. Pascal would have understood him, as would La Rochefoucauld and Boileau; so would Montaigne; so would Bayle. For the transition from the seventeenth century to the eighteenth was experiencing a revolution in ethical thought. "Rarely, if ever," says Brunetière, with perhaps too dogmatic assurance, "has so profound a transformation occurred more swiftly. Everything has changed." The pessimism of Pascal has given way to the optimism of Leibnitz; the theory of self-love of La Rochefoucauld to the theory of benevolence of Hutcheson and Hume; the scepticism of Montaigne to the rationalism of Locke, Toland, and Clarke; the dualism of Nature and Grace to a monistic inclusion of Nature under the rule of a beneficent God; the bold warfare between atheism and faith to a mere gentlemen's quarrel between revealed and natural religion. In fact, it is this revolutionary background which alone can explain Swift's purpose in writing *Gulliver's Travels.*

Swift's darker meaning, to be sure, does not lie on the surface, for, as Johnson noted in his biographical sketch, he was the most reticent of men. Rarely does he reveal his opinions or his feelings without a cloak of irony; rarely does he quote an author. Indeed an article of his artistic creed discouraged quotation. Pedantry is absent from his writings to a fault. While Bolingbroke, in the famous correspondence, overloads his page with learning, Swift turns out epigrams on Ireland or the weather. *Vive la bagatelle* was his motto. He might illustrate the saying of Joubert: "The wise man is serious about few things." Or he might have applied to himself his own maxim: "Some people take more care to hide their wisdom than their folly."

Yet the student of Swift is not left entirely without guidance as to his philosophical opinions. The *Tale of a Tub*, for example, furnishes plentiful evidence of his distrust of metaphysics on the one hand, of his hatred of mystical enthusiasm on the other. A stray remark in his *Letter to a Young Clergyman* tells us that he did not approve of Locke's attack upon innate ideas. His *Sermon on the Trinity*, thought by Wesley to be one of the great sermons of the age, helps, when read in the light of contemporary thought, to define the same antirationalism which appears in *Gulliver's Travels* and which animated his attacks upon the Deists. The *Sermon on Conscience*, in turn, defending religion against the upholders of mere moral honesty and honor, reads like a rebuttal of both Shaftesbury and Mandeville. The *Correspondence* yields more than one hint that Swift felt himself to be on the side of the opposition with reference to the growing optimism of Pope and Bolingbroke. In two letters, in particular, Swift plays the truant to his creed of reticence, giving us in round terms his formula of misanthropy. I shall quote the respective passages in full. The first, indeed, constitutes the *locus classicus* for the critic of Gulliver.

> I have ever hated all nations, professions, and communities, and all my love is toward individuals: for instance, I hate the tribe of lawyers, but I love Counsellor Such-a-one, and Judge Such-a-one. . . . But principally I hate and detest that animal called man, although I heartily love John, Peter, Thomas, and so forth. This is the system upon which I have governed myself many years, but do not tell, and so I shall go on till I have done with them. I have got materials toward a treatise, proving the falsity of that definition *animal rationale*, and to show it should be only *rationis capax*. Upon this great foundation of misanthropy, though not in Timon's manner, the whole building of my Travels is erected; and I will never have peace of mind till all honest men are of my opinion.

In the second and later letter Swift is dissuading Pope from undertaking a refutation of La Rochefoucauld, who, Swift says, "is my favourite, because I found my whole character in him."

> I desire you and all my friends will take a special care that my disaffection to the world may not be imputed to my age, for I have credible witnesses ready to depose that it has never varied

from the twenty-first to the fifty-eighth year of my life. . . . I tell you after all, that I do not hate mankind: it is *vous autres* who hate them, because you would have them reasonable animals, and are angry for being disappointed.

Finally, besides all such incidental aids for the critic, we have *Gulliver's Travels* itself—its views on education and politics; its attack on science; its satire on luxury, war, and commerce, bordering on a kind of primitivism; its dualism of Yahoos and Houyhnhnms; above all, its savage indignation at the animalism and pettiness of man, culminating in its magnificent peroration on pride.

And in trying to interpret in the light of the ethical revolution of his day, at least some of this provocative satire, I may begin with his misanthropic view in general, his hatred of the animal called man, his love for individuals—"a sentiment," so Thomas Warton thought, voicing the general opinion of posterity, "that dishonors him as a man, a Christian, and a philosopher." A hard view of man it is, clearly, yet no more severe than that of the seventeenth century as a whole. Parallels to Swift's very words can be found several times over. Listen, for example, to Pascal: "The nature of man may be viewed in two ways: the one according to its end, and then he is great and incomparable; the other, according to the multitude, just as we judge of the nature of the horse and the dog, popularly, . . . and then man is abject and vile. . . . The nature of man is wholly natural, *omne animal*." Or to a similar judgment of La Bruyère: "A reasonable man may hate mankind in general; he discovers in it so little of virtue. But he is ready to excuse the individual . . . and strives to deserve as little as possible a similar indulgence." One is tempted to quote by way of contrast Hazlitt's confession, equally typical of more recent centuries: "I believe in the theoretical benevolence, but the practical malignity of man."

In more general form, Swift's hard view of man could be duplicated scores of times even without resorting to the Ancients, the Fathers, or the Calvinists. Although, as we shall see, a more flattering doctrine had already appeared early in the seventeenth century, his is after all the prevailing judgment on human nature from Montaigne to Locke, among men of the world as well as ascetic Christians. Even Bayle at the turn of the new century, arch sceptic that he was, still clings to it. His article on Ovid, for example, in the *Dictionnaire,* quoting voluminously from Cicero and St. Augustine to Esprit and the Moderns, reads like a pedantic prospectus of *Gulliver's Travels.* In Bayle's view, man is still an ungovernable animal, ruled by self-love, given over to evil incomparably more than to good, the slight glimmering of reason which has been left him usually worsted in the fight against the passions, his only hope, apart from utilitarian virtue, being divine grace. Vauvenargues, a moralist writing in the middle of the eighteenth century, may well exclaim: "Man is at present in disgrace among all those who think; they heap upon him all manner of vices." Only he adds: "Perhaps he is soon to awake and to demand the restitution of his virtues." By the year 1726, in England at least, the restitution of man's virtues was already well under way. The dignity of human nature is already on everyone's lips. Locke and the Deists had given man a new trust in Reason; the Cambridge Platonists and Shaftesbury were discovering in him a moral sense, even in the hitherto despised realm of the passions. Nothing seems more certain to the new age than the existence of a beneficent deity, and the consequent goodness of his creation. Optimistic theodicies are being written on all sides, explaining away the evil from this best of all possible worlds.

> Place the mind in its right posture, [declares a *Spectator* paper,] it will immediately discover its innate propension to beneficence. Persons conscious of their own integrity, satisfied with themselves and their condition, and full of confidence in a Supreme Being, and the hope of immortality, survey all about them with a flow of goodwill. As trees which like their soil, they shoot out in expressions of kindness and bend beneath their own precious load, to the hand of the gatherer.

A popular article in the *Gentleman's Magazine* (1732) sets out to prove "that men are as generally good, as they are represented bad." Any other conclusion is declared to be a blasphemy against God; "for neither God nor man can be good but by their works."

Definitions of vice and virtue are at sixes and sevens. Evil and good, once set over against each other as equivalent to Nature and Grace, now oppose each other within the natural realm alone. Pride has become a virtue. When Pope proposed to refute La Rochefoucauld by dissolving vices into virtues, as the cynic of the seventeenth century had dissolved virtues into vices, he set himself a supernumerary task. The thing was being done all around him. An unworldly definition of virtue had become almost unintelligible. Tindal, the Deist, asserts that the Sermon on the Mount is absurd for practical life. "Pascal and La Rochefoucauld," says Voltaire, "who were read by everyone, have accustomed the French public to interpret the word self-love always in a bad sense. Only in the eighteenth century did a change come about, so that the ideas of vice and pride were no longer necessarily attached to the word." Precisely so. Mandeville gained a stormy hearing for his paradox of "private vices, public benefits" simply because at least half of his terminology was being dropped from the new vocabulary.

In theological terms, what was happening of course was the avowed, or tacit denial of the doctrine of Original Sin. Human nature was being absolved of corruption. The ancient Christian faith, in the words of Pascal, had rested on but two things, "the corruption of nature and redemption by Jesus Christ." Half at least of Pascal's formula is seldom spoken of after 1700. Even before that date optimism and orthodoxy jostle each other in unexpected places. Jeremy Taylor is already suspected of unorthodoxy on the subject of Original Sin. Tillotson, though he bows to the traditional dogma, became for the Deists a favorite prop for their rationalistic doctrines. A popular version of both the old and the new in theological thought is Bishop Burnet's naïve account (1680) of the death of the Earl of Rochester. Though Rochester's views can lay no claim to consistency, he is at least an optimist. Man's instincts must be restrained here and there perhaps, but they are not evil. The story of Adam's fall is absurd—one man cheating the whole world. The honest Bishop offers no rational explanation; he merely asserts in the name of Platonism and Augustinian Christianity that "common experience tells us there is a great disorder in our Nature, which is not easily rectified: all philosophers were sensible of it, and every man that designs to govern himself by Reason, feels the struggle between it and Nature. So that it is plain there is a lapse of the high powers of the Soul."

With the turn of the century, however, words like these are rarely heard. If anyone doubts that by the year 1700 a new philosophy was in the air, he need merely read a designedly orthodox work such as Locke's *Reasonableness of Christianity*. Christianity is no longer for Locke what it was for Pascal, a healer of souls, but a supernatural blunderbuss enforcing the police regulations of natural morality. Adam's fall, so Locke argues, brought the punishment of death upon the world but implies no corruption of nature. "If by death, threatened to Adam, were meant the corruption of human nature in his posterity, 'tis strange that the New Testament should not anywhere take notice of it." Locke's literalism is indeed daring in view of centuries of Pauline theology. And while occasionally a writer on divinity saw that here lay the chief danger to the old orthodoxy in Locke's appealing philosophy, the prevailing thought of the century passed on to other issues, busying itself with asserting the necessity of revelation for natural law, or in Samuel Johnson's phrase, defending the apostles against the charge of forgery once a week. Wesley, harking back to pagan antiquity for parallels to his own unflattering view of man, and glancing at the new gospel, exclaims: "But how much more knowing than these old pagans are the present generation of Christians! How many laboured panegyrics do we now read and hear on the dignity of human nature!" . . . "I cannot see that we have much need of Christianity. Nay, not any at all; for 'they that are whole have no need of a physician!' . . . Nor can Christian philosophy, whatever be thought of the pagan, be more properly defined than in Plato's words: 'the only true method of healing a distempered soul.' But what need of this if we are in perfect health?" And in refutation of contemporary optimism Wesley proceeds to unload upon the reader page upon page of *Gulliver*.

In the world of political thought, the clash between old and new is perhaps nowhere so concretely exhibited as in the contrasting theories regarding the state of nature. For not in *Gulliver* only are Yahoos set over against Houyhnhnms. In fact it looks like too simple a discovery to point out that in the last voyage of the *Travels* we have, designedly or not, Hobbes contrasted with Locke. And yet the parallel holds good surprisingly well. Men in Hobbes's state of nature, like Swift's Yahoos, are "in that condition which is called war; and such a war, as is of every man against every man . . . with no arts, no letters, no society, and, which is worst of all, continual fear of violent danger; and the life of man, solitary, poor, nasty, brutish, and short." And while Hobbes's brevity of description with regard to his state of war prevents elaboration of the parallel, the corresponding similarity between Locke and Swift is certainly tempting. Men in Locke's state of nature, like the Houyhnhnms, are rational creatures, "living together according to reason, without a common superior,"—in a state of liberty without license, every one administering the laws of nature for himself, laws of temperance and mutual benevolence. The relation of Swift to Hobbes and to Locke is a subject for separate investigation. On the whole, I think (and Swift's political writings would furnish evidence in abundance), he stands nearer to Hobbes. In *Gulliver's Travels,* however, Swift is clearly neither Hobbes nor Locke. Gulliver is neither Yahoo nor Houyhnhnm. He cannot attain to the rational felicity of the Houyhnhnms. Neither has he sunk to the level of the Yahoos, though this is a doubtful advantage. He lacks the strength of a healthy animal, and his glimmering of reason has unhappily burdened him with responsibility of conscience.

Indeed, if Swift's own hints regarding the meaning of his book are heeded, it is in the contrast between Yahoo and Houyhnhnm that his main thesis lies hid. Gulliver, occupying a position between the two, part beast, part reason, is Swift's allegorical picture of the dual nature of man. He is not Houyhnhnm, *animal rationale,* nor is he Yahoo. He is *rationis capax.*

One could apply to *Gulliver's Travels* a passage of Cicero, quoted with approval by both St. Augustine and Bayle: "Nature has been to man not a mother, but a step-mother—sending him into the world naked, frail, and infirm, toiling under a burden of care, fearful, slothful, and given over to lust, but not without a spark of divine reason."

Animal rationale—animal rationis capax! Swift's somewhat scholastic distinction turns out, in the light of seventeenth-century thought, to be by no means scholastic. It symbolises, in fact, the chief intellectual battle of the age. Swift seems to have seen clearly enough that in assaulting man's pride in reason, he was attacking the new optimism at its very root. His enmity to rationalistic dogmatising was the one enduring intellectual passion of his life. It animates his orthodoxy in his sermon on the Trinity; it prompts the dangerous laughter of *A Tale of a Tub;* it explains his merciless satire of the Deists.

The phrase *animal rationale* can be traced at least as far back as Seneca and ancient Stoicism. This fact alone explains much. For it is precisely the circle of ideas represented by Stoicism, however changed in form through centuries of filtration, which the seventeenth century, like the fifth, was still finding it difficult to assimilate. Stoicism has ever been associated with optimism. It is the Stoic who worships pride. And despite the noble appeal of its ethical heroism—or perhaps one had better say because of it—Stoicism has constituted one of Christianity's gravest dangers. *Corruptio optimi pessima est.* No Christian in the Augustinian sense could have said with Epictetus: "I was never hindered in my will or compelled against my wish. . . . Who can hinder me against my own judgments, or put compulsion on me? I am as safe as Zeus." The Stoic faith in a beneficent deity and a rational world robbed the universe of evil. To follow nature was to obey God and reason. The wise man, to be sure, had to conquer his passions; but the passions themselves were merely wrong opinion. The Stoic was still master of his fate.

It was Stoicism in the form of the Pelagian heresy against which St. Augustine threw the whole weight of his eloquence in the last great doctrinal war of his career. Man for Pelagius, too, was not by nature evil. "For they think," so St. Augustine defines the belief of his enemies, "that, by the strength of their own will, they will fulfill the commands of the law; and wrapped up in their pride, they are not converted to assisting grace." Conceive of God as goodness and benevolence, of nature as His creation, include man in nature, let the myth of the Fall imply, as it did for Locke, merely a legal death penalty laid upon otherwise innocent descendants of Adam, who are rational beings, free to choose good and evil, and you have the Pelagian heresy.

Of the popularity of Stoicism in this period there can be no doubt. According to Strowski, the author oftenest reprinted in the first half of the seventeenth century was Du Vair, whose *Philosophie Morale des Stoïques* was one of the chief Stoic texts, together with a similar compendium of Justus Lipsius. Coming to the fore by way of translation and paraphrase, Stoicism, as I shall try to show a little later, soon suffered a sea-change, and was destined in its new form, to conquer the world. For the moment, however, its victory was delayed, though the warfare against it was confused, and though many a skirmish was fought on secondary issues. The passions, for one thing, found defenders against the Stoic attitude of disdain. Positivistic observers of man simply denied that man was ruled by reason. Balzac ridicules the Stoics as "that inhuman sect which, in cutting off from man his passions and his feelings, desires to rob him of half of himself. In place of having created a wise man, the Stoics have merely created a statue." Or as Swift himself puts it in one of his maxims: "The Stoical scheme of supplying our wants by lopping off our desires is like cutting off our feet, when we want shoes." La Rochefoucauld, man of the world, sees human nature as merely the dupe of the ruling passion of self-love. As the century advances, optimism itself takes to throwing stones at the Stoics, actually defending the passions as good in themselves. Sénault writes a treatise proving the Stoic wise man a fiction and the passions useful in the moral life. A similar defense is found in the *Enchiridion Ethicum* of the Cambridge Platonist, Henry More. The Augustinian tradition, of course, is against the Stoics. Jansen's *Augustinus* is an attack upon them; so is Arnauld's *Fréquente Communion.* And Pascal, dualist always, accepts neither the man of the world's cynical acceptance of man as a creature of the passions, nor the Stoic's pride in having conquered them. It is he who expresses the conviction of the mystic: "The heart has its reasons, which the reason knows not of." Machiavellians, Epicureans, and Christians are at one in laughing at the Stoic's vain pretensions that the passions can be conquered, and that the will is free.

Combatants of divergent loyalties again united in attacking Stoic rationalism itself—Montaigne, Bayle, Pascal: Epicurean, sceptic, and Christian. Montaigne indeed may be said to be all three in one. And to understand Swift's own position, Montaigne is of particular importance. The best commentary on *Gulliver's Travels* is the great *Apologie de Raymond Sébonde.* According to Busson's recent study of rationalism in the Renaissance, Montaigne sums up in popular form the scepticism of the preceding centuries of enlightenment. Now the rationalism of the Renaissance differed from that of the eighteenth century precisely in that it was a sceptical balancing of reason against faith, including reason itself among the objects of doubt.

Que sais je? asks Montaigne. What do I know? Montaigne's *Apologie*, like *Gulliver's Travels* is a scathing attack upon Stoic pride. Man is placed on a level almost lower than that of the dog and the horse. In fact Montaigne's primitivism, imitated by Swift—his disgust with the pompous boasts of civilization—is a good deal softened in *Gulliver's Travels*. Montaigne mistrusts dogmatic theology on the one hand, man's reason on the other. Hence, like Bayle a century later, he falls back on faith. It is absurd for man, so Montaigne closes his *Apologie*, to attempt to raise himself above humanity.

> For to make the handful bigger than the hand, and the armful larger than the arm, and to hope to stride farther than our legs can reach, is impossible and monstrous; or that man should rise above himself and humanity; for he cannot see but with his own eyes, nor seize but with his power. He shall rise if God will extraordinarily lend him His hand; he shall rise by abandoning and renouncing his own proper means, and by suffering himself to be raised and elevated by means purely celestial. It belongs to our Christian faith, and not to his stoical virtue, to pretend to that divine and miraculous metamorphosis.

And however mystifying Montaigne's philosophy may be when viewed as a whole, it is, I think, a gross misunderstanding of the role which scepticism has played in religion to accuse either Montaigne or Bayle of entire bad faith. Upon the twin pillars of scepticism and the corruption of human nature Pascal built his own *apologie,* as did Newman in more recent times his defense of the Catholic church. Newman merely echoes Montaigne when he says: "Quarry the granite rock with razors, or moor the vessel with a thread of silk; then you may hope with such keen and delicate instruments as human knowledge and human reason to contend against those giants, the passion and the pride of man."

But by the time that Swift wrote his own treatise to vex the world, scepticism and the belief in the corruption of human nature had given way to rationalism and an optimistic faith in man. The Stoic creed had suffered its sea-change. Sceptic, Epicurean, dualistic Christian had surrendered.

And the founder of the new faith was no other than the father of modern philosophy, Descartes himself. To the layman, burrowing his way into the history of ideas in the seventeenth century, it is almost disconcerting to discover how all roads lead to the author of the *Discourse on Method.* Let any one, after reading Montaigne's *Apologie,* turn to Descartes's treatise on the passions and a new planet swims into his ken. For the first assumption of Descartes is precisely the Stoic faith in a beneficent God and an uncorrupted nature. A good God cannot deceive us, and our reason is from God; hence our reason is to be trusted. And while the Stoicism of Epictetus still left within man a dualism of reason and passion, this, too, is obliterated by Descartes. The passions become good. *Elles sont toutes bonnes.* Vicious and evil instincts are denied the name of passions—ingratitude, impudence, effrontery. Reversing the method of La Rochefoucauld, Descartes dissolves a bad passion into that good one which nearly resembles it. Envy, for example, becomes a praiseworthy love of distributive justice. Pride is good, except when wrongly applied. Humility is scored as evil when it persuades us that we are feeble or unable to exercise our free will. Descartes's treatise on the passions does not, of course, yet picture the man of sentiment of Vauvenargues, or Rousseau; man is still decidedly *animal rationale,* master over himself like the heroes of Corneille:

> Je suis, maître du moi, comme de l'univers;
> Je le suis, je veux l'être.

But one may perhaps already see the eighteenth century in the offing—Deism, Shaftesbury, even the new antirationalism of Rousseau.

Though Cartesianism, as we have seen, found plentiful enemies in the seventeenth century, its ultimate victory was a foregone conclusion. It became for a time the ally of orthodoxy itself. Deceived by the firstfruits of the Cartesian method, resulting as it did in a dogmatic faith in God and immortality, the Church, fifty years later, discovered that she had fallen victim to seduction. The Deism of Toland, for example, is almost pure Descartes. Eighteenth-century orthodoxy, itself turned rationalist and optimist, found no weapons adequate to fight the Deists. Swift was one of few bold enough to oppose them squarely with an appeal to the weakness of human reason. Bossuet still saw the danger, as did the lighthearted Bayle. And Pascal rested his dualism precisely on the necessity of reconciling Montaigne and Descartes. Nowhere, perhaps, is the issue fought out in the seventeenth century more clearly expressed than in Pascal's little dialogue between himself and M. de Saci, in which Montaigne is set over against Epictetus—Montaigne, for whom man was on a level with the beasts; Epictetus (Descartes), for whom man was a god.

Clearly Swift belongs with Montaigne, La Rochefoucauld, and Bayle, among those who see man without illusion. But can he also be said to be a disciple of Pascal, the Christian? I do not think so. He did not, like Montaigne, achieve Epicurean tranquillity. He was decidedly not at ease in his inn. Neither could he feel kinship with the saints as could Pascal. Swift was not a mystic. One might apply to *Gulliver's Travels* Pascal's words: "It is dangerous to make man see too clearly his equality with the brutes, without showing him his greatness." Even Swift's Utopia is the Utopia of Locke, not Plato's philosopher's kingdom, nor St. Augustine's City of God. He was a rationalist with no faith in reason. Against the language of the heart he harbored an almost Freudian complex. Wesley, we may be sure, would have found him strange company. Sceptic and misanthrope, Swift fell back upon *saeva indignatio* and the established religion of his country.

Yet Swift's view of man, as Wesley perceived, and as Professor Bernbaum has pointed out in our own time, is essentially the view of the classical and Christian tradition. Almost any fair definition of that tradition would absolve *Gulliver's Travels* from the charge of being an isolated example of misanthropy. I can, in truth, find no better closing comment on *Gulliver's Travels* than a passage from Sainte-Beuve's *Port-Royal*. It is a definition of Christianity, written by one who was not himself a Christian, who throughout his sympathetic study of seventeenth-century mysticism preserved the calm detachment of the critic.

> One of the most direct ways to conceive the essence of Christianity is to accept the view of human nature as a fallen human nature, exactly as do Hobbes, La Rochefoucauld, and Machiavelli [and Sainte-Beuve might surely have added Swift], those great positive observers of life. The more such a view arouses a feeling of sadness, either in a soul not too hardened, or in a soul which, in spite of being hardened, is capable of compassion and which yearns for happiness, the more it disposes and provokes such a soul to accept the extreme remedy, the remedy of hope. Such a soul will ask itself if this is the true and final view of life, and will seek a way of escape beyond this earth and this state of misery, even in the vastnesses of heaven, in the awful infinite silences. This entering by the narrow gate, this unhoped-for way of escape to safety, this is Christianity. And I speak of that which is verifiable.

Gulliver and Swift

Phyllis Greenacre

Gulliver's Travels is generally considered Swift's masterpiece. It is said to have been written largely in a period of four years, 1721–25, and was published in 1726. These were years of paramount importance in Swift's personal life. Vanessa had died in 1723; and he had reacted with wandering and sleeping excessively, such a sleep as indicates a need for denial and deep repression. Just how much of the *Travels* had been written or thought out at this time is unclear. The narrative had certainly been forecast much earlier. It is to be expected under any circumstances that some imprint of Swift's own emotional struggle will be found in this, his greatest literary creation. But with his capacity to turn away from his conflicts and to recover balance through particularly strong inner defensive maneuvers, it was inevitable that Swift's tale of himself should appear in a thoroughly disguised and symbolic form. How much he wrote of himself was hidden probably even from his own awareness. It is likely that the latter part of the *Travels,* the fourth and most terrifying voyage, was elaborated after Vanessa's death, in June, 1723.

A fairly definite idea of the period of Swift's writing the *Travels* is contained in his letters to Charles Ford, none of which were published until 1896. Apparently he wrote consistently and intimately to Ford. A letter of April 1721 announced that he had begun the *Travels* and planned to publish them in a larger volume—a statement which certainly suggests that he had had them well in mind before this. In January, 1724 he wrote accusingly

From *Swift and Carroll: A Psychoanalytic Study of Two Lives.* © 1955 by International Universities Press, Inc.

to Ford, who was in France, and who had told Bolingbroke of Swift's essay
on the Brobdingnags and on the Yahoos (or at least Swift thought that
Ford had done so). He wrote:

> Else how should he [Bolingbroke] know anything of Stella and
> the Horses? 'T is hard that folks in France will not let us in
> Ireland be quiet. I would have him and you know that I hate
> Yahoos of both sexes, and that Stella and Madame de Villette
> are only tolerable at best, for want of Houyhnhnms. My greatest
> want here is of somebody qualified to censure and correct what
> I write . . . I have left the country of Horses, and am in the
> Flying Island where I shall not stay long, and my two last Jour-
> nyes will soon be over.

The date of this, early in 1724, certainly suggests that Swift may have been
preoccupied with the *Travels* during or immediately after his return from
his horseback journey following Vanessa's death, a period at least part of
which Stella spent with Dingley at Ford's estate. Successive letters to Ford
in 1724 repeated the charge that Ford had betrayed him to Bolingbroke. In
April, 1724, he wrote that he would soon finish the *Travels;* in August,
1725, he reported that he *had* finished them and described them as "admirable things, and will wonderfully mend the world." From the sequence
of letters, it seems that their writing also helped to mend Jonathan Swift.

The book is manifestly an adventure story, burlesquing the reports of
world explorations at a time when new areas of this strange world were
being opened up, and the explorer was a romantic storyteller, a conqueror
and a chronicler of anthropological mysteries. It was also an era in which
other writers, e.g., Defoe, used this form as an allegorical medium. Perhaps
in these particular aspects *Gulliver's Travels* might be compared to the better
comic science fiction of today. But the *Travels* has endured as a fairy-tale
classic as well, and obviously its universal appeal must be based on its
closeness to profound and unconscious problems of mankind. In addition,
it contains bold satirical attacks upon political and governmental policies
of the day, and students of history point out sly darts of ridicule directed
at certain individuals whom Swift honored with a particular contempt. It
is clearly not its specific historical political significance, however, which
has made an appeal to children.

The *Travels* consists of four voyages: the first to Lilliput, the land of
the little people; the second to Brobdingnag, the land of the giants; the third
to five places, Laputa, Balnibarbi, Glubbdubdrib, Luggnagg, and Japan;
and the fourth, final journey to the strangest land of all, that of the

Houyhnhnms. Lemuel Gulliver, the traveler, was a young man of Nottinghamshire, the third among five sons and recently apprenticed to a surgeon, Mr. James Bates. But he had always an interest in travel and prepared himself, in addition to his medical training, by studying navigation, mathematics, and two years of physics at Leyden. His master, Bates, then recommended him as a ship's surgeon on the *Swallow,* where he served for three years on voyages to the Levant. Later, again under the influence of Bates, he undertook to settle in London and practice his profession. Accordingly he married Mrs. Mary Burton, second daughter of a hosier, who brought him a modest dowry. But his good master, Bates, dying within two years, left Lemuel with few friends, a fast-failing business, and a strong conscience which did not permit him to imitate the bad practice of others of his profession. He went back to sea and started his maritime career which was to last for more than fifteen years. He sailed on the *Antelope,* leaving Bristol in May, 1699 and returned from his fourth and last voyage arriving at his home on December 5, 1715.

It is interesting and fitting to compare the lives of Lemuel Gulliver and Jonathan Swift, his creator, both as to sequences of events and the occurrences at specific dates in the two lives. Gulliver was a few years older than Swift. Unlike Gulliver, Swift never traveled far, though he several times planned to; but he was a constant voyager between Ireland and England, sometimes dividing the year between the two countries. Swift was a clergyman, preoccupied with the ills of his own body and the political ills of the state but could hardly bear to consider the bodies of others. Gulliver was a surgeon's apprentice, who went on to explore the topography of foreign lands and peoples. Gulliver went to Cambridge at fourteen, the age at which Swift entered Trinity. While Gulliver was being apprenticed to his master Bates, Swift at a corresponding time was working for his Master's degree. Both left their native soil at the age of twenty-one, Gulliver going to Leyden to prepare for travel, and Swift to England to find his mother. At twenty-seven, Gulliver married and attempted to settle down in London. At the same age, Swift was wishing to marry Jane Waring and settle into the life of a clergyman. Both men lost their benefactors, Mr. Bates and Sir William Temple respectively, at the age of thirty-two. Gulliver then returned to the sea, and Swift to the Church. The year 1699, in which Gulliver set out on his first recorded voyage, was a landmark in the life of Swift, being the time of Sir William Temple's death, of Swift's final rupture with Jane Waring, and of the marriage of Jane Swift. The date, December, 1715, of Gulliver's return from his last voyage in a state in which he abhorred his wife, was only a few months before Swift's supposed marriage to Stella.

If one may summarize the qualities and contents in the voyages very briefly, it can be pointed out that the first two are much concerned with relative body size. In the first, Gulliver is the giant in the land of tiny folk; in the second, he is comparatively tiny in the land of the giants. In the third voyage, changes of size, but especially the movement of inanimate objects in a land of abstract geometric fantasies not subject to reality testing, are striking elements. The land of the fourth voyage is inhabited by ideal creatures and foul creatures, and the interrelations between these and their relation to the *Travels* comprise the climax of the tales.

The voyage to the Lilliputians, the best known of the *Travels,* extended from May, 1699 to April, 1702. Heading for the East Indies, the ship was wrecked by storms in November, 1699, and Gulliver alone was saved. He dragged himself ashore on a strange island and fell asleep. On awakening, he found himself pinioned by a lacing of ropes fastened to pegs driven into the ground. He soon found he was in a land of tiny people, who thus sought to restrain him and hold him down. They first attacked him, then brought him to a temple which had been profaned by the murder of a man. Here he was placed in full view of the populace, tethered by a chain to make escape impossible. Thus he found it difficult to achieve excretory relief inoffensively. In panic he defecated once indoors within the temple, but later went into the open air for this purpose. He explains all this in detail, and remarks with a Swiftian preoccupation with cleanliness: "I would not have dwelt so long upon a circumstance that perhaps, at first sight, may appear not very momentous, if I had not thought it necessary to justify my character in point of cleanliness to the world, which I am told some of my maligners have been pleased upon this and other occasions to call into question." (Involuntary moral guilt and unavoidable physical dirtiness are clearly associated.)

There are several general motifs in the tale of Gulliver's life among the Lilliputians. The most pervasive one is the problem of disparity in size between Gulliver and the Lilliputians. The latter are afraid that Gulliver, now called the Man Mountain, will impoverish them with his need for food and the expense of his clothing. He in turn pretends that he may eat up some of the little folk himself. Finally accepting the burden and responsibility of his care, they set out to train him in their language and ways. Thus they tentatively adopt him. Most conspicuous of all, however, is the effect of awe or offensiveness to the Lilliputians, of Gulliver's mountainous body. He sneezes and creates a tornado; his urination produces a torrent of "noise and violence"; his defecation causes a national health problem. He brandishes his sword, and the sunlight on the blade causes them to kneel down in blinded awe. When he shoots his pistol in the air, a hundred men fall down as though struck dead.

The mutual sport between Gulliver and the Lilliputians is interesting. Threads, ropes, and cords are important in their games. Not only is there the opening incident of Gulliver finding himself bound, but he is later to find that feats of tightrope walking and exhibitions of ropedancing are required for great employments and high favors at court. In other games, colored cords or threads are the prizes given for skill in jumping over hurdles held by the Emperor. The ropes were of different color, and were worn around the waists of the recipients, indicating different degrees of distinction, like colored ribbons of merit in an exhibition or race. Gulliver, in his turn, staked out a small parade ground or arena for the exercise of the King's cavalry, and played with the horsemen much like a child playing with toy soldiers.

The interest in, awe at, and revulsion from the human body is played actively and passively between Gulliver and his tiny hosts. While Gulliver watched the games, antics, and movements of the Lilliputians, they in turn were repeatedly impressed with his body structure and primitive functions. So with a reversal of the toy cavalry game situation, the Emperor directed Gulliver to stand like a Colossus with his legs apart, while the soldiers paraded through the arch thus formed. To the soldiers, the Emperor issued orders to "observe the strictest decency" with regard to Gulliver's person, but this did not prevent the younger ones from looking heavenward as they passed under him, and the state of his breeches was such that the sight "afforded opportunities for laughter and admiration." Further, in a kind of treaty between the Emperor and Gulliver, it was agreed among other things that Gulliver should survey the Island of the Lilliputians by means of a computation of his paces around its border. They in turn guaranteed him food equal to that consumed by 1728 Lilliputians, this figure being arrived at by their computations of his body size. Under the terms of the treaty, Gulliver was permitted to visit the capital city. This, too, was a mutual sight-seeing expedition in which the populace gathered to view the Man Mountain, and he showed ingenuity in getting his oversized eye to the window of the Emperor's private apartment. Since this was an authorized peeping, the Empress threw him a kiss.

Presently the problem of relative size appears in other guises, as Gulliver learns that the country has for a long time tended to split into factions. Currently a struggle was going on between the conservative High-Heels and the progressive Low-Heels. While the Emperor appointed only Low-Heels in his administration, it was observed that the Emperor himself had heels of uneven height which caused him to hobble and brought disturbance into his cabinet. As a background to such struggles, there was a low-grade chronic warfare between Lilliput and the neighboring country of Blefuscu, concerning whether an egg should be opened at the large or the small end in preparation for eating. This had assumed the quality of a religious war. The Big Endians, having suffered persecution and massacre and the outlawing of their books, found refuge and help among the Blefuscudians. Now the Lilliputians sought Gulliver's aid. Here again he played the benevolent oversized child-god, manipulating the enemy's fleet but in such a way as not to destroy it. He simply waded into the channel, fastened a cord to each Blefuscudian ship and hooked it to a long crossbar big enough to be the lead for the entire fleet. Then cutting the individual anchor cables, he could draw the entire fleet after him like a child dragging a number of toys.

With a Swiftian passion for fairness, however, Gulliver did not permit his services to the Lilliputian Emperor to be exploited for the destruction of the Blefuscudians. At this point he had, because of his great size, a chance to do a further service to the Lilliputian monarch. This was by the adaptive use of the most primitive and impressive function at his disposal. Thus the royal household was saved from complete destruction by fire when Gulliver, having been well dined and especially wined by the Blefuscudians, found himself, in the heat of the fire, to be the generator of extraordinary urinary pressure, and by the adroit use and direction of this heightened ability, he put out the fire in three minutes. Although urinating within the palace grounds was ordinarily a capital offense, naturally under these conditions of emergency use, this behavior would be expected to bring praise and congratulations. Yet the Empress reacted with such horror (and envy?) that she vowed revenge.

Certain customs and value scales among the Lilliputians are described by Gulliver, especially the emphasis on morals rather than ability. The system of education was founded on the principle that parents begot children purely from drives of biological instinct. Consequently, children were considered to owe their parents nothing, and the parents to be ill chosen to educate their children. The educational system provided schools of different ranks, which were also separate for the two sexes. Boys were brought up by men, with older women performing only the most menial tasks. Parents might visit for two hours throughout the year but must give no indication of endearment. At no time might the boys converse with any servant. Girls were educated after the fashion of boys, only by their own sex. They were, however, schooled "to despise all personal ornaments beyond decency and cleanliness." No difference was permitted to exist in the training of the two sexes, under the maxim that a wife "should always be a reasonable and agreeable Companion, because she cannot always be young." These communal training centers were supported by levies upon the parents, for the Lilliputians considered nothing so unjust as people who would bring children into the world and leave the burden of supporting them on the public. In this highly moral country, however, Gulliver found himself about to be impeached, since the court people were afraid of his abilities. He escaped then to Blefuscu, and from there sailed homewards.

The second voyage was undertaken (June, 1702) within two months after Gulliver had returned from the first. Again the ship was diverted from its course by storms, and after a complete year of wandering (no account is given of the drain upon the provisions), the entire crew landed on a new continent. Here, separating himself from the others, the better to view the lay of the land, Gulliver found himself permanently separated from them, as they had swum back to their boat and returned to the ship, after being frightened by a monstrous creature found wading in the water. Thus Gulliver finds the tables exactly turned, with a reversal of the situation in which he so recently waded into the channel himself and gathered up the entire fleet. Indeed he finds that he is now a tiny person in the land of giants, fears being trampled under foot, cut by their scythes, or even eaten up by them. This is the land of Brobdingnag. Here the contact with children, nurses, and small animals (large in this land of oversized creatures) played a much greater part than had been true in Lilliput, and the fear of being eaten or mistreated by them is a recurrent theme. The appearance of the nurse as an important figure is also significant. Two types of nurses appear: the revolting adult nurse who bared her dry nipple to quiet the baby offering him suck and, in doing so, reminded Gulliver of how the Lilliputians had found his skin revolting with its monstrous pores and stumps of hairs; and the little girl nurse who protected him and taught him the language and called him "mannikin." The impression of the revolting breast was later reinforced by the sight of a woman with a cancerous breast where the holes were so great that Gulliver could have hidden in any one of them.

When Gulliver suffered a passive exhibition, being shown as a curio at county fairs, his young nurse carried him in a kind of doll cage dangling from a cord around her waist. He was taken to the Royal Court, purchased by the Queen, and scientifically examined by the King and the wise men, one of whom at first considered him a clockwork toy, then suggested that he might be an embryo or an abortion; and finally decided he was a *lusus naturae,* a sport or freak of nature, although Gulliver protested that he came from a country in which he was a standard product. Particularly difficult in this monstrous country was the behavior of the oversize insects who left unpleasant trails upon his food or carried it away with them.

Ultimately, too, the Queen prepared for him a secure small closet in which he might ride on horseback strapped to the belt of the rider, or in a sedan, upon the lap of the child nurse who remained with him. In this manner he traveled on sight-seeing tours over the country, being himself also the object of much curiosity even as had been true in Lilliput. Interestingly enough, however, he was unimpressed by the tallest steeple tower in the land, and computed its height to be relatively less than that of Salisbury steeple in England. Gulliver also found himself in situations of extraordinary mutual exposure with the Maids of Honor, to whose apartments he was taken by his child nurse. Here they stripped themselves and him, and held him close to their bodies until he could scarcely endure the smell, though this, too, forced him to recall that the Lilliputians had sometimes complained of his body smell. These maids certainly used him for their own erotic amusement, one of them setting him astride her nipple—which completely disgusted and horrified him, as did their copious urination. In the next paragraph we have the report of how he was prevailed upon to witness the execution by beheading of a murderer, in such a manner that the blood spurted prodigiously.

Two incidents following this are also of some import: the Queen provided Gulliver with a small pleasure boat especially fitted to his size, and ordered the building of a trough filled with water, in which the boat might be propelled, sometimes by oars, and sometimes by the breeze from the ladies' fans, thus giving pleasure to both himself and them. A further indication of this unexpected relationship to one of the ladies, governess to his nurse, is given in an anecdote as follows: This lady lifted him up to place him in the boat, but he slipped through her fingers and plunged downward, his fall being stopped by a corking-pin that stuck in the gentlewoman's stomacher, the head of the pin passing between his skin and the waistband of his breeches. He was thus suspended in the air, more or less attached to the governess, until he was rescued by his little nurse. At another time he was attacked in the trough by an odious frog which deposited slime on him while hopping over him.

During this period in Brobdingnag, Gulliver suffered three near kidnappings, all by animals. First a dog took him in his mouth and carried him to his master, the gardener, who returned him to his little girl nurse. A little later, a kite hovering over the garden swooped down and would have carried him away, had he not saved himself by running under an espalier. Finally, some time later a monkey came chattering to his box home and, after spying him from every angle, reached in and grabbed him out. Holding him "as a nurse does a child she is about to suckle" and "squeezed . . . so hard that [it was] more prudent to submit." The monkey is described as a male monkey who probably took Gulliver for a young monkey, and being startled, ran out of the palace and to the roof of an adjoining one, where he sat on the ridgepole, holding Gulliver with one hand while he crammed food into him with the other, squeezing the food out from a bag on one side of his chaps. Finally the monkey became frightened by pursuers and let Gulliver drop upon the ridge tile until he was rescued by a young boy, footman to the child nurse. Gulliver was so sickened by the stuff which had been put into his mouth by the evil monkey, that the dear little nurse had to pick it out with a needle. When the King later chaffed him about this, Gulliver was forced to see how really diminutive a figure he was in the land of these giant people, and how much even his misfortunes became a matter of diversion among the Big Ones. Finally, in an effort to be impressive despite his minute stature, he gave the King an account of English laws and customs but found to his dismay that the King had only become convinced of the ignorance, idleness, and vice prevailing in England, and hoped that the traveler had profited by being so much away from his own country. Gulliver felt extremely bad about this, and explained that he had really tried most artfully to elude the King's careful questioning and make his answers as favorable as possible.

In a final effort to convince the King of the glories and the power of England, Gulliver told him of the invention of gun powder and how it might be used, offering to him the secret of its composition. But the monarch, horrified by the proposal, replied that "he was amazed how so impotent and groveling an Insect . . . could entertain such inhuman Ideas" and appear so unmoved by them. In spite of the shortsightedness of this view, it was to appear that the country was not without its own impressive show of might, and that the members of the militia, spread out in a field twenty miles square, would on command all brandish their swords at once, producing an effect of ten thousand flashes of lightning in the sky. (A reversal, certainly, of Gulliver's situation with the Lilliputians.) Gulliver ultimately found that even this isolated country had suffered from "the same disease to which the whole race of mankind is subject: the nobility often contending for power, the people for liberty, and the King for absolute dominion."

The traveler, having been about two years in the land of Brobdingnag, began to wish to return home, especially as the King was eager to find him a mate his own size with whom he might found a family. Unable to bear the thought of propagating a race so diminutive that it would inevitably be laughable, he sought to escape. In this he had the unexpected cooperation of an eagle, which swooped down upon his box house while the pages had wandered away, and kidnapped him in it, carrying it by the ring that was fastened to its top. After approximately two hours of flight, the bird, being chased by other eagles, dropped the box into the sea where it was tossed about by the waves until it was sighted and taken aboard an English vessel, on which Gulliver returned to England, not before the sailing captain had questioned him carefully to see whether he had committed some great crime for which he was being cast away to perish at sea. This return voyage took exactly nine months. On board the ship and for some time after his return home, Gulliver suffered from a kind of sensory unreality feeling, due to the discrepancy between the sensory impressions of those around him and those giants with whom he had lived for two years. He thought his wife and children had starved because they were so small, and at first thought he was back in the land of Lilliput. He had arrived home early in June, 1706. His residence was at Redriff.

While the first voyage had been undertaken for economic gain, the second one was frankly because of Gulliver's "insatiable desire of seeing foreign countries," and was begun only two months after the return from the first. At this time he left his wife, his son Johnny and his daughter Betty, then of school age, and embarked on a vessel called the *Adventure*. Gulliver opens his account of his second voyage, that to Brobdingnag, with the statement that he was "condemned by nature and fortune to an active and restless life." When Gulliver returned from his second voyage, he was confused, due in large measure to the difficulty in focusing his vision and accommodating to the idea of being the same size as other people. His wife was concerned about him and begged him never again to return to the sea. But "she had not the power to hinder" him and in ten days he was again under the influence of the "thirst . . . of seeing the world" and was negotiating with the Captain of the *Hopewell*, planning a voyage to the East Indies.

Consequently, on August 5, 1706, Gulliver set out on this third journey. Only a few days out at sea, the ship was attacked by Dutch and Japanese pirates in two ships. He spoke so imprudently to them that they cast him adrift in a canoe. This led to his discovery of a peculiar, exactly circular island up in the air, which was suspended over the body of a continent. The island, which rested on a lodestone so delicately balanced that a little child's hand could manipulate it, could be moved at will "to raise or sink or put it in progressive motion" by the inhabitants. This was the Island of Laputa, and might be described as the Island of Abstract Fantasy without Reality Testing. The movement of the Island, directed by the King, depended much upon mathematics and music. Ideas were often expressed in geometrical figures, although there was great contempt for practical geometry. Even the meat was cut in geometrical shapes rather than according to the principles of anatomical structure. The Laputians were chronically anxious and fearful of total destruction of the earth, the planets, and everything. The Island was also a place of peculiar marital relations. Here Gulliver stayed a month or more, feeling greatly neglected because the Laputians, being so absorbed in their geometry, paid him scant attention. The women, however, were mostly unsatisfied and restless, a condition which Gulliver likened to that of England.

Through the intervention of the stupidest man on the Island, Gulliver succeeded in getting away to the adjacent continent of Balnibarbi, with a metropolis called Lagado, and a kindly, lordly host, Munodi, who gave the traveler an apartment in his own house. The continent of Balnibarbi had at one time been a substantial and rather noble place, but in the past forty years it had been greatly affected by its local citizens' visits to the Island of Laputa, from which they returned with smatterings of mathematics and "volatile spirits acquired in that airy region." They had attempted to put these exquisite abstractions into practice, but had not completed their projects, and consequently left the country in waste and the people impoverished. It seems to have been a country of energetic promoters of abstractions. Here in the Grand Academy, a kind of Institute of Scientific Exhibits, one man was engaged in extracting sunbeams from cucumbers; another was engaged in an operation to reduce human excrement to its original food; another had written on the malleability of fire. A mixer of paint determined his color choice by feeling and smelling. A physician cured colic by pumping the bowel full of wind which, when released, brought the noxious out with it. On another side of the Academy were projectors in speculative learning. Here there was a machine for the indiscriminate mixing and grinding of words with which to produce books in philosophy, poetry, politics, law, theology, and mathematics. In another place there was a scheme for abolishing words altogether, which was considered an advantage in health, for each word uttered was held to be a diminution of the lungs by corrosion and consequently might shorten life. Thus it was considered advisable to supplant words by the *things* which they symbolized, which must then be carried by each person. Only the women rebelled and insisted on using their tongues. Further, a kind of lobotomy was practiced as well, but with the advantage of an interchange between individuals, of the amputated lobes. In this progressive country, Gulliver recommended a department made up of spies, informers, discoverers, accusers, witnesses, etc. Here it would be first agreed what suspected persons should be accused of, then all care was taken to procure all their papers and letters and to put the criminals in chains. The anagrammatic method was used in evaluating the evidence.

This country made Gulliver homesick for England. He seemed convinced that this Kingdom really might extend to America and to the land of California. He decided to go further to the Island of Luggnagg, but on his way had an involuntary stopover of a month, and went to the tiny Island of Glubbdubdrib, inhabited by sorcerers and magicians. The servants here were all ghosts, called up for a single stretch of twenty-four-hour duty, once every three months; but they might be dismissed into thin air by a twitch of the Governor's finger. Here fantasy could be readily and magically converted into reality. In his ten days' stay, Gulliver materialized as serviceable ghosts many illustrious people such as Alexander the Great, Hannibal, Caesar, Pompey, and others (incidentally, all men), as well as unmasking the villainy and wretched foulness of many of the supposed great.

The next stop was Luggnagg, where he arrived on April 21, 1709. There a *man* interpreter helped Gulliver who was then informed he might proceed to the King, where he could lick the dust before the royal footstool. Although this performance of a ritual was made antiseptic in honor of the visiting traveler, it was ordinarily a way of his majesty's dealing with his enemies. In the consummation of the ritual, the visitor was directed to say certain strange words signifying "My tongue is in the mouth of my friend."

After three months, Gulliver's lust for travel gave way to a desire to see his wife and children. Before he left, however, he was introduced to a strange group of immortals, the Struldbruggs, special variant creatures, human but not subject to death, distinguishable by a peculiar circular mark over one eye. To his disappointment, he found that these people lived like mortals till the age of thirty, then became increasingly dejected until they were eighty. But instead of then fading gracefully, they became opinionated, covetous, morose: envy and impotent desires supplanting affection until they sank into unending senility. The King wished to send a few Struldbruggs with Gulliver to arm the people of England against the fear of death. The traveler left Luggnagg in May, 1709, for Japan where he stayed but briefly and returned thence to his native England, arriving on April 16, 1710.

In August, 1710, having remained at home four to five months and his wife being already well advanced in another pregnancy, Gulliver decided to go, not as a surgeon, but as Captain—again of the *Adventure*. After some months of sailing under adverse conditions, the sailors mutinied, held their captain prisoner, and deposited him abruptly in a desolate land inhabited by strangely evil and by noble creatures. The former were dirty, hairy, nightmarish animals that scampered about and climbed trees, persecuting and tormenting the traveler by letting excrement drop upon his head. In contrast to these were the reasonable, gentle horses who were the natural aristocrats of the land. Soon he was taken in charge by a pair of them who taught him much of the language and gave him a home. From them he learned that the dirty creatures were called Yahoos and the horses were Houyhnhnms. From the way in which the various Houyhnhnms looked at his face and hands, he observed that they considered him some sort of special Yahoo, although they marveled at his cleanliness, his teachableness, and his civility, as these qualities were opposite to the character of the Yahoos.

At one time they discovered him at night when his clothing had slipped off, uncovering especially the lower part of his body. Now they were sure he was a Yahoo, as earlier his clothing had caused them to think him at least somewhat different. However, a complete examination of Gulliver's body convinced the Houyhnhnms that he was really a very perfect Yahoo, distinguished by his fine white skin, a characterization which did not entirely please Gulliver, and aroused him to protest against it. His subsequent attempts to explain to his benefactors the nature of the customs and laws of the country from which he came only verified their impression of his Yahoo origin. They considered that in some respects he was even at a disadvantage, compared with the hardier Yahoos of their own country. However, after a year's residence in the country of the Houyhnhnms, Gulliver resolved not to return to humankind. The master Houyhnhnm explained that "*the Yahoos were known to hate one another more than they did any different species of animals; and the reason usually assigned was the odiousness of their own shapes, which all could see in the rest but none in themselves.*" The greediness and lack of discrimination in their appetites was truly appalling. The sexuality of the Yahoos was aggressively foul, as was their system of medicine, the sick depending for cure on the eating of the body excreta. Gulliver himself, attempting to study the Yahoos, confirmed their unteachability but attributed it interestingly enough to a perverse, restive disposition rather than to inherent defect.

After Gulliver had been in the country three years, he became convinced of his own indubitable Yahoo origin when a Yahoo girl of eleven fell in love with him when she saw him bathing, and was so energetic in her embraces that he had to be rescued by his sorrel nag.

In contrast to this Yahoo passion, the Houyhnhnms were governed entirely by reasonable justice and friendliness, educating their own offspring out of reasonableness rather than love, and showing no preference for their own young over those of their neighbors. The number of offspring was also equably determined and couples remained together only until the required number of young was produced, but during the period of the marriage the relationship was one of mutual friendship and benevolence, which was, however, no greater for the mate than for all others of the species. It was noteworthy that the Houyhnhnms trained their youths by exercising them in running up and down hills, and in competitive races.

It is thus apparent that in this land the Houyhnhnms embodied completely equable reason and impersonal good will, while the Yahoos were the creatures of primordial hate and passion. The Houyhnhnms showed minuteness and exactness in descriptions, and a justness of similes in their poetry that was truly remarkable. Further, when they died, which came about through the passage of time resulting in painless decay, and not as the result of disease, there was no mourning or show of emotion, and the dead person was said to have "retired to his first mother." Before this reasonable departure from earth, the dying ones called upon all their friends, meticulously repaying past visits.

Gulliver, having been forced, by the behavior of the Yahoo girl, to recognize his own Yahoo identity, settled down to stay in this extraordinary country, hating himself more than any ordinary Yahoo, contrary to the fashion among them, and meanwhile taking on, by a kind of primary emulation, the speech, behavior, and attitudes of the noble Houyhnhnms. But after he had been there five years, he found his stay terminated by the decision of the Houyhnhnms' General Council, many of whom feared him as a special and potentially most dangerous Yahoo. He was therefore forced to leave, and aided by his constant benefactor built a boat in which he got away. He was ultimately picked up by a Portuguese vessel whose captain regarded the exiled Gulliver as a man quite out of his mind, especially when he heard the traveler's account of his experiences. Gulliver was then only desirous of retiring to a solitary island to spend the rest of his days, but the captain prevailed upon him to return to his wife and children. Still under the influence of the noble and reasonable Houyhnhnm ideals, Gulliver could not bear the thought that he had cohabited with a Yahoo and even produced Yahoo children. Indeed, he recoiled from the affection of his wife, and so odious an animal did he feel her to be that he fell in a swoon, and it was more than a year before he could tolerate so much as to eat in the same room with her and the children. Never afterward could he tolerate their drinking from the same cup with him, or allow them to touch his hand. He perpetuated the memory of the reasonable Houyhnhnms by the purchase of a pair of horses which, with their groom, became his favorites and lived in amiable friendship with him; the smell of their stable invariably reviving his sagging spirits.

No account of *Gulliver's Travels* in relation to the life of Swift would be reasonably complete without a reference to the forecast of the *Travels* which was written as early as 1711–1714. At this time Swift, together with Pope, Gay, Oxford, Parnell, and Arbuthnot, formed a club, first called the Tory Club, later the Scriblerus Club, whose members planned to write in collaboration a comprehensive satire on the abuses of learning. In these writings Scriblerus, who is frankly identified as Swift, reveals certain fantasies concerning his birth, his grandiose ideas, and his attitude towards his own genius. Swift projects the *Travels* (later given to Gulliver) as the *Secession of Martinus Scriblerus* and outlines quite clearly the four voyages in a way that indicates he has definitely in mind the first voyage to the land of the pygmies, the second to the giants, the third to the land of the philosophers and mathematicians (which at this time are conceived of as beneficial), and the fourth, in which there is a "vein of melancholy proceeding almost to a Disgust of his Species." At this time, too, he forecast his cannibalistic scheme for relieving the conditions of the poor, which was not to be actually written until 1729.

Animal Rationis Capax

Kathleen Williams

Gulliver's Travels is Swift's most complete and most masterly summing-up of the nature of man and of his proper behavior in a difficult world. As in so much of his writing, he works partly through parody, parody of travel literature and its authors, parody of the conclusions of the philosophic voyagers; but here as in *A Tale of a Tub*, the antiromantic poems, or the *Modest Proposal*, parody is only a means to a moral end, serving, especially in the fourth voyage, to make Swift's point in the most economical way by a sharp reversal of the findings common in travels to Utopia. The "Voyage to the Houyhnhnms" is so much the most striking and effective that it has often been considered in isolation, but in fact it is the climax towards which the whole work moves. Swift claimed, in his humorous but wholly serious letter to Pope, that the *Travels* in its entirety was built upon the same "great foundation of misanthropy, though not in Timon's manner," and it is true that a consistent purpose is visible throughout. Even the "Voyage to Laputa," once scorned as untidy, superficial, boring, a book of leftovers, can now be seen in its proper eighteenth-century context as highly relevant to Swift's general purpose. The whole of *Gulliver's Travels*, though it is timeless in its vision of the unchanging condition of man, is at the same time contemporary, presenting humanity in the particular situation of Swift's scientific, system-making, Deistic, and rationalistic age. Compared with *A Tale of a Tub*, the *Travels* is a model of clarity and order, but it is more inclusive than the earlier work, for Swift's perfect choice of

From *Jonathan Swift and the Age of Compromise.* © 1958 by the University of Kansas Press.

vehicle enables him to deal without confusion, often in the same incident or character, with science, philosophy, politics, morals. The third voyage is conceived in terms of contemporary science, but it has also political connotations and relevance to Swift's primary theme of the proper activity of man; the voyages to Lilliput and Brobdingnag are moral and political, but Swift's chosen allegory of the giants and pygmies, the enormous and the microscopic, has great significance for the new scientific age. Book IV is less concerned with science or with politics, for here we have reached the primary theme itself, and Swift treats openly of the different attitudes to man which underlie differences on the political or scientific level; but the moral lesson, with its basis in Christian tradition, is related to the ideas of Hobbes and Locke, Shaftesbury and Bolingbroke and Descartes, and the progressive and Deistic perfectionism of the philosophic voyagers. Satiric method can never, in Swift, be considered apart from his theme, but here form and content are even more beautifully integrated than in his other work. The "Voyage to Laputa," it is true, is a partial exception, but even here commentators have in the past exaggerated its untidiness and its episodic quality. Miss Nicolson and Miss Mohler have demonstrated the unity of theme which had been lost to the readers of the nineteenth and twentieth centuries, and it is not, I think, special pleading to suggest that here as in *A Tale of a Tub* an air of confusion and wrongheadedness is part of the theme, for the Laputans have plunged into unreality as delightedly as the author of the *Tale*. Structurally it is perhaps a fault to revert to another and earlier method in the midst of an ostensibly factual and sober work, but the psychological effect of this book, placed as it is before the "Voyage to the Houyhnhnms," is well calculated.

The satiric basis of the voyages to Lilliput and Brobdingnag is the conception known as relative size, and regarded purely as a satiric device this is apt and successful: man is seen more clearly and with more detachment when seen from a far lower or far higher physical position. But Swift's methods never can be regarded purely as satiric devices, and in these first voyages he is setting his readers into the context of eighteenth-century insecurity. For this is the age of the telescope and the microscope, displaying so excitingly and yet so alarmingly the huge spaces around man, planets perhaps with other living beings, and the world of insects beneath him, tiny yet, to its inhabitants, as infinite as man's world is to himself. The literature of the early eighteenth century is full of awed references to the revelations of these two machines: to the disconcerting animal world of the sceptical Raleigh or Montaigne, incomprehensible to man, are added these other planes of being, the life of the insects and the life of the possibly inhabited worlds. "Relative size" is an aspect of the atmosphere of relativity in which man found himself, no longer the center of the universe but, perhaps, as unimportant and absurd as the insects, who no doubt believe themselves to be valuable creatures. "I dare engage," says the Giant King, speaking of Gulliver's race, "these Creatures have their Titles and Distinctions of Honour; they contrive little Nests and Burrows, that they call Houses and Cities; they make a Figure in Dress and Equipage; they love, they fight, they dispute, they cheat, they betray." Similarly Voltaire, later in the century, brought to earth from Saturn the giant Micromégas, who strides unaware across the world until he chances to look through a diamond and sees the tiny animalcules who are men and women, as the scientists had seen through the first microscopes the teeming life of leaf and puddle. Many men of the period were disconcerted by these new discoveries; many wrote of the wonders newly displayed and thought uneasily of the relation of these things to the position of man. Glanvill felt that the new knowledge gave more grounds for his "fear, that we scarce yet see anything as it is," since it is now even more plain that "our Senses extremely deceive us in their reports, and informations." But only Swift saw how relativity could be used, not merely to exhilarate or to shock, but to express in contemporary terms a moral view of man; only Swift turned the idea of man the insect into the clear-sighted condemnation of the King of Brobdingnag: "I cannot but conclude the Bulk of your Natives, to be the most pernicious Race of little odious Vermin that Nature ever suffered to crawl upon the Surface of the Earth." In Swift's hands, what the microscope reveals is related to the ancient Christian and Judaic vision of proud and insignificant man, to Job and Ecclesiastes and Corinthians, to the grasshoppers of Isaiah and to the serpents and snails of the Psalms. The pride shaken by relativity is essentially the same as the pride of the "wicked" of the Old Testament; it is vanity and delusion.

But the denunciation of man by the Giant King can only be accepted as the climax of Swift's insect imagery because it has been prepared for with such care and skill. Throughout the first two books there is a steady accumulation of hints and pressures, slight in themselves but preparing us gradually for the King's response to Gulliver's eager praise of European man. The insect and animal suggestions at first are harmless, even charming; in Book I Gulliver feels a small creature, "something alive moving on my left Leg," which turns out to be "a human Creature not six Inches high," one of the Lilliputians whom he calls, at first, "the Creatures." Actual insect reference is hardly necessary in Book I, for we take up our position with Gulliver and naturally regard these tiny human beings much as we would particularly accomplished mice. Much of the effect of relativity is gained through the description of the Lilliputians' own animals, their tiny sheep and geese, "and so the several Gradations downwards, till you come to the smallest, which, to my Sight, were almost invisible." But in Book II the comparison must be more firmly made, for here we must be gradually detached from Gulliver, and must look at him, as representative of mankind, from the point of view of the Brobdingnagians, seeing him as before we had seen the Lilliputians. Accordingly Gulliver is to the giants a "small dangerous Animal" like a weasel, as alarming as a toad or a spider: he fears that the children may torment him as ours do "Sparrows, Rabbits, young Kittens, and Puppy-Dogs." He is carried about by an affectionate monkey, who "took me for a young one of his own Species," and petted by the giant ladies as if he were something quite inhuman. At best he is a pet, at worst one of a "Race of little odious Vermin," and he is so insignificant that the giants find it difficult to recognize him as a rational creature, though in Book I Gulliver himself had quickly seen that the Lilliputians, small as they were, were human. The charm of insectlike man gives way to the frightened malignancy of the small beast, weasel, toad, or vermin, and as the animal world steadily closes us in we see ourselves, in Gulliver, as the animal man.

Relativity provides Swift, too, with a means of stressing the effect on the mind and character of such physical accidents as size, so that we gain the impression that man's intellectual and moral achievement is to a considerable extent dependent on his physical nature and situation. All the characters in Books I and II are subject to the influence of bodily circumstance on mental qualities. The Lilliputian mind is precise but petty and limited, just as their vision is; Gulliver tells us with the accuracy of a scientific observer reporting on the fly's "microscopic eye": "Nature hath adapted the Eyes of the Lilliputians to all Objects proper for their View: They see with great Exactness, but at no great Distance." They are neat, efficient, and in their narrow, insectlike way well adapted to their environment, but the arrival of the giant Gulliver brings out their most cruel and treacherous qualities in their efforts to assert themselves, and with the necessary exception of the lord who warns Gulliver of his danger, they show neither generosity nor gratitude. Despite all that Gulliver has done for them, the Emperor and his Empress—the grandiloquent titles are typical—harbor a malicious resentment for the offenses given to their petty dignity, and Gulliver is finally sentenced to be blinded, though this is represented as an act of great clemency on the Emperor's part. All this is, of course, partly a comment on the immorality of man as a political animal, for one aspect of the insectlike, organized efficiency of Lilliput is political, and this comment is carried further in Book II, in the giant King's opinion of European behavior and also in the sharp contrast between him and the Emperor. The Emperor has no regard for the ordinary human obligations where his schemes of wealth and power are concerned, whereas the King sees cruelty as no more justified in public matters than it is in dealing with private persons. Gulliver, for his part, is at his most attractive, and at his most consistent, in Book I, behaving towards his small captors with great humanity and kindness, and his own gratitude and constancy throw into relief the small-minded selfishness of the Emperor:

> Once I was strongly bent upon Resistance: For while I had Liberty, the whole Strength of that Empire could hardly subdue me, and I might easily with Stones pelt the Metropolis to Pieces: But I soon rejected that Project with Horror, by remembering the Oath I had made to the Emperor, the Favours I received from him, and the high Title of Nardac he conferred upon me. Neither had I so soon learned the Gratitude of Courtiers, to persuade myself that his Majesty's present Severities acquitted me of all past Obligations.

Yet this same Gulliver in Book II becomes very like a Lilliputian himself, for in his new situation magnanimity is impossible and he feels a constant need to insist on "the Dignity of human Kind" by behavior which he later recognizes as absurd. After being ignominiously carried off by the pet monkey, he tells the King:

> And as for that monstrous Animal with whom I was so lately engaged, (it was indeed as large as an Elephant) if my Fears had suffered me to think so far as to make Use of my Hanger (looking fiercely, and clapping my Hand upon the Hilt as I spoke) when he poked his Paw into my Chamber, perhaps I should have given him such a Wound, as would have made him glad to withdraw it with more Haste than he put it in. This I delivered in a firm Tone, like a Person who was jealous lest his Courage should be called in Question. However, my Speech produced nothing else besides a loud Laughter.

This conceited posturing little creature is a different person from the kindly, humble Gulliver of Book I, so much has his character changed with his physical situation. In Brobdingnag he is constantly subjected to great danger both to life and to character from causes in themselves trifling, and the resulting sense of the precariousness of human life and virtue is reinforced by his account of an old Brobdingnagian treatise which he found in the possession of Glumdalclitch's governess, "a grave elderly Gentlewoman, who dealt in Writings of Morality and Devotion." Gulliver's condescending attitude towards this "little old Treatise" warns us that we are to take the passage seriously. The book treats, he says, "of the Weakness of Human kind; and is in little Esteem except among Women and the Vulgar." Certainly the ideas put forward are not new or progressive, being familiar to us as to Swift from countless of the more old-fashioned moral works of the seventeenth century. But though the ideas are trite, and naïvely expressed, the writer's intention, to bring down man's pride by showing him as, "in his own Nature," a weak and helpless animal, is a serious matter. Montaigne is an obvious source, and Godfrey Goodman's *The Fall of Man, or the Corruption of Nature* (1616), a work which presents in the form of a straightforward treatise the view of mankind which Swift found it necessary to express in the poems and *Gulliver's Travels* through attack and indirection, makes much of man's natural weakness. Such notions are likely to be dismissed by Gulliver, who is at this point inclined to be complacent about human achievement and is a great lover of mankind. For the writer "went through all the usual Topicks of European Moralists; shewing how diminutive, contemptible, and helpless an Animal was Man in his own Nature; how unable to defend himself from Inclemencies of the Air, or the Fury of wild Beasts: How much he was excelled by one Creature in Strength, by another in Speed, by a third in Foresight, by a fourth in Industry." The author is also convinced of the physical degeneracy of giant man, and believes that at one time he was "not so liable to Destruction from every little Accident of a Tile falling from a House, or a Stone cast from the Hand of a Boy, or of being drowned in a little Brook." From all this were drawn "several moral Applications useful in the Conduct of Life," but Gulliver thinks it needless to repeat them, and shows how ill he has learned the lesson of relativity when he assumes that the large size of the giants, and of their stones and their brooks, invalidates the author's arguments and so, by implication, the view of European moralists that fallen man is insecure, weak, a stranger on the earth. For the author of the treatise is really underlining the theme of the first two voyages, the lesson which the King, with his firm sane moral standards, is so quick to draw from his contemplation of diminutive man: "he observed, how contemptible a Thing was human Grandeur, which could be mimicked by such diminutive Insects as I."

The giants themselves are the third element in the complicated relationships of Lilliput and Brobdingnag, and it is in them that the physical or animal aspects of humanity are most forcibly thrust upon our attention. Their enormous bodies are insisted upon; there are descriptions of their skin and beards and gestures and of the horrors of disease and dirt in the beggars, infested by vermin whose limbs Gulliver could see "much better than those of an European Louse through a Microscope; and their Snouts with which they rooted like Swine." The nastiness of these creatures brings additional force to the King's condemnation of the little odious vermin, man, and the reference to a microscope relates the Brobdingnagians to ourselves, as does the magnifying glass which, Gulliver supposes, would make the fine skin of English ladies look as coarse as that of the giants. The behavior of the Queen's maids of honor brings us close to the anti-romantic poems with their plea for a decent reticence; in both the human body is being used deliberately, not as an outlet for physical disgust in Swift himself but to present a moral truth. The Brobdingnagians are akin to the Yahoos in that they embody the physical and its senses and passions, but they differ from the Yahoos in the same way that Gulliver does; they are not a part of man, but man. In their case the physical is deliberately stressed because through his handling of relativity Swift intends to impress upon us man's weakness and limitations and above all the power of flesh and blood which must always be reckoned with. But the Brobdingnagians are not simple creatures like the Yahoos, or even like the Lilliputians. In Lilliput, everyone is much the same: one can generalize easily enough about the Lilliputian character. In Brobdingnag, there is considerable variation among the people, and as individuals they are more complex than any of the creatures of the *Travels* except the Europeans of Book IV. The giants can be cruel through selfishness and avarice, like Gulliver's first owner the farmer, who wears him out by constant showing and then makes haste to sell him before he dies; they can be jealous like Gulliver's enemy the dwarf, or playfully lascivious like the maids of honor, or stupid through vanity like the scholars. They are, in fact, very like ourselves, easily swayed by self-love and the desires and passions common to humanity. But it is not only our tendency to brutishness and selfishness that is displayed in them; they also possess human warmth, sympathy, and affection; the animal side of man is shown in its capacity for good as well as for evil, and the huge size of the giants can impress upon us not only animality but expansive good humor, magnanimity, and a breadth of moral understanding. The motherliness of the farmer's wife, the graciousness of the Queen, the loyal, protective affection of Gulliver's young "nurse," are attractive examples of human goodness, and Glumdalclitch in particular, so enormous and yet so delicately understanding of the feelings of her difficult charge, is as admirable an illustration of the value of well-regulated affections in human relationships as is the delightful Mrs. Robert Cope of "The First of April." The people of Brobdingnag have the same bearing on human behavior as the government of Brobdingnag has upon human states: there is nothing utopian or ideal about them, but they are the best that man can attain. They have come to terms with reality, and in them mind and body have established a fruitful relationship. They are not interested in abstract reasoning—"as to Ideas, Entities, Abstractions and Transcendentals, I could never drive the least Conception into their Heads"—they are well aware of man's limitations and attempt only what they are capable of. Their reasoning powers are used for practical and benevolent purposes, to ameliorate human conditions, to "make two Ears of Corn, or Two Blades of Grass to grow upon a Spot of Ground where only one grew before."

The wisest and best of the Brobdingnagians is the King, who, as Gulliver admits, is "a Prince of excellent Understanding," but whose intelligence exercises itself strictly within the limits of a firmly moral conception of life. It is because of this that Gulliver regards him as narrowminded; his contempt for what he has heard of Europe is the result of moral condemnation. No amount of achievement or ingenuity can impress the King if it leads to evil results, to cruelty and inhumanity, and Gulliver is accordingly moved to tell him that this attitude of contempt and disgust "did not seem answerable to those excellent Qualities of Mind, that he was Master of." His own government is essentially moral, based on his human and kingly duties to the governed and concerned with their welfare, and his comments on Europe are expressed in terms of practical morality. He is quick to see what Gulliver will not admit, that humanity on the whole is always ready to distort what seems, in the abstract, a good political scheme, through bribery and self-interest, and it is because he is aware of the need to prevent this that he is such a good ruler. "It doth not appear," he says at last, "from all you have said, how any one Perfection is required towards the Procurement of any one Station among you; much less that Men are ennobled on account of their Virtue, that Priests are advanced for their Piety or Learning, Soldiers for their Conduct or Valour, Judges for their Integrity, Senators for the Love of their Country, or Counsellors for their Wisdom." And it is a mark of his tolerance and charity that he delivers his judgment on the little vermin while gently stroking their representative, the "little friend Grildrig" to whom he shows such affectionate forbearance. The King has, indeed, attained that unillusioned view of man which Swift advocated and tried himself to achieve; his sober clear sight into the motives of mankind is to him a reason not for hatred but for pity and charity and practical help. The clearest instance of his moral thinking and his unfailing humanity is his response to Gulliver's offer to give him the secret of gunpowder: "although few Things delighted him so much as new Discoveries in Art or in Nature; yet he would rather lose Half his Kingdom than be privy to such a Secret." This time even the realistic and tolerant King is horrified at Gulliver's revelation of human depravity, and "amazed how so impotent and groveling an Insect as I (these were his Expressions) could entertain such inhuman Ideas, and in so familiar a Manner as to appear wholly unmoved at all the Scenes of Blood and Desolation, which I had painted as the common Effects of those destructive Machines." Gulliver's comment is "A Strange Effect of narrow Principles and short Views!" But after all, he considers, the remoteness of Brobdingnag necessarily produces "many Prejudices, and a certain Narrowness of Thinking; from which we and the politer Countries of Europe are wholly exempted. And it would be hard indeed, if so remote a Prince's Notions of Virtue and Vice were to be offered as a Standard for all Mankind." Through the disapproval of Gulliver we are made aware that the compassionate King of Brobdingnag is Swift's positive standard for man, and this hint is repeated by Gulliver in the twelfth and final chapter of the "Voyage to the Houyhnhnms," where Gulliver, now obsessed by the pure reason of the alien Houyhnhnm race, and loathing all men, whom he erroneously equates with Yahoos, grudgingly admits that "the least corrupted are the Brobdingnagians, whose wise Maxims in Morality and Government, it would be our Happiness to observe." One can put it that this indirect commendation is all that Swift's ironic method itself will allow him to make, but it is truer to say that the ironic method itself is the result of Swift's reluctance to put forward an unambiguous standard. For always he is saying not simply, "This is what man should aim at" but rather "This is all that man can aim at." Limitation, compromise, humility, must be inherent in his positives, and so they must be presented indirectly, almost grudgingly, as the best that can be had. Gulliver's words, while they express the supreme irony that in aiming too high he has fallen too low, and is blind to achievable goodness, are also accurate: the Brobdingnagians are not perfect; they are, precisely, the least corrupted of fallen humanity. But this limitation by no means implies despair. The King and the Queen and Glumdalclitch show that the best that corrupt mankind can attain to is high indeed, but that it can only be reached by a humble realism and a recognition that the passions, senses, instinctive affections, if guided by reason working within a moral context, can issue in true human goodness. Swift's ability to embody ideas in the persons of men and women stands him here in good stead, for the warmth and reality, the charm and the human responsibility, of the best of the Brobdingnagians can hardly fail not only to convey his conception of the goodness proper to man but to convince us that it is both admirable and true.

But of course we can only see the Brobdingnagian virtue, and its meaning in the whole structure, when we have read to the end of the *Travels*. The immediate effect of the first two books is of growing unease, not of acceptance of a standard, for the compromise standard has to be worked out when all the creatures are assembled and when what at first seems to be an absolute good—the life of the Houyhnhnms—has been shown to be a false simplification. The world of Brobdingnag is solid and sane, but we are not yet allowed to rest at ease in it. Our amusement and annoyance with the Lilliputians and their antlike organization, and our approval of the decency of unpolitical man as displayed in Gulliver, are turned to uncertainty as we find ourselves in the shifting world of relativity and discover that Gulliver is far from being a norm of behavior and that according to circumstances he can be as mean-minded and vain as a Lilliputian, and even more inhuman. Moreover, Gulliver, we begin to see, is apt to draw very wrong conclusions from his experiences. Even in Lilliput, where he is seen to best advantage, he too readily accepts Lilliputian standards, and talks quite seriously of the great nobles, and of the honors he has received in this ridiculous little state. For instance: "I should not have dwelt so long upon this Particular, if it had not been a Point wherein the Reputation of a great Lady is so nearly concerned; to say nothing of my own; although I had the Honour to be a Nardac, which the Treasurer himself is not; for all the World knows he is only a Clumglum, a Title inferior by one Degree, as that of a Marquess is to a Duke in England; yet I allow he preceded me in right of his Post." In Brobdingnag, his reactions to the King's opinions are quite clearly wrong, and he learns nothing from his visit except to be ill at ease at home, fancying his friends and relatives undersized, and looking at them "as if they had been Pigmies, and I a Giant." In a little time, he came to an understanding with his family and friends, but his wife protested he should never go to sea any more. She was in the right, for Gulliver's malleable character and his aptitude for enthusiastic misunderstanding were to lead to worse and more permanent difficulty after his last voyage, when the furthest accommodation he reports is that "I began last Week to permit my Wife to sit at Dinner with me, at the farthest End of a long Table; and to answer (but with the utmost Brevity) the few Questions I asked her." Thus the qualities necessary to a satiric mouthpiece—the inconsistency, the

palpable wrongheadedness and absurdity, that lack, indeed, of a positive
character, so essential if ironic comment is to be made on any but the
simplest scale—are turned with the greatest precision and economy to further purpose.

The insecurity and uncertainty of direction we feel at the end of the
"Voyage to Brobdingnag" is heightened in Book III. The success of this
book is not at all easy for a modern reader to gauge. Its sharp contrast in
method, with the grotesque figures of the Laputans and the excursions into
magic and immortality, certainly breaks the atmosphere of moral realism
which pervades the voyages to Lilliput, Brobdingnag, and Houyhnhnmland; even the rational horses belong to a world of morality, not of fantasy.
This third book, the latest written, would be, by us, the least missed. But
on the other hand the fantasy world of Laputa, in its madness and delusion,
still further shakes our wits and our confidence before the final resolution
of Book IV, and the Laputan lunacies have, after all, a moral connotation
as we can see if we remember *A Tale of a Tub*. But for us, to whom the
scientific outlook is a commonplace, it is not so easy to see the "Voyage
to Laputa" in terms of modern vice and traditional virtue, and we find it
less striking than the other voyages, where moral problems are more overtly
considered though their presentation is influenced by contemporary thinking. Only the episode of the Struldbruggs of Luggnagg, unencumbered as
it is by topical satire, strikes us with the immediate force and the moral
emphasis of the second and fourth books, for to a modern reader scientific
experiment is a less acceptable example of irrelevant thinking than are the
speculations of Burnet or of Thomas Vaughan. Swift's opinion of the scientific achievement of his day is, in itself, inadequate, and considered as an
attack on science the third book must seem wrongheaded and unfair. But
considered as what it really is, an allegorical presentation of the evils of a
frivolous attitude to life, it is consistent and effective, however unjust we
may consider Swift's chosen allegory to be.

For the visit to Laputa itself, and to the subject land of Balnibarbi, has
a more serious intention than the topical one of ridiculing the Royal Society.
The flying island, though it has a precise relationship—even as to size—
with William Gilbert's dipping-needle, and though it uses Gilbert's idea
"of the Earth's whole Body being but one great Magnet; and, lesser Magnets
being so many Terrella's sympathising with the Whole," presents through
this contemporary scientific interest a political philosophy and a comment
on man's relation to nature which go beyond the merely topical: beyond
particular scientific discoveries or the relation of the kingdoms of England
and Ireland. The flying island, "the King's Demesn," in its devious and

sensitive oblique movements, suggests the relationship of king and country. Laputa is ultimately dependent upon Balnibarbi, its motions only allowed by the magnetic quality of the "King's Dominions." It is this quality which has allowed the Laputan king to establish his power over the fixed land, but there is a reciprocal dependence, for if either side pressed its power too far the result would be general ruin. The King's last resource, in case of defiance from the populace of Balnibarbi, is to let the flying island drop upon their heads, but this, though it would certainly destroy both houses and men, would at the same time damage the adamant of Laputa itself.

> Of all this the People are well apprized, and understand how far to carry their Obstinacy, where their Liberty or Property is concerned. And the King, when he is highest provoked, and most determined to press a City to Rubbish, orders the Island to descend with great Gentleness, out of a Pretence of Tenderness to his People, but indeed for fear of breaking the Adamantine Bottom; in which Case it is the Opinion of all their Philosophers, that the Load-Stone could no longer hold it up, and the whole Mass would fall to the Ground.

As for the nobles and ministers, they are in part committed to the welfare of both lands, for while they attend at the Laputan court their estates lie on the continent below, so that they will never dare advise the King to make himself "the most absolute Prince in the Universe" by so ruthless and desperate a course. The balance of power, and the delicate relationships which subsist between a monarch and those whom he governs, could scarcely be better represented than by conditions in Laputa and Balnibarbi, and it is typical of Swift that these relationships, though given a color of respect for human life and liberties, are seen to be really dependent upon the exact adjustment of practical necessities; the self-love of each party is carried as far as it can go without that open conflict with the self-love of others which would bring it to destruction.

Further, the relation of the greater and lesser magnets, Laputa and Balnibarbi, suggests the limited usefulness of that understanding of the laws of the universe upon which the Newtonian era so prided itself, and which is one of the main objects of Swift's satiric comment in this book. The Laputan king, for all his knowledge of cosmic circumstance, for all the ingenuity of his flying island, is yet dependent upon the firm earth beneath him for every movement Laputa can make; for all his theoretic achievement man is, in practice, dependent upon and circumscribed by other men and by laws of nature, of which he can take a certain limited advantage but which he can neither alter nor, finally, explain. The astronomers of Laputa, although they have written "large Systems concerning the Stone" whose movements control the course of the flying island, can give no better reason for the inability of Laputa to rise above four miles, or to move beyond the extent of the King's continental dominions, than the self-evident one "That the Magnetick Virtue does not extend beyond the Distance of four Miles, and that the Mineral which acts upon the Stone in the Bowels of the Earth, and in the Sea about Six Leagues distant from the Shoar, is not diffused through the whole Globe, but terminated with the Limits of the King's Dominions." Their pursuit of second causes ends in inscrutable mystery, which their confident exposition can only conceal, not clarify. The allegory of Laputa and of Balnibarbi, "controlled by that which it alone controls," is indeed an epitome of the situation more fully explored in the detailed descriptions of the inhabitants of the flying island and of conditions on the mainland below; the neat, generalized relationships help us to find our way in the confusion of the Academy of Projectors and the alien clarities of the Laputan court.

The Laputans, though they are in human shape, are more obviously allegorical creatures than any in *Gulliver's Travels*. Their physical characteristics express their nature as do those of the Brobdingnagians or the Yahoos but in a different way. Their effect is made not through exaggeration or isolation but through distortion, of the physical, and though by this means much of the force of Swift's greatest figures is lost, this is in itself part of the meaning, since the Laputans have indeed lost their human quality in their abnormal absorption in things remote from the concerns of men. They make little physical effect upon us, for their outer aspect is as unnatural, as purely emblematic, as that of a personification like Spenser's Occasion: "One of their Eyes turned inward, and the other directly up to the Zenith" because they are completely absorbed in their own speculations and in the study of the stars. Their interests are entirely abstract, and they see nothing of the everyday practical world, ignoring the knowledge of the senses as totally as Jack or the philosopher of *A Tale of a Tub*. The Laputan is "always so wrapped up in Cogitation, that he is in manifest Danger of falling down every Precipice, and bouncing his Head against every Post; and in the Streets, of jostling others, or being jostled himself into the Kennel." Because they scorn the evidence of the senses, the Laputans are necessarily "very bad Reasoners," though very positive and dogmatic ones, for the senses are "so many Avenues to the Fort of Reason," which in them as in the mechanical operators of the spirit is wholly blocked up. These strange figures are akin not only to the mechanical operators but more closely to the spiderlike world-makers. Like the author of *A Tale of a Tub*, they are less consistent than inclusive, summing up various departures from the middle way. One eye looks outward, but only to a remote world of abstractions where, in the regular motions of the heavens, mathematics and music join. One eye looks inward, to the mind where systems are spun out of a "Native Stock," not built up from that basis of observed fact which, however faulty our senses, is yet the only material upon which our reason can work constructively and practically. Laputan thinking produces results as flimsy and useless as a cobweb—Gulliver's ill-fitting suit, the devastated countryside of Balnibarbi.

The King and his court are devoted entirely to two subjects, music and mathematics, the most abstract of sciences. There is a topical reference, in that an interest in these "two eternal and immutable verities" and in the analogies between them serves to identify the Laputans as members of the Royal Society, but for centuries an interest in the relationship of mathematics and music had existed, so that it was by no means an exclusively contemporary concern. In the Middle Ages music, regarded as a mathematical science, had been one of the purest embodiments of unchanging law, and the Laputans with their absorption in music, mathematics, and astronomy, represent specifically the members of the Royal Society but more generally all those who believe that, by turning away from the impressions of the senses and the ordinary concerns of human nature they can ignore sublunary confusion and reach eternal truth. Swift's reference to the music of the spheres emphasizes this more general meaning; the Laputans spend hours at their instruments, preparing themselves to join in the music of the spheres, which they claim to be able to hear. Since mankind is traditionally deaf to this music because of the grossness of the senses through sin, the claim implies that the Laputans believe themselves to have escaped from such tyranny. To their impracticality is added the presumption of ignoring the inherited wisdom which sees man as a fallen creature separated, through his own fault, from the order, truth, and justice figured in the celestial harmony of the nine enfolded spheres.

The narrowness, even to inhumanity, of the Laputans is indeed stressed throughout. They have cut themselves off completely from all that is humanly creative and constructive. Even their food approaches as nearly as possible to the rarefied atmosphere in which they live, for their meat is carved into geometrical shapes and their poultry trussed up "into the Form of Fiddles." Nor have they any conception of physical or sensuous beauty, since they see beauty only in mathematical abstractions, and judge not by sense impressions but by an arbitrary relation of animal forms to abstract shapes existing in their minds: "If they would, for Example, praise the Beauty of a Woman, or any other Animal, they describe it by Rhombs, Circles, Parallelograms, Ellipses, and other Geometrical Terms; or else by Words of Art drawn from Musick . . . the whole Compass of their Thoughts and Mind, being shut up within the two forementioned Sciences." But the world of human beings cannot be adequately dealt with in mathematical terms, and their wives, as a consequence, have fallen into matter, escaping whenever possible into a life altogether physical and degraded, as exaggeratedly animal as that of their husbands is exaggeratedly intellectual. The King has no interest in "the Laws, Government, History, Religion, or Manners of the Countries" Gulliver has visited, and his realm of Balnibarbi is chaotic. Gulliver "could not discover one Ear of Corn, or Blade of Grass" except in a few places, during his journeys, and our minds revert to the kingdom of Brobdingnag, the land which has been called a "simple Utopia of abundance," where government is conducted with practical good will and a due regard for traditional wisdom, and where the King regards his task as one of promoting increase and life, making "two Ears of Corn, or two Blades of Grass, to grow where only one grew before." The Laputans, on the other hand, produce a world of death, and the results of their efforts are purely destructive because their aims are impossibly high and are unrelated to real conditions. Some day, they say, "a Palace may be built in a Week, of Materials so durable as to last for ever without repairing. All the Fruits of the Earth shall come to Maturity at whatever Season we think fit to chuse, and increase an Hundred Fold more than they do at present; with innumerable other happy Proposals." In the meantime, houses are ruined, land uncultivated, and people starving, and the only result of Laputan enterprise on the prosperous estate of the old-fashioned Lord Munodi has been to destroy the mill which had long provided his family and tenants, in order to make way for one which should, on scientific principles, be better, but which somehow fails to work. Samuel Johnson sums up in similar terms the humanist sense of the Royal Society's irrelevance to true and living values:

When the philosophers of the last age were first congregated into the Royal Society, great expectations were raised of the sudden progress of useful arts; the time was supposed to be near, when engines should turn by a perpetual motion, and health be secured by the universal medicine; when learning should be facilitated by a real character, and commerce extended by ships which could reach their ports in defiance of the tempest.

> But improvement is naturally slow. The Society met and parted without any visible diminution of the miseries of life. The gout and stone were still painful, the ground that was not ploughed brought no harvest, and neither oranges nor grapes would grow upon the hawthorn.

That Munodi, the one successful landowner in Balnibarbi, should be a traditionalist is only to be expected; "being not of an enterprizing Spirit, he was content to go on in the old Forms; to live in the Houses his Ancestors had built, and act as they did in every Part of Life without Innovation."

The activities of the members of the Academy of Projectors, though they involve experiment, are yet related to the abstract thinking of the King. For the most part, they are based on some wrongheaded abstract conception, and are really examples of what Pope calls reasoning downward, taking "the High Priori Road"; they are aspects, therefore, of the great modern heresy of ignoring "the old Forms" and relying on a spiderlike spinning of thought. By blending experiment and High Priori reasoning in the Academy at Lagado, Swift is able to show scientific "projects" as yet another example of that whole development of thinking which leads away from the ways of a Christian and humanist tradition, and Pope's lines would refer as well to the mathematicians of Laputa and the scientists of Lagado as they do to Hobbes, Descartes, Spinoza, and Samuel Clarke:

> Let others creep by timid steps, and slow,
> On plain Experience lay foundations low,
> By common sense to common knowledge bred,
> And last, to Nature's Cause through Nature led.

Indeed one of the projects is an exact allegorical equivalent of the process of reasoning downward to, instead of upward from, the foundations of plain experience: "There was a most ingenious Architect who had contrived a new Method for building Houses, by beginning at the Roof, and working downwards to the Foundation; which he justified to me by the like Practice of those two prudent Insects the Bee and the Spider." We are not told the results of this method, but in other cases the ideas of the projectors do not well stand up to experiment; for instance, the notion of "plowing the Ground with Hogs to save the Charges of Plows, Cattle, and Labour" results, "upon Experiment," in no crop and a great deal of trouble and expense.

The experiments and their results allow Swift to collect together various images which, as so often, express his meaning through producing a

certain atmosphere which must affect our response to Laputa and Balnibarbi. These projects leave an impression of uselessness, dirt, ephemerality,
or death; the Academicians present for our inspection a spider web, a hog
rooting up acorns, a muddle of painters' colors, a dead dog. Their efforts
are summed up in an illustrious member who has been given the title of
"the Universal Artist," and who has been for thirty years directing his
followers in various ways of converting things into their opposites, thus
turning the useful into the unusable and the vital into the atrophied. Air is
made tangible and marble soft, land is sown with chaff and naked sheep
are bred; and perhaps most exact of all as an epitome of the achievements
of the Academy, the hooves of a living horse are being petrified. The
projects of Lagado are, in fact, conducted in an atmosphere similar to that
of *A Tale of a Tub,* an atmosphere of aimless activity, distorted values, and
a perversion of things from their proper purpose even to the point of
removing all life and meaning from them. The results produced are woolless
sheep, dead dogs, horses whose living hooves are turned to stone. The
mechanism of the *Tale* exists in Lagado, too, in the machine which is to
replace the thinking and creating mind of man and will, by pure chance,
eventually produce "Books in Philosophy, Poetry, Politicks, Law, Math-
ematicks and Theology." While the prevailing effect of the images we
associate with Lilliput and, especially, Brobdingnag is of man and other
animals as vigorous physical presences, the effect of Laputa and its subject
kingdom is of a wilful abandoning of the physical and of the vital for the
abstract, the mechanical, and the unproductive. The prevailing images here
are not of real people and animals, even "little odious vermin," but of ruins,
mechanical constructions, men who look like allegorical figures, and
women who are thought of as rhomboids or parallelograms. Animals are
only negatively present, as in the pathetic horses and sheep of the Academy.
Even Laputa itself is a mechanical device, and the flying island expresses
not only the Laputans' desertion of the common earth of reality but their
conversion of the universe to a mechanism and of living to a mechanical
process.

From Lagado Gulliver makes his way to Glubbdubdrib, where again
he is in a world of no-meaning, of delusion and death, darker and more
shadowy than Laputa. In the palace of the sorcerer who is governor of the
island he has a series of singularly uninformative interviews with the ghosts
of the famous dead, and Alexander and Hannibal, who as conquerors and
destroyers had little to recommend them to Swift, make particularly trivial
replies. We are given a gloomy enough picture of both the ancient and the
modern world, and upon this ghostly history follows the most somber

episode of all, that of the Struldbruggs of Luggnagg, in which the lesson of Laputa with its naïve hopes, its misplaced ambition, and its eventual sterility is repeated with more open seriousness. A right sense of values, a proper attitude to living, is here suggested not through the handling of contemporary aims and habits of thought but through the figure of man, immortal yet still painfully recognizable, and perhaps owing some of its power and poignancy to Swift's own fear of death and, still more, of decay, of a lingering old age giving way at last to helpless lunacy. Gulliver, hearing of the immortals, cries out "as in a Rapture," exclaiming upon the wisdom and happiness which they must have achieved. They must, he says, "being born exempt from that universal Calamity of human Nature, have their Minds free and disingaged, without the Weight and Depression of Spirits caused by the continual Apprehension of Death," and he is only too willing to tell his hearers how he would plan his life, if he were a Struldbrugg, to bring the greatest possible benefit to himself and his country. In fact, of course, the immortal and aged creatures, though free from the fear of death, are yet as full of fears and wretchedness as any other men: being what we are, we will always find occasion to display those vices which as human beings we will always have, however long we may live. The Struldbruggs certainly do not keep their minds free and disengaged, and for them the prospect of endless life does not conjure up visions of endless improvement in wisdom and virtue. They regard their immortality as a "dreadful Prospect" even as other men regard their death, and indeed they long to die as did the wretched Sibyl in Petronius's *Satyricon,* regarding with great jealousy those of their acquaintance who go "to an Harbour of Rest, to which they themselves never can hope to arrive." Immortal man is still man, limited in his capacity for growth, sinful, fearful, dissatisfied; the somber simplicity of the passage, and indeed of the whole of the visit to Glubbdubdrib, is reminiscent of Johnson's methods rather than of Swift's, and the message is essentially similar. Gulliver, who has dreamed of being a king, a general, or a great lord, and now dreams of being a Struldbrugg, has to learn the same lesson as the Prince of Abyssinia: that life is a serious, difficult, and above all a moral undertaking, that whatever excuses we may find for ourselves, however we may dream of the greatness we could have achieved under other conditions, we will realize at last that humanity is always the same, and that there is no escape from our vices and our trivialities. Gulliver says that he grew "heartily ashamed of the pleasing Visions I had formed; and thought no Tyrant could invent a Death into which I would not run with Pleasure from such a Life," and that he would have been willing, if it had not been forbidden by the laws of Luggnagg, to send a couple of

Struldbruggs to England to arm the people against that fear of death which is natural to mankind.

So the "Voyage to Laputa," which opens among a people essentially frivolous in its refusal to face the facts of human existence, ends face to face with inescapable reality. Laputa, where the search for the clarity of abstractions involves such confusion in the living world, seems at first merely hilarious and absurd, but as confusion turns to mechanism and destruction this remoteness and unreality becomes not only ludicrous but evil, and the countries about Laputa and Balnibarbi are seen to be places of superstition, sorcery, and tyranny, of ghosts and the corpselike immortals of Luggnagg. The voyage to illusion, the escape from facts, ends in a darker reality than any Gulliver has yet encountered. Gulliver himself, in this book, becomes a part of the world of illusion and distorted values. Already in the earlier voyages the shifting, inconsistent quality which Gulliver shares with all Swift's satiric mouthpieces has been made to contribute to effects of relativity, and to suggest the hold of physical circumstances over mankind. That he is, generally, a different man in Brobdingnag and in Lilliput is made into part of Swift's presentation of human nature. In the "Voyage to Laputa," any still surviving notion that Gulliver is a safe guide through these strange countries is ended. He ceases to have any character and, in effect, vanishes, so that for the most part the satire speaks directly to us; the "mouthpiece" performs no real function. The transparent account of "Tribnia, by the Natives called Langden," where "the Bulk of the People consisted wholly of Discoverers, Witnesses, Informers, Accusers, Prosecutors, Evidences, Swearers," owes nothing to Gulliver, and would be quite inconceivable from what we have known of him before; in the second voyage he had "wished for the Tongue of Demosthenes or Cicero, that might have enabled me to celebrate the Praise of my own dear native Country in a Style equal to its Merits and Felicity." Here he is being frankly used for ironic comment, as his exaggerated enthusiasm shows; in the description of Tribnia, he is not being used at all. From time to time he is given a momentary reality, but of the most perfunctory kind; there is no attempt to endow him even with the one or two dominant characteristics that he is given elsewhere. His approval of projects, or his tendency to dream about impossible situations instead of getting on with the business of living, his dismissal of obviously desirable political reforms as "wild impossible Chimaeras," are, quite openly, mentioned for satiric purposes of a very simple kind. The handling of Gulliver is in fact far less interesting, and his contribution is far slighter, than in any other book, probably because his function had been worked to its limits in the voyages already written, which included the "Voyage to the Houyhnhnms." But whether or not Swift planned it so, Gulliver's virtual lack of function, indeed of existence, in the "Voyage to Laputa" has a certain effectiveness in contributing to the atmosphere of meaningless activity and self-deceit, leading to a shadowy despair. The gradual undermining of the comparatively solid worlds of Lilliput and Brobdingnag was achieved partly through a shift in Gulliver's position; here he merges completely into his surroundings, and serves merely to describe what he sees, so that we cannot take him seriously as an interpreter. When he reappears in Book IV, we are well prepared to find that his function will not be a simple one either of sensible comment on the vagaries of a strange country, or of admiration for a Utopia, for we have accepted him as one of the many figures in the *Travels*, expressing meaning by his relationship to them, and no more exempt than they from satiric treatment. As a completion of the processes begun in Lilliput and Brobdingnag, and as a preparation for the resolution in Houyhnhnmland, the Laputan voyage performs its task adequately, though without the formal elegance and neatness of the other books.

Of all the voyages, the fourth is perhaps the most satisfying, both in its fullness of content and in the completeness of its expression. It is also the voyage about which there has been most divergency of view, and though there is no longer any question of its being regarded, as it once was, as the splenetic outburst of a man consumed by hatred of "Human Name, and Face," critical opinion is still divided on the question of Swift's precise meaning. It was formerly assumed that the Houyhnhnms were intended as perfected human beings whom man should try to copy, or alternatively as faultless rational creatures whose nobility serves to show up the evil of mankind. But if the Houyhnhnms are Swift's positive ideal, attainable by man or not, many difficulties arise; for this interpretation must mean that his satiric method is much more simple and direct than elsewhere, and that the attitude of mind is quite different from that which his other work has led us to expect. In recent years there has been increasing support for the view that Swift did not intend his Houyhnhnms as a simple positive standard, and various possible alternatives have been put forward. Opinion varies, also, as to the success of this book; it is sometimes said that it fails to make its meaning effective and clear, and that Swift has mishandled his allegorical narrative and the creatures within it. But in fact it is, I believe, the most perfectly managed of all Swift's satires. Of course it is partly dependent on the earlier books for its success, but Swift takes full advantage of the meanings established, and the psychological effect made, in them, and in the "Voyage to the Houyhnhnms" he sums up, with the utmost economy of means, the suggestions made in Laputa, Lilliput, and Brobdingnag. In a way, it is a summing up of all his work, for it is his most complete and effective presentation of that central conviction from which his moral, political, and social views arise, a conviction about the nature of man. Implicit in all his work, this preoccupation here becomes explicit in the creatures of Houyhnhnmland, in the Houyhnhnms themselves, the Yahoos, Gulliver, the Portuguese sea captain Don Pedro, and, by association, the Brobdingnagians. But though Swift's concern with the moral nature of man here becomes explicit, and is no longer seen through particular human activities such as science, politics, literature, it is still indirectly expressed. The components of meaning are given plainly enough, but the conclusion, though present, is present by implication as the middle way, the acceptable and vital compromise between two sterile extremes. The meticulous balance of figures expresses meaning, and gives shape and point to the more discursive methods of the earlier voyages, while the figures themselves are the most perfectly conceived of all Swift's symbols.

Clear and precise though it is in its main outlines, the fourth voyage carries a great weight of meaning, and though it is less obviously tight-packed with learning than *A Tale of a Tub,* much of Swift's reading, as well as of his thinking and his conversation, lies behind it. Part of its force is due, indeed, to the fact that in it the experience of a lifetime, whether personal or public, the experience of political and social life or of solitary reading and thinking, is ordered into complete expression, so that it relates at many points to his other writings. By reference, imagery, parody, the clear issues of Houyhnhnmland are linked with the actual life of civilized man. The literary connections of this voyage are particularly obvious and, of course, vital to its understanding. The voyages to Lilliput and Brobdingnag owe little of importance to travel literature; the matter-of-fact tone and the detailed exactness of description may have been borrowed from it, but these were effects Swift had always been able to produce for satiric purpose, and the possible debts to Cyrano or to Francis Godwin are hardly significant. The "Voyage to Laputa," the least original of all, is in the tradition of the fantastic and satiric voyages, but its relation to them is simple and derivative; the complications of Laputa depend on the handling of topical interests, not in the handling of an existing literary form. But in the "Voyage to the Houyhnhnms," we have to deal with an ancient, formidable, and ambiguous tradition, that of the rational Utopia; and on our interpretation of the relationship between Houyhnhnmland and that tradition depends our interpretation of meaning. In considering this, we must remember what had been made of the Utopia tradition in Swift's own time, for in all his writing he is a man of his age, concerned as an Augustan writer was always concerned with the attitudes of his own contemporaries. He deals with the fundamental concerns of humanity, but his way of dealing with them is conditioned by what other men are making of them, and this is as true of the "Voyage to the Houyhnhnms" as of the visit to Laputa, or of *A Tale of a Tub*.

In the later seventeenth century the Utopian voyage, in the general sense of an account of a visit to a land of perfect or near perfect beings who are then used as a standard to condemn societies of men, was often used, especially by the *libertins* of France, as a convenient and comparatively safe method of attacking Christianity. The primitivism which had resulted from tales of the noble savages discovered by explorers lent color to such accounts; and though these voyages are necessarily ambiguous and sprinkled with pious comments the conclusion really meant to be drawn from contemplation of the virtuous pagans is, often, not that since they have reached such goodness without the aid of revelation Christian societies should be able to achieve far more, but that their goodness shows the moral failure and the falsity of revealed religion. For the freethinkers their purpose is, in fact, the same as that of the philosophers of the ancient world as set out by Swift in his sermon "Upon the Excellency of Christianity"; from their superior wisdom and virtue reached "purely upon the strength of their own reason and liberty of thinking," we are intended to draw the conclusion that "either all Revelation is false, or what is worse, that it hath depraved the nature of man, and left him worse than it found him." These Utopian races were generally guided by reason, like the *"Hommes raisonnables"* of Claude Gilbert, who are truly happy, their happiness being *"conforme à la nature et à la raison, qui ont établi les règles qui doivent l'assurer."* Denis Veiras's *Histoire des Sevarambes,* which after appearing in England and France in the late 1670's was printed as part of a spurious third volume of *Gulliver's Travels* in 1727, attacks religion through its presentation of the virtuous Australian Sevarambes, akin to men but living in a society based on reason and natural law. One of the most extreme of these voyages is that of Gabriel de Foigny, free-liver as well as freethinker, who as an unfrocked monk later expelled from Geneva doubtless conceived a particular spite against revealed religion. Foigny's *La Terre Australe Connue* was published in 1676, recast in 1692, and translated into English in 1693. There is no indication that Swift had read this, or any of the voyages I have mentioned, but it is at least possible that he had, since we know that he read travel literature and since *Gulliver's Travels* itself displays a thorough familiarity with "voyages" of various kinds. The fourth voyage above all, with its easy handling of the conventions and ideas of the philosophic or Utopian voyage, could scarcely have been written in ignorance of the tradition as it had continued through the seventeenth century, whether or not these particular examples of it were known to Swift. Certainly there are likenesses between this voyage and *La Terre Australe Connue* as far as its materials are concerned, likenesses both in particular instances and in the general arrangement of figures; but Foigny's book is only a typical example of such voyages, though in the sharp contrast between the rational inhabitants of Australia on the one hand and man, regarded by the Australians as near-bestial, on the other, the point of this kind of travel literature is made with a peculiar sharpness. The striking difference between Swift's version of the seventeenth-century Utopian voyage and that of Foigny is that the gulf is bridged: Yahoo and Houyhnhnm are as far apart as Fondin and Australian, but between them stands a third figure, that of man as he can be, animal indeed, but not bestial for all his irrationality. For the destructiveness of Foigny and Veiras is substituted a positive approach. Swift supplies what they have left out, and so by his manipulation of an existing form finds an economic means of expression. The fourth book is therefore in one of its aspects a comment on the opinions implied in a well-known form, the philosophic voyage of the seventeenth century, with its rationalist, Deist, or anti-Christian pictures of mankind perfected in goodness through the exercise of reason in an untrammeled state of nature; and one way—among several converging ways—towards an understanding of the book is to see it as a significant variation on a familiar theme, and so to set it against its appropriate background. Foigny's account of la Terre Australe, so like and yet in its total effect so different from the account of Houyhnhnmland, may serve as an example of the genre which is here used to present Swift's summing-up of mankind.

The race which Foigny's traveler Sadeur meets in Australia, and which he regards with such reverence, is a race of tall, six-fingered hermaphrodites, their physical peculiarity being a sign of their completeness and perfection, of their lack of passion, and of the love and unity which exist among them. They regard themselves as *"hommes entiers,"* *"vrais hommes,"* an opinion in which Sadeur soon concurs, for these people are the perfection of human nature. They look upon other races as *"demi-hommes,"* and though they at first suppose that Sadeur, who happens also to be a hermaphrodite, is one of themselves they soon realize from his behavior that he, too, is a half-man, having *"de petites étincelles de raison"* but ruled for the most part by passion and so sharing the nature of the beasts; and he narrowly escapes being put to death. According to the old man through whose conversation

Sadeur learns most about the Australians, "L'homme véritablement homme étoit toujours homme, c'est-à-dire humain, raisonnable, débonnaire, sans passion, par ce que c'est en ce point que consiste la nature de l'homme." Man cannot be truly man if he does not differ completely from the beasts, full as they are of passions and of those faults, arising from the passions, from which man must be wholly free. Sadeur is most impressed by this uncompromising view, which has been reached entirely by the light of nature and reason, and which is certainly startlingly different from the traditional acceptances of the Christianity he professes to embrace. The virtuous Australians are of course total strangers to revelation, though nature and reason have led them, as they led the European Deists of the seventeenth and eighteenth centuries, to belief in a Supreme Being, or First Cause, regarded as something remote and ultimately incomprehensible, never to be discussed because reason can form no clear idea of it beyond the fact of its existence. The conception of a more personal relationship between God and man they regard as absurd, and the old Australian dismisses revelation on those rational grounds which Swift ridicules in his parody of the Deist Anthony Collins, that it cannot reasonably be supposed that a benevolent God would declare the truth only to a few. Sadeur soon decides that he would be wise to say no more about Christianity, since the old man's reasonable mind is sure to make it seem ridiculous.

As might be expected, the Australians live simply. They eat no flesh, for this might contaminate them with the animal nature they regard with such horror. They have all things in common and, since they are all completely reasonable and therefore think rightly and uniformly on all subjects, they live in unbroken amity and so in freedom and equality, no government being necessary. With this rational uniformity and equality in virtue there is no cause for them to prefer one to another, and so they have an equal benevolence towards all of their kind. "Ils s'aiment tous d'un amour cordial, et l'amour est égal pour tous." Not being ruled by self-love, they have no sense of personal ownership, and their rational benevolence is not disturbed by any instinctive preference for their own kin. They have, of course, no wars among themselves, since no possible cause of war exists among them, but they carry out extensive massacres among the other inhabitants of the country, a race of ordinary though uncivilized human beings of the same nature as Sadeur. These people are regarded as bestial creatures whose numbers it is only reasonable to keep down, and Sadeur finds himself in trouble through his sense of kinship with them and consequent reluctance to kill them. From the nature of the "true men" it is not to be wondered at that they wear no clothes, which they regard as contrary to nature. Their nakedness, like their bisexuality, is a sign of their lack of passion, their purely reasonable nature, the absence in them of any sense of sin or, consequently, of shame. Sadeur points out the symbolic nature of this characteristic: "Il n'est que le péché qui nous ait donné de l'horreur de nous-même et qui, ayant sali notre âme devant Dieu, nous ait rendus insupportables." Whether the real intention is to accept the existence of Original Sin or, as seems far more likely from the context, to jibe at religion for having inculcated a sense of sin, clothes are here being used as a symbol for man's conviction that he is sinful, a conviction wholly lacking in the Australians. The signification was an old one among Christian moralists, who inferred from Genesis that the urge to clothe ourselves is an urge to cover our nakedness both of body and of mind, and a direct consequence of the Fall.

It is clear enough that the adventures of Sadeur have something in common with those of Gulliver, and that the inhabitants of the two countries which these travelers visit have certain similarities. In each there is a virtuous race guided by nature and reason, an inferior race regarded by the other as subhuman, and a human visitor. The materials of Swift's fourth book are those of a rationalist philosophic voyage, but it is hardly to be expected that his handling of these materials should be straightforward. Voyages of this kind present a view of man and an attitude towards religion which Swift constantly opposed; in the terms of his day reason and nature were the catchwords of the Deist, not of the Christian moralist. It is his frequent habit, moreover, to adopt an established form to satiric purpose, as he does in *A Modest Proposal* and in *An Argument against Abolishing Christianity*, through parody involving a sharp twist of meaning. Swift's habit of mind, and the satiric methods which result from it, do not predispose us to expect a simple Utopian voyage in which the actual depravity of humanity is contrasted with the virtue of "true man," nor do Gulliver's earlier voyages raise such an expectation. And in fact the characters, and their relation to one another, are so handled as to suggest that the philosophic voyagers have rather misunderstood the situation, and have contrived to find the wrong answer to the problem set them in the land they visit. Swift uses their materials as an economical and typically indirect way of giving the right answer, which is less simple than theirs.

The Houyhnhnms, though physically quite different from the people of Foigny's Australia, are of similar nature. The fact that they are in the shape of horses, instead of in that of more complete human beings like the Australians, is in itself significant, and not a matter of satiric distance alone. Foigny's rationally virtuous creatures are improved men, men whose phys-

ical completeness is a sign of their wholeness and self-sufficiency. Swift's
are beings whose physical difference from man is thrust upon our notice
to suggest that they are of quite a different order, and that their rational
virtue is alien to mankind; the efforts of Deists, rationalists, haters of Christianity, or believers in the innate nobility of man are all irrelevant to the
true situation. As symbols they are curiously effective, both suggesting and
contradicting certain traditional associations; they are both familiar and
disconcerting. The horse is one of the noblest of animals, one of the most
perfect creations of the natural world; it is also a symbol of passion and
power, to be held in check by reason as, in poetic theory, the winged
Pegasus must be checked and guided by judgment. That the creature which
we expect to represent passion and force is here in no need of domestication
and control strikes us with a certain oddity and even disappointment: the
Houyhnhnms lack the life and force that their shape would lead us to expect,
and it is with a sense of loss that we see them sitting quietly at their mangers,
drawn in their sledges, threading needles, and drinking milk. These are
symbols which have a negative as well as a positive connotation.

Like Foigny's Australians, the Houyhnhnms are creatures of nature
and reason, but Swift takes some pains to impress upon us what their shape
suggests, that they are not simply more virtuous and rational, more fully
in control of their passions than we; they are not human beings at all. The
contrast between the Houyhnhnms and the other characters is very marked
and firmly sustained. The Houyhnhnms are by nature virtuous: "As these
noble Houyhnhnms are endowed by Nature with a general Disposition to
all Virtues, and have no Conceptions or Ideas of what is evil in a rational
Creature; so their grand Maxim is, to cultivate Reason, and to be wholly
governed by it." The point of the description lies in "as" and "so." The
Houyhnhnms can live by reason because their nature is different from ours;
they have no shame, no temptations, no conception of sin. They are totally
unable to comprehend the purpose of lying, for they define the ends of
speech in purely rational terms and argue that "if any one said the Thing
which was not, those Ends were defeated." That speech could be used to
further other than rational ends—to satisfy self-love, for instance—is inconceivable to them. It is the same with the other common temptations of
man, and Gulliver takes days to explain to his master the ravages, among
human beings, of the passions, "of the Desire of Power and Riches; of the
terrible Effects of Lust, Intemperance, Malice, and Envy." Nature and
reason, in the Houyhnhnms, are one and the same, and no passions exist
in them to complicate the business of living. They have no "natural affections" in our sense; nature, they say, has taught them to be equally benev-

olent to everyone, and to make distinction of persons only on the rational grounds of "a superior Degree of Virtue." "They have no Fondness for their Colts or Foles: but the Care they take in educating them proceedeth entirely from the Dictates of Reason. And, I observed my Master to shew the same Affection to his Neighbour's Issue that he had for his own. They will have it that Nature teaches them to love the whole Species, and it is Reason only that maketh a Distinction of Persons, where there is a superior Degree of Virtue." Marriage is undertaken simply as "one of the necessary Actions in a reasonable Being," and their mates are chosen by their parents and friends with due regard to color, strength, and comeliness. They select such colors as will not produce a disagreeable mixture in the breed, and further "Strength is chiefly valued in the Male, and Comeliness in the Female; not upon the Account of Love, but to preserve the Race from degenerating." These considerations are entirely for the good of "the whole Species," so that matches are made on the purely rational principles according to which, among human beings, animals are bred. And perhaps most striking of all, they have no fear of death, that passion which Swift believed to be implanted, together with the passion of love, in all men, perhaps through the deliberate action of Providence so that mankind might be the less likely to die out. In this as in so much else, the Houyhnhnms are like Foigny's hermaphrodites, who regard death as a good because the agitations of life will then give way to repose, and who take Sadeur's unreasonable fear of death as an additional proof that he is not truly human. The Houyhnhnms carry Stoic indifference even further, and look forward to death no more than they fear it. Rather they accept it as casually as a journey, and call it retiring to their "first Mother." This term, with its pagan air, suggests the complete naturalness of death, as of life, to the Houyhnhnm mind; they are buried as obscurely as possible, and their relations express "neither Joy nor Grief at their Departure; nor does the dying Person discover the least Regret that he is leaving the World, any more than if he were upon returning home from a Visit to one of his Neighbours." They die only of old age, or occasionally from some accident, and are never ill: indeed their bodies seem only an extension of their minds, as though the physical in them were not merely under the control of the reason, but not differentiated from the reason. Since they have no bodily passions, none of the tensions native to man, in whom reason and passion struggle for mastery, are visible in them. They live as easily and naturally in their state of reason as do the beasts in their state of instinct, for reason is, in them, instinctive, inborn, and all-embracing, reason "true and perfect," as it is "in itself." Whereas for us the exercise of reason leads to controversy and dispute, Houyhnhnm reason leads to unanimity, as with the people of la Terre Australe who will consider only those things of which they have clear and distinct ideas. Gulliver tells us:

> Neither is Reason among them a Point problematical as with us, where Men can argue with Plausibility on both sides of a Question; but strikes you with immediate Conviction; as it must needs do where it is not mingled, obscured, or discoloured by Passion and Interest. I remember it was with extreme Difficulty that I could bring my Master to understand the Meaning of the Word Opinion, or how a Point could be disputable; because Reason taught us to affirm or deny only where we are certain; and beyond our Knowledge we cannot do either.

Indeed the Houyhnhnms are what Gulliver says their name implies, the "Perfection of Nature," and it is nature or reason (in them identical) which alone "teaches" and "guides" them. This is constantly insisted on; they assert that "Reason alone is sufficient to govern a Rational Creature" and again that "Nature and Reason were sufficient Guides for a reasonable Animal." For Foigny's Australian likewise "sa raison c'est la loy, c'est la règle, c'est son unique guide." Being sinless they are, like the Australians, naked, and when Gulliver, who is desperately concerned to keep on his clothes as a distinguishing mark from the Yahoos, begs that he may not be compelled to "expose those Parts that Nature taught us to conceal," his master replies that "he could not understand why Nature should teach us to conceal what Nature had given." To him, of course, the covering of human nakedness as a consequence of sin would be incomprehensible, and the contrast between his use of the term "nature" and Gulliver's sharply points the difference between human nature, only to be explained by the "Scripture-system of man's creation," and that of the Houyhnhnms. The Yahoos, too, are naked and in a way sinless, for they as much as the Houyhnhnms act according to their nature, and are no more to be blamed for their odiousness than a beast. The sin and shame which are anciently symbolized by the covering of our bodies are the distinguishing marks of humanity: nature indeed cannot teach us to conceal what she herself has given, but man, whether for good or ill, is not a child of nature in the same sense as Houyhnhnm and Yahoo.

The Houyhnhnms, then, are of the same order as the reasonable beings of the Utopian voyagers, but more clearly and consistently drawn than they, and more sharply differentiated from man. They are conceived entirely in terms of nature and reason, and their actions are a logical consequence from this, while the total result is carefully shown as different not in degree simply, but in kind, from anything possible to man. They are precisely "*animalia rationalia*," natural creatures which are reasonable, and therefore they are given animal shape; Swift's choice of one of the noblest of the animal creation as a symbol of self-sufficient reason is based upon a traditional view of the uniqueness of man. The Houyhnhnms are the dream of the Deist and the rationalist, and so are, like other of Swift's creations, composite beings embodying different aspects of that belief which underlies the conclusions of Plato or Shaftesbury, Zeno or Bolingbroke, the "scheme of virtue without religion," the assumption that man is self-sufficient and able to achieve virtue under the sole guidance of reason and of "Nature, who worketh all things to Perfection." Thus their life, with its poems of friendship and benevolence and praise of athletic achievement, its diet of milk and oats, its lack of iron, has the simplicity of the Golden Age, the dream of the virtuous pagans; their scorn of systems of natural philosophy reminds Gulliver of the sentiments of Socrates as delivered to us by Plato; they are rational creatures as defined by Marcus Aurelius: "To the rational creature the same act is at once according to nature and according to reason." But all such daydreams merge in the various forms of Deistic thinking current in Swift's own day, and it is in these that the significant parallels may be found.

The insistence on reason as a sufficient guide is of course the chief characteristic of Deism, but many of the polemical Deists or freethinkers were content to use it merely as an argument against Christianity, showing revealed religion as an affront to human reason and also as unnecessary, since reason is a sufficient and even a more successful guide for a rational being. But to find a more detailed account of the effects of living by nature and reason Swift had only to turn to the writings of Shaftesbury and to the letters and conversation of his own friend Bolingbroke. Shaftesbury, with his denial of the power of self-love, and his certainty that man has an inborn moral sense which will lead him to benevolence if it is left free to do so, certainly has his place here. Mandeville, in common with many of Shaftesbury's contemporaries, may have underestimated the amount of self-discipline which he thought necessary to the achievement of virtue, but none the less he is essentially right in his criticism of Shaftesbury as requiring and expecting "Goodness in his Species, as we do a sweet Taste in Grapes and China Oranges, of which, if any of them are sour, we boldly pronounce that they are not come to that Perfection their Nature is capable of." For him man is a natural creature, at home in the universe and finding his true happiness in living in harmony with the whole, loving not individual men but the species; this is to live "according to Nature," and this is what the Houyhnhnms do. Shaftesbury's good men, like Theocles, are very much rational creatures, but he makes less use of the word itself than do many of his contemporaries, substituting for it the term "moral sense" and so freeing himself from the difficulties which surrounded the definition of reason. But the more thoroughgoing Bolingbroke, finding this phrase too enthusiastic, prefers to ground his philosophy on reason, which shows man the "essential differences of things" and that "virtue is the perfection of his nature." Reason, he believes, is the faculty which can lead us to universal benevolence.

> [God] has made us happy, and he has put it into our power to make ourselves happier by a due use of our reason, which leads us to the practice of moral virtue and of all the duties of society. We are designed to be social, not solitary, creatures. Mutual wants unite us: and natural benevolence and political order, on which our happiness depends, are founded in them. This is the law of our nature; and tho every man is not able for different reasons to discern it, or discerning it to apply it, yet so many are able to do this, that they serve as guides to the rest.

Bolingbroke's philosophical writings are full of such phrases as "nature and reason," "sound, unprejudiced reason," the guides of the great ancients who are his ideals of virtue. In the letter to Swift, in September 1724, in which he rather angrily and sarcastically defines the term "freethinker," he writes thus of reason: "If indeed by *esprit fort,* or free-thinker, you only mean a man who makes a free use of his reason, who searches after truth without passion or prejudice, and adheres inviolably to it, you mean a wise and honest man, and such a one as I labour to be. The faculty of distinguishing between right and wrong, true and false, which we call reason or common sense, which is given to every man by our bountiful Creator, and which most men lose by neglect, is the light of the mind, and ought to guide all the operations of it." This, put in typical Deist phraseology, is very like the infallible reason of the Houyhnhnms, which "strikes you with immediate Conviction" and which is sufficient to guide them aright in all questions of morality; it is also, despite the difference in terminology, very like Shaftesbury's moral sense in its almost intuitive immediacy; and there is a similarity between Houyhnhnm reason and the Cartesian "rational intuition" of clear and distinct ideas, by which Foigny's Australians appear to be ruled. All these conceptions would seem to Swift equally remote from reality, but in view of the standing argument which was conducted in the letters of Swift and Bolingbroke during the period when *Gulliver's Travels* was being written it seems likely that Bolingbroke's views were much in Swift's mind at this time. Bolingbroke, after all, affected a Stoic serenity during his retirement, and in another letter, in March 1731, he sounds absurdly like a Houyhnhnm in his claim that indifference to death can be achieved simply by following nature: "But we may, nay, if we will follow nature, and do not work up imagination against her plainest dictates, we shall of course grow every year more indifferent to life." No doubt such attitudes had been affected by Bolingbroke before the 1730's, and it is surely to him as much as to Pope that Swift's systematic rebuttal of rational benevolence, the love of the species, is made in 1725: "I hate and detest that animal called man, although I heartily love John, Peter, Thomas and so forth." The Houyhnhnms are "humanity living that law of nature which Bolingbroke describes," supposing that such a thing were possible, but Swift was certain that it was not. "Passion and prejudice" cannot be so easily dismissed, and nature, in Swift's opinion, does not teach man detachment, serenity, benevolence, nor does his reason teach him the difference between right and wrong. Nature teaches man fear and anger and selfishness, and our nature is not to be fulfilled but controlled and guided by the help of religion. Reason and "moral sense" are alike fallible in man; "there is no solid, firm Foundation of Virtue, but in a Conscience directed by the Principles of Religion."

Since this is what the Houyhnhnms stand for, it is not surprising that, for all their monolithic impressiveness and for all the nostalgic charm of the simple untroubled life they lead, readers of the fourth voyage have found them remote, unsympathetic, and in the end profoundly unsatisfying. They are made so because the philosophy they represent is so, and Swift ensures that we will find them unsatisfying not by telling us that they are, but by the narrative methods proper to the form he is using. He puts them into situations in which they must seem unsympathetic or sometimes faintly absurd; situations which could easily have been avoided and whose tendency Swift, with his sensitivity and humor and his skill in managing his characters, could not have failed to see. The Houyhnhnms are as much subject to ironic treatment as any other of his creations, and there is no need, I think, to suppress a feeling of amusement as we read of their placid, awkward domesticity, or of irritation at their solemn assumption of superiority over all other creatures. Still less should we complain that Swift has blundered; it is we who blunder in expecting, against all the evidence of this and his other works, that he should set us, simply and unequivocally, a standard to follow and admire, especially a standard like that which the

Houyhnhnms represent. He deliberately emphasizes their least attractive characteristic, their coldness: a natural result of their purely reasonable nature but one that he would have done well, if he meant to gain our admiration for them, not to thrust upon our notice for the sake of emphasizing their poor opinion of Gulliver. For example, the master Houyhnhnm, Gulliver tells us, "brought me into all Company, and made them treat me with Civility, because, as he told them privately, this would put me into good Humour, and make me more diverting." Again this characteristic coldness and lack of sympathy are displayed in the dispassionate debate of the assembly about the nature and the future fate of Gulliver and the Yahoos, issuing in the calm resolve, on irreproachably rational grounds, to send Gulliver to an almost certain death. Rational benevolence, which teaches them to regard the good of their own species, can find no place for the representative of man. Gulliver finds it impossible to refute their conclusions, but even he, adoring as he is, uneasily feels that his idols lack something of the humane, and that reason might be tempered by pity. Within the framework which Swift has adopted, the limitations of a virtue founded upon reason could scarcely be more forcibly put than in Gulliver's comment: "In my weak and corrupt Judgment, I thought it might consist with Reason to have been less rigorous. . . . I knew too well upon what solid Reasons all the Determinations of the wise Houyhnhnms were founded, not to be shaken by Arguments of mine, a miserable Yahoo."

For all the corruption of his reason, Gulliver is considerably more humane than the wise Houyhnhnms, whose purely reasonable nature has none of the qualities from which humanity can arise. Of course the Houyhnhnms are in many ways admirable enough; to follow reason must produce much that is good, and as far as reason can take them these creatures have gone. Swift uses them not only as a satiric norm against which to show up the lamentable activities of mankind as reported to his master by Gulliver but to embody the reasonable virtues, such as truthfulness and honesty, which we would do well to follow so far as we may. Their customs and institutions—their disapproval of "systems," their education of females—are often those which Swift would approve. But in their blamelessness there is something lacking, the positive goodness of love, pity, gratitude, kindness, which makes life bearable in man's fallen world. Elsewhere in the *Travels* Swift treats with sympathy that deliberate intervention of one man in the life of another which is so different from the Houyhnhnms' equal benevolence, detachment, and rational respect for virtue, but among them the nearest approach to human warmth is the touching devotion of the humble sorrel nag, one of the servant breeds who were "not born with equal Talents of Mind." The nag, with his incompletely rational mind, is the only creature in Houyhnhnmland to show any affection, and Gulliver's last link with the country as he sails away is the voice of the "Sorrel Nag (who always loved me) crying out—Take Care of thy self, gentle Yahoo."

While the Houyhnhnms lack human warmth because they lack passions and affections, all that the rationalists summed up as the misleading effects of our unfortunate possession of bodies, the Yahoos are at the opposite extreme, inhuman because they have nothing but bodily senses and passions, and are altogether lacking in reason; in them there is nothing to control passion or to shape it into human affection. In them as in the Houyhnhnms one aspect of man's complex nature is isolated. Of all Swift's allegorical figures these are perhaps the most perfectly adapted to their purpose: the physical representation exactly embodies the moral meaning because the Yahoos are that part of human nature which arises from the physical. They embody in visible shape the animal passions of man, in the degenerate form that these passions would assume if isolated from reason, and it is because of this unity of expression and meaning that they achieve such haunting conviction. The sense of man's limitation by his animal nature, which has grown stronger throughout the whole work, here becomes overwhelming, and the more vivid and repulsive these apelike creatures are made, the more physically present they are to us, the more fully Swift's meaning is conveyed. There is no doubt that we are meant to share Gulliver's disgust with the Yahoos, for though Gulliver's own reactions (or those of any of Swift's characters) are not necessarily to be trusted, we are shown enough to judge for ourselves, and are moreover given a further pointer in the carefully chosen associations of uncleanness which surround them. The Yahoos feed upon things which under the Levitical code are forbidden as polluting or unclean—asses' flesh, meat from dead carcasses, rodents, dogs—and they are treated in those terms in which Christian moralists had for so long written of the flesh, the unregenerate man. In a state of nature and with reason totally absent, the animal part of man is entirely given over to sin, or what would be sin in a creature gifted with reason and responsibility, though in a Yahoo it can hardly be called so. The extreme contrast between the hideously physical Yahoos, with their brutish parodies of human behavior, and the Houyhnhnms in whom the body is merely a vehicle for the expression of reason, is an important part of Swift's meaning. To those who consider "Reason alone" as sufficient guide for humanity he is displaying, isolated and therefore exaggerated, those things in us with which reason has to contend. The Yahoos show why man could never be a Houyhnhnm, why the Stoic or the Deist solution to the human problem must always be a failure. But the suggestion of inhumanity in the Houyhnhnms, and the connotations of sin in the Yahoos, indicate also, however lightly, that though the Deist answer will not do there is another answer which can take into account the whole nature of man, resolving the absolute contrast of Houyhnhnm and Yahoo. The biblical images of uncleanness relate to another dimension in which all the strange beings of *Gulliver's Travels* can be placed in proper relationship. As T. O. Wedel long ago pointed out, the Yahoos live in a "state of nature" nearer to that envisaged by Hobbes than to that of Locke's *Two Treatises of Government,* and infinitely far from that perfection of nature which the Deists believed the churches had done so much to prevent. Their state of nature is a state of war, of unbridled self-love: this is the natural condition of man according to such observers as Hobbes, La Rochefoucauld, Mandeville, and, as the Deists saw, this view was less remote from the traditions of the church than was their own, though it could support only a part of Christian teaching. Swift's handling of the Yahoos is in the tradition of Christian homiletic literature; they are not only examples of the Hobbist state of nature which is a state of war; they are "the body of this death," though their traditional message is adapted to the age of rationalism and dualism, and the new problems that it brought. By the terms in which they are described they imply a context in which brutish self-love is not the whole truth about man, and in which he can be more fully comprehended than by Houyhnhnm reason, which so signally fails to find, in its world of neat and simplified extremes, a place for mankind. These hints are followed up through the relationship of Gulliver to the creatures of Houyhnhnmland, a relationship which is crucial to Swift's meaning, since it is through his handling of it that his carefully established contrast is finally to be resolved.

The most humiliating experience which Gulliver, that stout upholder of the dignity of human kind, has to endure in all his adventures is the recognition that he is akin to the Yahoos. Only with the greatest reluctance and shame is he brought to admit this kinship even to himself, for he is, like so many of us, deliberately blind to the treasure of baseness in man. Yet the physical likeness is strong and continually stressed, and it is apparent to us while Gulliver is still refusing to recognize it. Being expressed in physical terms, it makes much more impression on us than does the likeness between Gulliver and the Houyhnhnms, which consists in his possession of a tincture of that reason which constitutes the whole of their nature. This of course is what Swift intends, since he wishes to convey the faintness of reason in us, and the strength of our passions, but he is also at pains to show us that Gulliver is different from the Yahoos. For Gulliver can reason, and though he and his fellows share all the selfish instincts of the Yahoos, and though the master Houyhnhnm, like the Brobdingnagian king, recognizes that men too often use their reason to conceal their passions or to gratify them more subtly, the difference is still very great. The Houyhnhnm sums up the situation from his own point of view when he tells the Assembly, according to Gulliver, "That, he observed in me all the Qualities of a Yahoo, only a little more civilised by some Tincture of Reason; which however was in a Degree as far inferior to the Houyhnhnm Race, as the Yahoos of their Country were to me." The Houyhnhnms judge by their own standard of reason, but the inadequacy of their comments on Gulliver and on Gulliver's account of human behavior suggests that this standard is not altogether an appropriate one to apply to mankind. For instance, Gulliver's master, having heard of the distorted ingenuity with which the science of law is conducted in England, remarks that creatures "endowed with such prodigious Abilities of mind" as these lawyers must be, ought to instruct others in wisdom and knowledge: a specific satiric point is made about the state of the law in England, but the Houyhnhnm standard of judgment—"Abilities of mind"—is incidentally shown to be faulty. Indeed the very fact that the Houyhnhnms are used, like any of Swift's characters, to make satiric points even if this involves inadequacy or obtuseness on their part, is an indication that we are not to accept them uncritically, and that they are no more to be regarded as perfect than Gulliver, or the King of Brobdingnag. Again the ineptitude of Houyhnhnm standards of nature and reason when applied to man and used as anything more than a temporary position of satiric vantage, is seen in the passage where Gulliver tries to explain the relative positions of Yahoo and Houyhnhnm (really of man and horse, quite a different matter) in his native country. The Houyhnhnm must, of course, admit that "if it were possible there could be any Country where Yahoos alone were endued with Reason, they certainly must be the governing Animal, because Reason will in Time always prevail against Brutal Strength." But he has to consider man as a natural creature, a being fulfilling its nature in a world in which it is at home, and he goes on to point out that Gulliver is physically ill equipped to employ that reason in the common offices of life. A horse, he implies, is in bodily shape much more fit than a man to live the life of nature and reason, and as far as it goes this criticism is just enough. For man is not, like a horse or a Houyhnhnm, a creature of nature; as such he is more imperfect even than a Yahoo "in point of real Advantage," as the Houyhnhnm points out almost in the same words on two separate occasions. Man indeed is a most imperfect animal, but then he must be judged by quite different standards, and the effect of the Houyhnhnm's painstakingly logical remarks is to show us that, understandably enough, he has no conception of what man really is. *Gulliver's Travels* is, in part, an examination of the definition of man as a reasoning animal, an examination which the conditions of the time made peculiarly necessary. Swift is concerned to explore not only in what sense man can be called rational but also, through the continuing play of animal imagery, in what sense he can be defined as an animal. The Houyhnhnms, like the Deists, misinterpret the definition in both its parts, and so in the whole which those parts compose. All that constitutes humanity in its curious mixture of reason and passion, all the complexity of a fallen being ill at ease in a world in which his fellow creatures are at home and yet capable of great good and great achievement: all this lies outside Houyhnhnm standards of judgment. But Gulliver understands none of this; he blindly accepts his master's condemnation, and so adds a further twist to the meaning, for it is in this book that Gulliver makes his greatest contribution, not as a simple mouthpiece but as an example of the disaster to which man can be led through a misunderstanding of his own nature. Gulliver's progress throughout the *Travels* has been in the direction of an increasing fluidity and untrustworthiness; contributing to relativity in the first two books, in the third he is so tenuous a character that we scarcely feel his presence, and by the time Book IV is reached we are well aware that Gulliver, as much as anyone else, is being manipulated in the service of his creator's moral and satiric intention. This is further impressed upon us in the detail of the fourth book itself; for instance, the lengthy condemnation, in Chapters V and VI, of Swift's hated sciences of war, medicine, and law reads like direct satiric attack upon familiar subjects, the stock subjects of satire, and we have no sense that it is being put forward through Gulliver. Rather we feel ourselves to be directly addressed, with the exaggeration usual in a simple attack of this kind, and with an open irony hardly to be expected of Gulliver. The following passage is difficult to relate to any notion we may earlier have formed of Gulliver's character, and not particularly consistent in itself save as the rather heavily and conventionally ironic comment of a satirist. Gulliver has, for the moment, vanished into the brain which conceived him:

> I had formerly upon Occasion discoursed with my Master upon the Nature of Government in general, and particularly of our own excellent Constitution, deservedly the Wonder and Envy of the whole World. But having here accidentally mentioned a Minister of State; he commanded me some Time after to inform

him, what Species of Yahoo I particularly meant by that Appellation.

I told him, that a First or Chief Minister of State, whom I intended to describe, was a Creature wholly exempt from Joy and Grief, Love and Hatred, Pity and Anger; at least makes use of no other Passions but a violent Desire of Wealth, Power, and Titles.

And so the passage, with its curious comments on the passions, so ill adapted to Houyhnhnm understanding or Houyhnhnm standards, proceeds to open invective against the political and moral character of Robert Walpole. After this, Gulliver's later claim that he has done all he can to set his countrymen in the best possible light can only add to our feeling that he is now frankly an instrument in his creator's hands; having first told us that the virtues of the Houyhnhnms have opened his eyes to the vices of men, and also taught him "an utter Detestation of all Falsehood or Disguise," he goes on somewhat inconsistently: "However, it is now some Comfort to reflect that in what I said of my Countrymen, I extenuated their Faults as much as I durst before so strict an Examiner; and upon every Article, gave as favourable a Turn as the Matter would bear. For, indeed, who is there alive that will not be swayed by his Byass and Partiality to the Place of his Birth?" Thus Gulliver is shown, in Book IV as earlier, to be himself part of the satire; meaning is expressed not through any one character but through the relationship of them all and through Gulliver's misunderstanding of that relationship when he identifies mankind with the Yahoos and at the same time tries to live like a Houyhnhnm, rejecting completely the bodily instincts and passions which the Yahoos represent. Gulliver is always too prone to take on the color of his surroundings, and here he accepts uncritically the rational standards of the Houyhnhnms, with the result that he, like his predecessor the Author of *A Tale of a Tub,* loses himself in a world of extremes, seeing nothing of the larger, more inclusive truth to be gained by moving between them. And as always the truth is only suggested, though more clearly and with more conviction than in the *Tale;* there is now less delight in absurdity, through experience of the disaster to which absurdity can lead, and correspondingly a stronger certainty of the importance of the one answer to the dangers and confusions of life.

Gulliver's first refusal to recognize what man has in common with the Yahoos is of a piece with his earlier concern for the dignity of humankind in Book II, and it is in these two closely connected books that human pride, in the shape of Gulliver himself, is most insisted upon. The same pride, when he is at last forced to recognize the likeness between mankind and the Yahoos, causes him to identify himself, as far as he may, with the Houyhnhnms, accepting their views on himself and his fellows and striving to be like them. The opening of Chapter VII shows how completely he has misunderstood the situation. It is true that he has lost his former pride in humanity, sees human vices more plainly, and thinks less of the honor of his own kind; he has lost his illusions and the pride they nurtured, and he is right to condemn certain human institutions against the standard of Houyhnhnm truthfulness and honesty. As so often with Swift, an extreme standard, a merciless stripping away of illusions, can be temporarily useful for satiric purposes. But Gulliver makes the extreme standard a permanent one, and removes, along with the illusions and the prejudices, those things which are not truly prejudices at all. He judges by pure reason, according to which no good can come of the passions which also exist in man; and because man is not a Houyhnhnm he supposes, as does his master, that he must be a Yahoo:

> The Reader may be disposed to wonder how I could prevail on myself to give so free a Representation of my own Species, among a Race of Mortals who were already too apt to conceive the vilest Opinion of Human Kind, from that entire Congruity betwixt me and their Yahoos. But I must freely confess, that the many Virtues of those excellent Quadrupeds placed in opposite View to human Corruptions, had so far opened mine Eyes, and enlarged my Understanding, that I began to view the Actions and Passions of Man in a very different Light; and to think the Honour of my own Kind not worth managing.

The tone of this—and it is by his sensitive modulation of tone that Swift produces some of his subtlest satiric effects—shows us where Gulliver is heading. He has accepted the simple dualism of Houyhnhnmland not as a satiric device but as a permanent truth, placing Houyhnhnm reason "in opposite View to human Corruptions," and as a result he is disgusted with mankind, whom he falsely identifies with the Yahoos. But his disgust does not really extend to himself, though he calls himself a Yahoo. He has already learned to hate all falsehood and hopes to live with the Houyhnhnms forever; a certain condescension and self-approval, a certain pompous absurdity even—"the many Virtues of those excellent Quadrupeds"—indicates that for one illusion, one source of pride, is being substituted another. Gulliver now sees himself as a potential Houyhnhnm, a correct choice certainly as between Houyhnhnm and Yahoo but hopelessly unrealistic because, for mankind, the choice does not exist. And when Gulliver tries to live the life of "Reason alone" the results are disastrous, since what is harmless and unavoidable self-satisfaction in a Houyhnhnm becomes in him a fanatical pride, an illusion more dangerous than any he has had before. The demands of the life of reason do not, in fact, allow in man even the blameless and negative virtue of the Houyhnhnms, for like Stoic indifference it can only be sustained through pride. The effort to support his chosen role forces Gulliver into isolation from his fellows, and the charming fondness for his own family which he had earlier shown is replaced not by the equal benevolence of reason but by hatred and contempt. "During the first Year I could not endure my Wife or Children in my Presence, the very Smell of them was intolerable; much less could I suffer them to eat in the same Room. To this Hour they dare not presume to touch my Bread, or drink out of the same Cup." Gulliver has in fact become, through choosing to judge mankind by an alien standard, a ludicrous yet terrible misanthrope, one of "*vous autres*" of Swift's letter to Bolingbroke and Pope, who can only end by hating mankind for its failure to live by inapplicable rules. This, one might say, is what the Utopian voyagers, what Bolingbroke, must come to. The only way to avoid such savage disillusion is to have no illusions in the first place, to recognize the Yahoo in man and to expect of him no more "than such an animal is capable of." Gulliver's course leads him into a self-deceit more complete and disastrous than that of any of Swift's representative figures, even than Peter or Jack, the Author of the *Tale* or the heroes of the antiromantic poems: he is immersed in chaos, the maddest of them all. In his last inhuman state, he is used to make valid satiric points; we are, no doubt, to accept as justified his strictures on the ridiculous vice of pride in such a creature as man, since that is one of the chief themes of the *Travels*, but it is a further irony that it is Gulliver who makes them in these last proud words: "and therefore I here intreat those who have any Tincture of this absurd Vice, that they will not presume to appear in my Sight."

To make even more clear the unreliability of Gulliver's views, his infinite capacity for getting things wrong by oversimplifying the issues, we are shown him in converse with his horses, who understand him tolerably well, and whom he regards as degenerate Houyhnhnms, and with his groom, because he smells of the stable; while his wife, who from what we hear of her is a very good sort of woman, is detested. This is plain foolishness, and indeed the whole of Gulliver's behavior after he leaves Houyhnhnmland is so obviously ridiculous that it is impossible he should be taken seriously. The tendency he has always shown to accept the point of view of his hosts is here very marked: he trots like a horse, speaks in a neighing tone, and finds it unnatural that the sailors should talk, "as monstrous as if a Dog or a Cow should speak in England, or a Yahoo in Houyhnhnm-Land." He still thinks of himself as different in kind from his fellows, telling us of Don Pedro that he "spoke so very movingly, that at last I descended to treat him like an Animal which had some little Portion of Reason." Even so, he will wear none of the captain's clothes, except "two clean Shirts, which having been washed since he wore them, I believed would not so much defile me." As though to impress even more forcibly upon the reader that Gulliver's conclusions are themselves the objects of satire, Swift prefaced to his work, in Faulkner's edition in 1735, "A Letter from Capt. Gulliver to his Cousin Sympson," in which Gulliver writes with extreme harshness, arrogance, and self-esteem, still differentiating himself from the Yahoos, "your Species," and preferring to the praise of the whole human race "the neighing of those two degenerate Houyhnhnms I keep in my Stable." His criticisms of party and faction, bad writing, faulty education, and the rest are valid, for he still has his topically satiric function to perform, but that he should suppose that all these things could be reformed within seven months of the publication of his *Travels,* because such reformations "were plainly deducible from the Precepts delivered in my Book," and that "seven Months were a sufficient Time to correct every Vice and Folly to which Yahoos are subject," so that their failure proves them incapable of "the least Disposition to Virtue or Wisdom": all this extremism, with its unrealistic view of what man can achieve followed by utter pessimism when he does not achieve it, shows clearly where Gulliver's error lies. Throughout the "Letter," Gulliver is handled with a markedly heavy irony; perhaps Swift had already found that his meaning had to be underlined.

Yet Gulliver's mistake was avoidable, for he had met on his previous voyages, especially during his stay in Brobdingnag, several examples of that kind of goodness to which it is possible for man to attain. His blindness is part of the satire, but we have no excuse for joining him in it, since there is plentiful evidence throughout *Gulliver's Travels* that man and Yahoo have not an "entire Congruity," and that some members of the human race are far more satisfactory models for Gulliver than are the Houyhnhnms. The King of Brobdingnag, Glumdalclitch, Lord Munodi, even Gulliver's wife or Gulliver himself as we see him in the first voyage, have qualities of kindness or friendliness or generosity, qualities which arise from the passions and affections of man, however controlled or purified, and which cannot exist in the rational Houyhnhnms. Moreover, in the fourth voyage itself Swift takes particular care to set against the inhuman Gulliver human figures of great goodness and tenderness, the Portuguese sailors. In earlier books, the sailors with whom Gulliver comes into contact have been an ordinarily mixed collection of men; Mr. John Biddel, captain of the vessel which picked him up after his departure from Blefuscu, was "a very civil Man," and Mr. Thomas Wilcocks, of the Brobdingnagian rescue, was honest and kindly. In the "Voyage to Laputa" there is a courteous Japanese pirate and an abominable Dutch one—here Swift's private prejudices are coming into play—and in the final voyage Gulliver is abandoned in Houyhnhnmland by his mutinous crew. All these people are mere narrative devices for getting Gulliver to and from the countries where the satire is carried on, except in the case of the Japanese and the Dutch, whose characteristics are a little more developed to make a particular satiric point. But the captain and crew of the Portuguese ship, which puts in for water on the island where Gulliver is hiding from his kind after his banishment from Houyhnhnmland, are more fully developed, and we hear much of Gulliver's reactions to their admirable qualities. He behaves very churlishly, displaying only an extreme anxiety to get away from them, but they treat him none the less, as he has to admit, with great humanity, and force him to be saved in spite of himself. Their captain, Don Pedro de Mendez, is particularly humane, compassionate, and forbearing, and Swift emphasizes in him those very qualities which the Houyhnhnms neither possess nor would understand, and which the obsessed Gulliver no longer values, though it is satirically necessary that he should perceive them. Of Don Pedro's goodness Gulliver remarks merely, with the cold and scornful surprise now to be expected of him, that "he was a very courteous and generous Person; he entreated me to give some Account of my self, and desired to know what I would eat or drink; said, I should be used as well as himself, and spoke so many obliging Things, that I wondered to find such Civilities from a Yahoo. However, I remained silent and sullen; I was ready to faint at the very Smell of him and his Men." That it is a physical disgust which Gulliver feels for these sailors and even for his own family, whose smell similarly distresses him, emphasizes the nature of his delusion.

The behavior of the seamen toward Gulliver is quite different from the curiosity of the Houyhnhnms. They regard themselves as responsible for him in spite of the rebuffs they receive; they forcibly prevent him from leaping overboard in an attempt to escape to his former solitude; and Don Pedro persuades him to abandon his design of living as a recluse, following so far as he can the life of rational self-sufficient virtue which the Houyhnhnms have taught him to admire, and instead to commit himself once more to the human relationships proper to mankind. Gulliver's duty as Don Pedro sees it is to return to a life of tolerance and affection among his own kind, and he tries to persuade him on grounds of "Honour and Conscience." As we know from the sermons, conscience for Swift was not a natural sense of right and wrong but a faculty which must itself be guided, by divine law only to be known from a source outside ourselves, from revelation; only a conscience guided by the principles of religion can give us a firm foundation for virtue. And indeed the Portuguese sailors, with their kindness and compassion, their deliberate and responsible intervention in the lives of the unfortunate, form a strong and attractive contrast to the Houyhnhnms' rational benevolence, as well as to the misanthropy of Gulliver. The long-suffering, charitable Don Pedro is perhaps the closest of all Swift's characters to his account, in the sermon "Upon the Excellency of Christianity," of the ideal Christian, who is "affable and courteous, gentle and kind, without any morose leaven of pride or vanity, which entered into the composition of most Heathen schemes." The "scheme" which Gulliver has learned from the Houyhnhnms has certainly an element of that self-sufficient pride which Swift and other churchmen saw both in Stoicism and in the modern schemes of the Deists. Don Pedro, placed in so prominent a position, must make a strong impression on our minds, and the tone of Gulliver's references to him would seem further to suggest that here, among the various figures of the fourth voyage, is to be found the embodiment of the course man should follow. Gulliver speaks of his benefactor with a grudging approval, tinged with contempt for an unenlightened Yahoo, and never accepts the standards by which Don Pedro lives and by which he tries to persuade Gulliver to live. For Gulliver only agrees to go back to England because he can do nothing else: "I complied at last, finding I could not do better." And his comment on Don Pedro, that he had "very good *human* Understanding," is typical of Swift's methods of ironic commendation, made by means of an uncomprehending mouthpiece. Again, through Gulliver, he commends to us the Brobdingnagians, as the poor best that humanity, as contrasted with those truly rational animals the Houyhnhnms, can achieve, and again the grudging, the almost negative, tone is a familiar element of Swift's ironic method: "I shall say nothing of those remote Nations where Yahoos preside; amongst which the least corrupted are the Brobdingnagians, whose wise Maxims in Morality and Government, it would be our Happiness to observe. But I forbear descanting further, and rather leave the judicious Reader to his own Remarks and Applications."

In Don Pedro and the Brobdingnagians we have, then, our positive standard, put forward, as always, ironically and indirectly according to Swift's habit. It is not an ideal standard—that Swift would ever have written a simple Utopia is almost inconceivable—and the indirection itself, the reluctance with which Gulliver recognizes the good qualities of the people he regards as a very poor second best, helps to pin down the meaning precisely. Swift is telling us, as always, not to expect too much and not to simplify what is essentially a difficult matter. The proper life for man is not that of Yahoo or of Houyhnhnm, for he has in him something of both, and in the blending of passion and reason, body and mind, something different from these simple, natural creatures is engendered. The Brobdingnagians and Don Pedro are, in a way, a compromise between extremes, and therefore they are indirectly presented, because we are to understand that we should not aim too high, as Gulliver does when, in trying to ignore part of his human nature, he becomes less than a human being. The best that man can achieve is considerable, but he can achieve it only through acceptance of the truth about himself as a fallen and degenerate creature who if he is to be good must base his endeavors on the whole of his complex nature. Though we cannot be Houyhnhnms we can be something better, and far more suited to the condition of fallen human beings who, as Bishop Butler said, "naturally, and from the condition we are placed in, necessarily depend upon each other." We need not, nor can we, escape that side of our nature which includes passions and affections; carefully guided by conscience and religion, to which reason must be subject, these qualities in man can issue in virtuous action, especially that compassionate assistance to our fellowmen, whether or not our reason judges them worthy of it, which Swift valued so highly and which "the Gentile philosophy" fails to produce. "If our Brother . . . is not in a Condition to preserve his Being, we ought to support him to the best of our Power, without reflecting over seriously on the Causes that brought him to his Misery."

In Gulliver's last voyage utter chaos is thrust sharply against absolute order, and it is this clashing contrast which, in the shape of the Yahoos and the Houyhnhnms, makes the first and strongest impression upon us. But this is not Swift's last word upon the predicament of man. If we cannot escape from confusion to a world of clarity and simplicity, yet we need not, either, be overwhelmed in the meaningless. We must accept and work upon it, each of us making our own order as best we can. Swift sets the extremes firmly before us, but the right course can, by its very nature, be only indirectly shown. For the right course is to avoid extremes and the distortions to which they give rise; and it is also the difficult course, involving a scrupulous balancing of values, a weighing of experience, a determination to include in one's solutions the elements of rightness which exist in the drastic and clamorous claims of Hobbes and Mandeville, Shaftesbury and Bolingbroke. To give too plain an answer would be to defeat Swift's very purpose, which is, in part, to deny that any simple and ready-made answer exists. Don Pedro and the giant king cannot be simply summed up; theirs is the goodness of humility and adaptiveness, tolerance and human warmth, an imaginative response to the needs of others. In the terms of the satire this positive standard can only be hinted at, but the terms of the satire are themselves chosen as those which express Swift's meaning most exactly, and part of that meaning is that the standard for man is not easy to find or to follow. In *Gulliver's Travels,* as in life itself, we must work out our solution, not denying but wrestling with the chaos we are born to, and refusing any of the tempting simplifications which prove, as in Gulliver's own case, so dangerous. As in *A Tale of a Tub,* the truth lies in what the ostensible author leaves out, in the compromise which includes all partial truths; and though here the true answer is reached, while in the *Tale* we must deduce it from our own examination of the Author's negatives, it can still not be put too plainly before us. In an age of false simplicities it is the chaos of man's life and the paradox of his nature which must be stressed. When that is accepted, we can work upon the whole of our nature for good, with the guidance of conscience and of Swift's one certainty, the Church.

The guidance of religion is not, of course, overtly mentioned in *Gulliver's Travels.* But in relation to the controversies of the day, it is seen to be present by implication. If "Reason alone" is not a sufficient guide for man, seen as a creature of mixed nature: if the good human beings are examples of a particular kind of virtue, which is not to be defined in purely rational terms: then Swift's position is opposed to Deism and neo-Stoicism, and this would in itself suggest, even without the biblical associations which surround the Yahoos, that definition of man's nature which Christian tradition has handed down. The conclusion is as natural as for Montaigne, who at the close of the *Apologie de Raymond Sebond* places Stoic pride in a firmly Christian context with his comment on the mingled nobility and absurdity of the heathen cry, "Oh what a vile and abject thing is man unless he raise himselfe above humanity!"

> Observe here a notable speech, and a profitable desire; but likewise absurd. For to make the handfull greater then the hand, and the embraced greater then the arme; and to hope to straddle more then our legs length; is impossible and monstrous: nor

that man should mount over and above himselfe or humanity; for he cannot see but with his owne eyes, nor take hold but with his owne armes. He shall raise himselfe up, if it please God extraordinarily to lend him his helping hand. He may elevate himselfe by forsaking and renouncing his owne meanes, and suffering himselfe to be elevated and raised by meere heavenly meanes. It is for our Christian faith, not for his Stoicke vertue to pretend or aspire to this divine Metamorphosis, or miraculous transmutation.

To assert the dual nature of man was still, in the early eighteenth century, the traditional defense against the partial truths of philosophical systems: Pascal's *Entretien avec Saci* appeared in 1728, and its argument that the notions both of Epictetus and of Montaigne were incomplete because they regarded only one aspect of our nature—"l'un la grandeur de l'homme, l'autre la foiblesse"—and that these can only be reconciled in the Christian faith, was followed in 1734 by John Arbuthnot's one serious poem, "Know Yourself," based on Pascal's theme. Arbuthnot contrasts, more topically, the theories of the Stoics and the Epicureans, both of which had their modern counterparts, and shows that while the former recognizes only man's strength, and ignores the instincts and passions which hamper it, the latter commits the opposite error of ignoring human possibilities for good. It is only to be expected, however, in the circumstances and particular dangers of the time, that Arbuthnot's comments on the nature of man, like those of his friends Pope and Swift, seem to stress human weakness rather than human strength, senses and instincts more than reason:

> These Godlike Thoughts while eager I pursue,
> Some glitt'ring Trifle offer'd to my view,
> A Gnat, an Insect of the meanest kind,
> Erase the new-born Image from my Mind,
> Some beastly Want, craving, importunate,
> Vile as the grinning Mastiffs at my Gate,
> Calls off from heav'nly Truth this reas'ning Me,
> And tells me I'm a Brute as much as He . . .
> So Man, amongst his Fellow-Brutes expos'd
> Sees he's a King, but 'tis a King depos'd:
> Pity him, Beasts! you by no Law confin'd,
> Are barr'd from devious Paths, by being blind;
> Whilst Man, through op'ning Views of various Ways
> Confounded by the Aid of Knowledge, strays.

One creed calls man a god, one a "two-legg'd Beast," and revelation alone can reconcile such "wide Extremes":

> Marks of my Birth, which I had worn in vain,
> Too hard for worldly Sages to explain:
> Zeno's were vain, vain Epicurus' Schemes,
> Their systems false, delusive were their Dreams;
> Unskill'd my two-fold Nature to divide,
> One nurs'd my Pleasure, and one nurs'd my Pride;
> Those jarring Truths which Human Art beguile,
> Thy sacred Page thus bids me reconcile.

For these traditional writers, whether divines like Butler and Swift or laymen like Pope and Arbuthnot, it is only in the Christian positive that the contradictions in man can be reconciled, his strength and weakness, his reason and passion, so that the whole of his nature, even his self-love, can be turned to affection and an active desire for the good of others. Anything simpler than this, any neater system, can be attained only by omission: compromise alone will avoid the opposed errors of *Gulliver's Travels* and *A Tale of a Tub,* and lead from delusion and death to a full, inclusive, and vital truth, to the fruitful life of Don Pedro and the Brobdingnagian king, and of Martin, who has best sustained the tradition of the primitive church. As Pascal believed, and as Swift demonstrates in the story of Gulliver, any one-sided account of the nature of man, any scheme that denies the paradoxical reality in favor of simplicity, will lead to disastrous practical results, to pride or despair or cynicism; and in its view of humanity Christianity approximates to a middle way between contemporary "wide Extremes," "jarring Truths which Human Art beguile." Swift's careful selecting and adjusting among opposing systems brings him, time and again, to his one certainty in the traditional teachings of his church and the morality which they support. Only thus can chaos be organized without loss, and the dangers of life surmounted. The words of Joseph Glanvill, sceptic follower of the middle way, form an apt comment on the task which faced Swift and his contemporaries: "Every Truth is near an Errour; for it lies between two Falsehoods: and he that goes far from One is apt to slip into the other; and while he flies from a Bear, a Lyon meets him. So that the best way to avoid the danger is to steer the middle Course; in which way we may be sure there is Charity and Peace, and very probably, Truth in their company." For only by countering one extreme opinion with another, "bending a crooked stick as much the other way, to straighten it," setting Yahoo against Houyhnhnm, can we reach that "discreet modest aequipoize of Judgment, that becomes the sons of Adam."

Order and Obligation: *Gulliver's Travels*

Martin Price

In *Gulliver's Travels* Swift carries the conflict of orders to its sharpest expression. Lemuel Gulliver is the most famous of Swift's masks or personae, and as always, it is important to see these masks in their fictional integrity first of all. Swift may not be consistent in maintaining them; they become at moments transparencies through which his irony shines in full intensity, but much of the nonsense that has been written about Swift's works derives from a failure to observe the character of their spokesmen. Gulliver is obtuse in a plausible and often attractive way. He is a matter-of-fact man, capable of minute accuracy of detail in what he reports but equally capable of total indifference to the "value tone" of experience. His deadpan style is consistent understatement through much of the book. It is not knowing understatement such as we find in Hemingway, conscious of all it refuses to mention. It is, rather, unconscious irony—a style that is calculated (by Swift and not by Gulliver) to reveal sharply just those values it fails to observe or mention; a style that gives itself away. Swift's spokesmen are always chosen for this useful service: they cheerfully systematize, they avow what is commonly suppressed, they scandalize where wiser or more cautious men would draw back and reconsider.

Gulliver is invented as the hero of a comedy of incomprehension. This is only one dimension of *Gulliver's Travels,* but it is an essential one. Why comedy rather than satire? Because, in this one dimension, Gulliver embodies the incorrigible tendency of the mind to oversimplify experience, a

From *To the Palace of Wisdom: Studies in Order and Energy from Dryden to Blake.* © 1964 by Martin Price. Southern Illinois University Press, 1964.

trait that takes, with equal ease, the form of complacency or of misanthropy. Given his tendency to see man as either a rational animal or an irrational beast, given his expectation that man will be essentially good or essentially evil, Gulliver can never comprehend the problematic nature of man as he really is. As Swift sees him, man is both blessed and cursed with the condition of *animal rationis capax*. Because he is capable of reason man can at least glimpse moral truth, because he is less than perfect in it he can lose the vision or pervert its meaning. The book raises the question of how much that we call civilization is an imperfect disguise of our lowest appetites (rather than a true sublimation or transformation of them), and also how far this civilization is necessary to the man who lives a purely moral life, adhering rigorously to the precepts of nature and reason alone (revelation apart). This is the same problem raised at least in passing by the *Argument against Abolishing Christianity*.

Finally, the book considers fundamental questions about the nature of politics, like the ideal reconciliation of duty and interest among the Houyhnhnms and the less perfect, but more humanly feasible, reconciliation in Brobdingnag. To these political orders are opposed such societies as that of the Lilliputians, which is elaborately administered disorder, the tyrannies of Laputa and Maldonada, and the savage democracy of the Yahoos. *Gulliver's Travels* is a tribute to the mixed state in which order is reconciled with freedom and yet made stable. To achieve such an order, one must come to terms with the nature of power, and the most essential feature of power is its tendency to become absolute.

Let us consider the political order. In Lilliput, Gulliver becomes the absolute weapon of an Emperor whose only wish is to conquer the world (that his world consists of two small islands makes the desire depressingly petty in its object but hardly petty in its intensity). The "spirit of opposition" governs the world of Lilliput; there is "a violent faction at home, and the danger [largely imaginary, a self-induced terror which unites the state, as in Orwell's *1984*] of an invasion by a most potent enemy from abroad" (I, iv). The occasions for dispute (like those for conquest) are so trivial as to be meaningless; the power drive creates its own pretexts. Within the state, the factions are rivals for influence and favor. Ministers are chosen by their agility—skill in walking a tightrope or jumping over sticks—and their subservience. The language of the court is a constant exercise in obfuscation. When the King's clemency is declared, his subjects run for cover. When Gulliver hastily puts out the fire in the Empress' palace by the quickest means available, the court accusation is a wonderful farrago of insinuation, self-importance, and intolerable legal jargon:

Whereas . . . it is enacted that whoever shall make water within
the precincts of the royal palace shall be liable to the pains and
penalties of high treason: notwithstanding, the said Quinbus
Flestrin [i.e., Gulliver], in open breach of the said law, under
color of extinguishing the fire kindled in the apartment of his
Majesty's most dear imperial consort, did maliciously, traito-
rously, and devilishly, by discharge of his urine, put out the said
fire kindled in the said apartment, lying and being within the
precincts of the said royal palace, against the statute in that case
provided, etc., against the duty, etc.

(I, vii)

Or again Gulliver is accused of preparing to make a voyage to Blefuscu,
"for which he hath received only verbal licence from his Imperial Majesty."

What is even more telling than the crazy mock logic of Lilliputian
politics is Gulliver's readiness to adapt to it. A bluff, well-meaning Englishman, twelve times their size and able to destroy them with ease, he
becomes dazzled by the honors paid him and the high status he has won
at court. Gulliver is restrained in part by oaths, in part by a sense of
gratitude, but in part, too, by a naïve readiness to assume that power confers
right. This becomes clear when, at the court of Brobdingnag, he reveals
his belated schooling in Machiavellian statecraft and offers the horrified
King the gift of gunpowder. Gulliver's disappointment at the rejection of
this proposal is strong:

A strange effect of narrow principles and short views! That a
prince . . . should from a nice, unnecessary scruple, whereof in
Europe we can have no conception, let slip an opportunity put
into his hands, that would have made him absolute master of
the lives, the liberties, and the fortunes of his people.

(II, vii)

In contrast to Lilliput, the Brobdingnagians have laws of no more than
twenty-two words, and "to write a comment upon any law is a capital
crime." Instead of a professional army they have a citizen militia, where
"every farmer is under the command of his own landlord, and every citizen
under that of the principal men in his own city, chosen after the manner
of Venice by ballot" (II, vii). The militia fixes power in the whole body
of the people rather than permitting the army to become an uncontrollable
bloc such as we know in Latin-American politics today, and controls the
disease that has attacked Brobdingnag, as it has every other nation: "the

nobility often contending for power, the people for liberty, and the King for absolute dominion."

In the land of the Houyhnhnms we find an anarchy of reasonable creatures, such as William Godwin admired. The rational horses need no government; they immediately intuit their duties and perform them. Only in a rare instance, where a novel situation is created—as by Gulliver's presence—must they deliberate. They control any dissidence by rational persuasion and "exhortation," for they need no compulsion. George Orwell is interesting but, I think, mistaken when he sees in this exhortation the "totalitarian tendency which is explicit in the anarchist or pacifist vision of Society. In a Society in which there is no law, and in theory no compulsion, the only arbiter of behavior is public opinion,"—which, Orwell shrewdly remarks, "is less tolerant than any system of law." This might be true if the Houyhnhnms cultivated a "general will," or if they carried on the kind of virtuous terrorism that in schools often goes by the name of "honor system." But there is no need to exert "continuous pressure" for conformity among the Houyhnhnms. They cannot but agree in all but an occasional matter, and even in the case Swift presents the Houyhnhnm master hesitates to assent only because of Gulliver's furious resistance to being sent away. Other critics have made similar objections about the religion of the Houyhnhnms. But one cannot call them conformists, as Orwell does, or Deists, as others do. Their reason inevitably produces agreement, and their piety is exemplary within the limits of their purely natural reason. We cannot blame them for finding fulfillment in what, for us, would be defects of liberty or failures of Christian faith.

Why should Swift have created these problems for us? Clearly he is demanding of his readers what he never grants to Gulliver, the power to make necessary distinctions. We must separate the intuitive rightness of the Houyhnhnms' choice from the tyranny of conformity, and we must separate natural piety from rationalistic or anticlerical deism. Gulliver fails to make the most important distinction of all—between *animal rationale* and *animal rationis capax*. Only after long exposure to human folly and perversity does he give up the dream of man as a rational animal, but instead of coming to terms with what in fact he is, Gulliver immediately turns to truly rational animals, the Houyhnhnms, and hopes to become one of them. His pathetic whinny and canter betray the fantasy of a literal-minded convert.

The same kind of problem occurs in the realm of politics. Gulliver's account of English institutions to the King of Brobdingnag betrays the corruptibility they invite: English laws are extremely complex, and they "are best explained, interpreted, and applied by those whose interest and abilities lie in perverting, confounding, and eluding them" (II, vi). There is no reconciliation of duty and interest but instead a systematic perversion of duty by interest. In his account of Europe to his Houyhnhnm master, Gulliver makes explicit all that he has earlier unconsciously revealed. Lawyers are now "equally disposed to pervert the general reason of mankind in every other subject of discourse, as in that of their own profession" (IV, v). This single instance is typical of all the rest. Gulliver has come to recognize the nature of corruption, but his recognition is so belated and so passionate that he despairs of all politics. When he writes an account of his travels, he expects the world to reform at once. But, in this case at least, we have a third possibility firmly sketched in: the reformed mixed state of the Brobdingnagians, which mediates between duty and interest, conformity and freedom, and accepts the need for a power structure but diffuses its control.

Parallel to the political issues in the book is the relationship of a body and reason. In Lilliput, Gulliver's body is grosser than he can imagine (although he senses it), and the Lilliputians seem more delicate than in fact they are. In Brobdingnag the human body becomes monstrous, as Gulliver confronts with microscopic acuteness its ugliness and its noisome smells. In both the Struldbruggs and the Yahoos we see bodies that are completely without control or cleanliness; in fact, the Yahoos revel in filth and use excrement as a weapon. The body becomes a physical symbol of the power drives that are seen in the body politic; in Brobdingnag there is ugliness (simply more visible to Gulliver because of his diminutive size, as his own normal human ugliness was apparent to the Lilliputians) as there is cruelty and at least some measure of corruption (the farmer's turning Gulliver into a profitable show, the court dwarf's malice), but there is also a saving control of both corruption and physical nastiness. In the Struldbruggs old age has produced physical deterioration, avarice, contentiousness, and irrationality; in the Yahoos (who seem to have degenerated from an original couple, like the human race) there is sheer abandoned animality. The Yahoos are particularly nasty animals, it should be noted, not because Swift "in his fury . . . is shouting at his fellow-creatures: 'You are filthier than you are!' " (Orwell's view) but because they are a degenerate species, which neither possesses the instinctive controls of other animals (such as seasonal mating) nor preserves the faculties by which the human animal controls itself—its rational powers. Recent experiments have shown us animals that lose the power to identify with their proper kind and cannot acquire the traits of the kind they are raised among. Something of the sort has happened to the Yahoos; and their nastiness is only a further tribute to the importance of man's rational powers of self-control.

A third pattern, related to both politics and the control of the physical body, is that of simplicity and complexity. The Brobdingnagian laws are transparently simple; the Houyhnhnms need no laws at all. So it is with their cultures. The King, whose largeness of vision has the generosity of a Renaissance humanist, reminds us that Brobdingnag is a place of cultivation. But his people do not create books in great quantity; their largest library has a thousand volumes. In their writing "they avoid nothing more than multiplying unnecessary words, or using various expressions." They are skilled in practical arts but utterly resistant to "ideas, entities, transcendentals, and abstractions." We see the reverse of this throughout the third voyage—the elaborate astronomy of Laputa is coupled with infantile superstition, the futile ingenuity of the experiments of Lagado is set against the simple adherence to traditional forms of Lord Munodi, the wisdom of Homer or Aristotle is swallowed up by the host of commentators that has battened on each. In place of the typical conqueror-heroes of history, Gulliver learns to admire the destroyers of tyrants and the defenders of liberty, the men who retrench corruption and win persecution in the process.

In the fourth voyage, the complexity of European civilization is traced in the Yahoos' savage behavior: they have a Prime Minister, they have court flirtations, they are acquisitive hoarders of shining stones, they become drunk and diseased, they even have a fashionable psychosomatic malady like the spleen. All the evils of civilization, and many of its professed glories, are caught in their elaborate behavior. In contrast, the Houyhnhnms perform "the necessary actions" of "a reasonable being" (IV, viii). They believe that "*reason* alone is sufficient to govern a *rational* creature"; they cannot even comprehend the nature of lies, let alone worse vices. "Neither is *reason* among them a point problematical as with us, where man can argue with plausibility on both sides of a question; but strikes you with immediate conviction, as it must needs do where it is not mingled, obscured, or discolored by passion and interest" (IV, viii). The consequences of perfect rational intuition are acute. They have no parental partiality nor do they mate except to bear children, and their choice of a marriage partner is based on cool eugenic principles. They accept death as natural ripeness and a return to the first mother. What are we to make of this passionless simplicity, where all is governed by the impartial virtues of friendship and benevolence?

In recent years critics have tended increasingly to find in the Houyhnhnms a satire upon the neo-Stoic humanism of Shaftesbury or the Deists. It is true that Swift mocks those who would base their lives on the belief that virtue is its own reward, but he does not mock the moral intuition that the Houyhnhnms live by. Of course, the Houyhnhnms are not human, and Swift never could have intended that we treat them as models. They are like that return to the System of the Gospels with which the *Argument against Abolishing Christianity* teases us. It would be disastrous to "our present schemes of wealth and power." But could we, in fact, return to primitive Christianity? In *A Tale of a Tub,* when the two brothers reject the corruptions introduced by the third, Jack performs a thorough reformation on his coat and tears it to shreds. Martin, on the other hand, preserves those additions that cannot be removed without destroying the fabric. So here, Swift mocks us with all we are not, with the simplicity and direct acceptance of obligation that is given all the more weight in the teaching of the Gospels (unknown to the merely "natural" Houyhnhnms), and with the close resemblance of our vaunted civilization to the bestiality of the Yahoos. But it is Gulliver, in his despair, who draws from this recognition the resolution to become a Houyhnhnm, and it is this that makes him shrink as if from a Yahoo when he encounters the generous and humane Portuguese sea captain who brings him back to Europe. At the last, even with his family, he is alienated, morose, contemptuous, although he has slowly begun to adapt himself once more to the human condition.

Swift is neither offering the Houyhnhnms as a model nor holding them up for satire. They have, it is true, some telltale complacency in the conclusions they draw without sufficient fact. But when Swift defends the ancient poets against ridicule, he points out that their moral teachings were altogether admirable within the limits of their awareness.

The Houyhnhnms would make a ludicrous model for man, but it is Gulliver who makes them that. They remain an embodiment—in alien animal form—of the life of unclouded moral intuition; a simple life because there are no passions to produce conflict or to generate "opinion." In most telling contrast to them is the Academy of Lagado, with its technical extravagance, its furious dedication to doing the unnecessary with the most dazzling ingenuity, its constant rediscovery of brute fact through ludicrous failure. The scientist who places the bellows to the posterior of a dog and inflates the beast until it explodes in a torrent of excrement serves as a link between the learning of Lagado and the filth of the Yahoos.

The Houyhnhnms represent the order of mind at its purest, free of rationalistic system-building or of pride in intellectual constructions. Conceived in this way, it contains much that is given to humans only in the order of charity—a moral sureness and serenity, a spontaneous goodness such as is bred in men by a "daily vision of God." But to achieve the equivalent in the world of men requires the arduous self-scrutiny, the courageous defiance of the world, the saving humility that Pope seeks to dramatize in the *Imitations of Horace.*

The Paradox of Man

Paul Fussell

Man is thus a mighty curious creature. A flesh-machine of self-destructive depravity fraught with ignorance and vanity, and at the same time inspirited somehow with an *anima* which has it in its power to redeem all defects except, perhaps, mortality, he is a wandering paradox perpetually looking for a place now to hide and now to exhibit himself. He both is and is not like an angel; he both is and is not like a brute. It is his curse and his glory to be at home in a curious moral geography, "this isthmus of a middle state," as Pope puts it in the *Essay on Man;* and it is his nature that finally it can be suggested only by a series of the most outrageous paradoxes:

> A being darkly wise, and rudely great:
> With too much knowledge for the Sceptic side,
> With too much weakness for the Stoic's pride,
> He hangs between;

Perpetually in doubt, he can commit himself entirely to neither direction in which his dualistic being seems to invite him:

> in doubt to act, or rest,
> In doubt to deem himself a God, or Beast;
> In doubt his Mind or Body to prefer,

—and at this point in Pope's exhibition the pathos which is the usual attendant of the humanist view of man wells up:

From *The Rhetorical World of Augustan Humanism.* © 1965 by the Oxford University Press.

> Born but to die, and reas'ning but to err;

Knowledge is of very little use in pointing to a satisfactory direction:

> Alike in ignorance, his reason such,
> Whether he thinks too little, or too much:

There is additional pathos in man's imagining himself "rational" and orderly, when actually he is only rarely even *capax rationis* and more often is simply a

> Chaos of Thought and Passion, all confus'd;

and whether in a state of ignorance or enlightenment, always his own worst enemy:

> Still by himself abus'd, or disabus'd;

His situation in the general hierarchy of things is both tense and tenuous:

> Created half to rise, and half to fall;

As Adam learns before his Fall, he is the "Great Lord of all things," and yet, as he discovers just after it, he is "a prey to all." In short, he is the "Sole judge of Truth," but he is also "in endless Error hurl'd." Small wonder that to the humanist he is at once

> The glory, jest, and riddle of the world!
> (ii, 2–18)

After this demonstration of Pope's, it seems natural that the humanist, when contemplating man, will not know whether to laugh or to weep, and so will do both at once, as at the end of *Gulliver's Travels* or at the end of *The Dunciad.* Pope's version of man sounds familiar and even stale, but one reason why it does is that it occupies so central a position in human experience and in humanistic expression. Pope's "isthmus" recalls preeminently Hamlet's "sterile promontory," and Hamlet proceeds to lesson Rosencrantz and Guildenstern in a proto-Popian version of man which their mechanistic simplifications show them to be in need of:

> this most excellent canopy, the air, look you, this brave o'er-hanging firmament, this majestical roof fretted with golden fire—why, it appeareth no other thing to me than a foul and pestilent congregation of vapours.

Warming to his humanist theme, he proceeds to sketch such a paradoxical picture of man's dualistic capacities that we wonder whether we are being "abus'd, or disabus'd":

> What a piece of work is a man! how noble in reason! how infinite
> in faculties! in form and moving how express and admirable! in
> action how like an angel! in apprehension how like a god! the
> beauty of the world! the paragon of animals!

And yet:

> And yet to me what is this quintessence of dust?
>
> (II, ii)

But familiar as it is, the paradox of the angelic brute is still capable of giving
pause, as it does to poor slow-witted Parson Adams in *Joseph Andrews*. The
parson's son Dick is reading the story about "Lennard's" wife: " 'But, good
as this lady was, she was still a woman; that is to say, an angel, and not
an angel.'—'You must mistake, child,' cries the parson, 'for you read nonsense.' 'It is so in the book,' answered the son." This paradoxical wise child
owes something to a fusion of classical and Christian motifs, suggesting at
once the image of the blind Tiresias being led by a boy and the Christian
imagery of the innocent child leading the dull adults.

The cause of paradox is the juxtaposition of all but irreconcilable dualisms. This is the burden of Erwin Panofsky's definition of "humanism,"
which he locates in "man's proud and tragic consciousness of self-approved
and self-imposed principles, contrasting with his utter subjection to illness,
decay and all that is implied in the word 'mortality.' " It seems illuminating
that the humanistic dual view of man as at once angel and beast appears
allied to the paradox of satire in general. Perhaps more than any other kind
of literature, satire transmits a dualistic vision, for it offers us always a
surface of contempt, disparagement, and ridicule masking something quite
different, namely, an implicit faith in man's capacity for redemption through
the operation of choice. Satire works by taxing its targets with brutishness
in order to turn them angelward. In the Augustan instinct for satire as a
favourite literary action we can sense very powerfully the presence of the
dualistic vision of man which in varying degrees informs all humanist
literature of whatever age.

To those aware of the workings of the moral imagination, dualistic
feelings are inescapable, for, as Johnson writes in *Rambler* 169, "In proportion as perfection is more distinctly conceived, the pleasure of contemplating our own performances will be lessened." And it seems to be the
strength of his dualistic instinct that keeps Johnson's view of man, even
when highly satiric in tendency, from ever turning into a mere Mandevillian
cynicism. Thus he writes his friend John Ryland: "As a being subject to so
many wants Man has inevitably a strong tendency to self-interest, so I hope

as a Being capable of comparing good and evil he finds something to be preferred in good, and is, therefore, capable of benevolence. . . ." The subtlety and tenuousness of Johnson's mode of Christianity is also provided in part by his dualistic habit. He suggests to Mrs. Thrale that "It is good to speak dubiously about futurity. It is likewise not amiss to hope."

It would be hard to find a happier emblem of the humanist dualistic conception of man than the Master Houyhnhnm's solution to the problem of Gulliver's most appropriate lodging-place during his first night in Houyhnhnmland. Gulliver could be sent to harbour with the Yahoos, for he certainly looks rather like one; or he could remain in the house of the Houyhnhnms, for he is capable of a form of converse with them. What to do? Gulliver's master determines on a meaningful compromise: "When it grew towards Evening, the Master Horse ordered a Place for me to lodge in; it was but Six Yards from the House, and separated from the Stable of the *Yahoos*. Here I got some Straw, and covering myself with my own Cloaths, slept very sound." This characteristically empirical, positional image locates Gulliver just where he belongs, in his proper "middle state" from which he is free to move in either direction. It is as if Swift were mindful of the ancient centaur myth and bent on domesticating it within the homely eighteenth-century realities and "comforts." Geoffrey Scott observes that what "nature" means to the humanist is not what it means to the savage nor yet what it means to the scientist. Taking Yahoos as loosely expressive of savagery and Houyhnhnms of science—perhaps their want of wit qualifies them, at least—we can see that what Scott says about the humanist's relation to "nature" illuminates Gulliver's challenge in Houyhnhnmland, the challenge that he accepts but bungles so badly. After positing a savage's "nature" and a scientist's "nature," Scott goes on to suggest that "a third way is open. [The humanist] may construct, within the world as it is, a pattern of the world as he would have it. This is the way of humanism, in philosophy, in life, and in the arts." But it is just this "third way" that Gulliver fails to take, a way which would make a gesture towards reconciling the dualistic extremes with which he is presented. Given his choice of behaving like the generous Captain Pedro de Mendez who rescues him or like the coherent, stable Martin of *A Tale of a Tub*, he decides instead to play a version of Peter, and the crashing irony is that he ends a slavering Jack. As Pope says in the *Essay on Man*, poor man is

This hour a slave, the next a deity.

(i, 68)

Gulliver sails proudly for home determined to act the deity, and succeeds only in turning slave.

Two-directional imagery like this image of Gulliver's lodging we encounter very frequently in Swift, and within the humanist tradition it seems the most common method for embodying ethical issues. Once we call it something like the habit of moral antithesis, it is obvious how it naturally works to shape the conventions of Augustan sentence structure and the syntactical and prosodic habits of the heroic couplet. Pope's prefatory remarks to the *Essay on Man* ("The Design") illustrate the dualistic or antithetical habit in prose: "If I could flatter myself that this Essay has any merit, it is in steering betwixt the extremes of doctrines seemingly opposite, . . . in forming a *temperate* yet not *inconsistent,* and a *short* yet not *imperfect* system of Ethics." Pope seems remarkably sensitive to the conventional halving of prayers in epic poetry, and his dualistic habit of mind seems to move him to recover the image for his own narrative uses. Thus in *The Rape of the Lock*

> [Lord Petre] begs with ardent Eyes
> Soon to obtain, and long possess the Prize:
> The pow'rs gave Ear, and granted half his Pray'r,
> The rest, the Winds dispers'd in empty Air.
>
> (ii, 43–46)

And complimenting Martha Blount in *Moral Essay* II, Pope tells her that Phoebus

> Averted half your Parents simple Pray'r,
> And gave you Beauty, but deny'd the Pelf
> That buys your sex a Tyrant o'er itself.
>
> (286–88)

It is all quite a bit like Hamlet's similar rhetorical habit. "Look here upon this picture, and on this," he invites Gertrude, and he proceeds to dichotomize vigorously until even the Queen, gradually moving a step closer to Hamlet's ethical vision, seems to catch the mode. She cries out,

> O, Hamlet, thou hast cleft my heart in twain.

As if encouraged that she has sensed the principle, Hamlet rejoins immediately:

> O, throw away the worser part of it,
> And live the purer with the better half,
>
> (III, iv. 54 ff.)

and he then moves to show her how self-restraint can be developed into an actual habit, almost, in Augustan terms, a "prejudice." Dualism is the method of Renaissance ethics, and it is remarkable how profoundly the dualistic habit of mind persists in ethical conservatives through all the political and social vicissitudes of the eighteenth century. Antitheses swarm everywhere: *this* and *that*, wit and judgment, reason and passion, art and nature, city and country, ancient and modern, uniformity and variety, sublime and beautiful. There is even a sense in which it is correct to say that the general method of a standard "ancient"—that is, moral—eighteenth-century poem is severely dichotomous. An action like the following, from Pope's *Epistle to Miss Blount, on her Leaving the Town, after the Coronation,* is played over and over again, from *Windsor Forest* and *The Day of Judgement* to *The Vanity of Human Wishes:*

> In some fair evening, on your elbow laid,
> You dream of triumphs in the rural shade;
> In pensive thought recall the fancy'd [urban] scene,
> See Coronations rise on ev'ry green;
> Before you pass th' imaginary sights
> Of Lords, and Earls, and Dukes, and garter'd Knights;
> While the spread Fan o'ershades your closing Eyes;
> Then give one flirt, and all the vision flies.
> Thus vanish sceptres, coronets, and balls,
> And leave you in lone woods, and empty halls.
>
> (31–40)

It is hard to tell whether the irony of poems like this results from the initial dualism of the ethical assumptions, or whether the ethical assumptions are pushed further in a dualistic direction by the natural operations of irony. But whatever we decide, there can be little doubt that there is an intimate relation between the dualistic method of mind and the humanist obsession with the paradox of man, as especially Samuel Johnson's rhetorical practice indicates.

Indeed, Johnson's habit of conceiving of things dualistically seems to provide him with his basic literary mode, whether he is talking or writing. As Boswell reports: "He would begin thus: 'Why, Sir, as to the good or evil of card-playing—' 'Now, (said Garrick,) he is thinking which side he shall take.' " In looking about him at human actions, Johnson's sense of the depravity of human nature colours dualistic perceptions like this, from *Rambler* 131: "the race of men may be divided in a political estimate between those who are practising fraud, and those who are repelling it." In sentence structure a dualism like the following is customary: "Spring is the season of gaiety, and winter of terror" (*Rambler* 80). Vast stylistic complication occurs, but the dualistic vision remains constant. Here, in the *Journey to the Western Islands,* he is exercising himself on the topic of power and money:

> Power and wealth supply the place of each other. Power confers the ability of gratifying our desire without the consent of others. Wealth enables us to obtain the consent of others to our gratification. Power, simply considered, whatever it confers on one, must take from another. Wealth enables its owner to give to others, by taking only from himself. Power pleases the violent and proud: wealth delights the placid and the timorous. Youth therefore flies at power, and age grovels after riches.

In the *Life of Milton* we are given the dualistic view of *Lycidas,* in which "there is no nature, for there is no truth; there is no art, for there is nothing new." And we are given the dualistic view of the practice of biography in *Idler* 84: "He that writes the life of another is either his friend or his enemy. . . ." And when Johnson insists in *Rambler* 4 that virtue and vice be depicted in fiction as clearly distinct and separable, we see the same impulse towards moral dichotomy; we see it, too, in his advice to Boswell about calling whores by the right name: "My dear Sir, never accustom your mind to mingle virtue and vice." Now and then the dualisms become themselves the agents of irony and wit, as when Johnson says of the Third Letter of Jenyns's *Free Inquiry* that it contains "a mixture of borrowed truth, and native folly, of some notions just and trite, and others uncommon and ridiculous." Poor Jenyns!

Johnson conceives of man's paradoxical nature as the product of the conflicting dualisms of which he is constituted. "While the world was yet in its infancy," he pronounces in *Rambler* 96, "TRUTH came among mortals from above, and FALSEHOOD from below." The result is a hierarchical arrangement of the human faculties which involves a constant struggle between mind at the top and body underneath. The contrary directions in which these two capacities urge him will always produce in man a degree of self-division: as Johnson says in *Adventurer* 120, the mind of the virtuous man, "however elevated, inhabits a body subject to innumerable casualties." Part of man's ethical business is to find any means for keeping the mind, the upper part of the hierarchical dualism, in the ascendancy. To Johnson, even so slight an activity as forming virtuoso collections of coins and shells has some ethical value, for, "by fixing the thoughts upon intellectual pleasures, [it] resists the natural encroachments of sensuality, and maintains the mind in her lawful superiority" (*Idler* 56). The phrase "lawful superiority" has of course a distinctly old-fashioned ring, recalling as it does such classic Renaissance formulations of moral hierarchy as that in Sir Thomas Elyot's *Book of the Governor* (1531): "In every thyng is ordre: and without ordre may be nothing stable or permanent: And it may nat be called ordre excepte it do contayne in it degrees, high and base, accordynge to the merite or estimation of the thynge that is ordred."

Few things are clearer to Johnson than that even in his moral victories man by his nature has been doomed to choose, and thus to reject a treasured part of himself, and thus to be miserable. In *Idler* 52 he writes: "The general voice of mankind, civil and barbarous, confesses that the mind and body are at variance, and that neither can be made happy by its proper gratifications but at the expence of the other." And yet man's predicament ironic as it is offers him no avenue to satisfaction but to cede to the upper element in his personal hierarchy; Johnson continues: "And none have failed to confer their esteem on those who prefer intellect to sense, who control their lower by their higher faculties, and forget the wants and desires of animal life for rational disquisitions or pious contemplations." Self-division is a sad thing, but self-destruction is worse.

Reynolds's image of hierarchy seems, in Elyot's term, to admit more "degrees" than Johnson's. The end of the *Ninth Discourse* operates in the "noble" Augustan tradition of fusing artistic taste and moral value. The great use of "liberal" painting, by which Reynolds means history painting depicting heroic moral conflicts, is that it may be a vehicle for refining the taste of whole countries. Refinement of taste, he says, "if it does not lead directly to purity of manners, obviates at least their general depravation, by disentangling the mind from appetite, and conducting the thoughts through successive stages of excellence, till that contemplation of universal rectitude and harmony which began by Taste, may, as it is exalted and refined, conclude in Virtue." But even though the upward movement from one extreme to another, from "depravation" to "purity," necessitates pauses at "successive stages," we are still conscious of an objective dualism defined by the distance between "mind" and "appetite." As Reynolds confesses in his remarks on Shakespeare, "If I was to judge from my own experience, the mind always desires to double, to entertain two objects at a time."

In Gibbon the dualistic tendency takes the form of an appreciation of something very like duplicity as fundamental to the uniform nature of man. In an observation like the following, from Chapter II of the *Decline and Fall*, we are invited to prefer the disingenuous dualism of the ancient philosophers to the naïve monism ("sincerity") of the early Christians: "In their writings and conversation the philosophers of antiquity asserted the independent dignity of reason; but they resigned their actions to the commands of law and of custom. Viewing with a smile of pity and indulgence the various errors of the vulgar, they diligently practised the ceremonies of their fathers . . . they approached with the same inward contempt and the same external reverence the altars of the Libyan, the Olympian, or the Capitoline Jupiter." Dissimulation thus becomes something close to an obligation for those deeply aware of the requirements of human nature. Gibbon's sense of the vast difference between inner and outer corresponds to Johnson's scepticism about literary "sincerity," and the Gibbonian relation between philosophers and Christians is very like that between the eighteenth-century literary "ancients" and "moderns."

From these examples of the humanist instinct for dualistic images we can gauge the distance of the humanist ethical and rhetorical world from the monistic or transcendental world, with its impulse towards erasing disparities and distinctions rather than asserting and emphasizing them. It is a fundamental humanist assumption that nothing is equal to anything else. It follows as we have seen that man's obligations to the life of value require of him a constant exercise of hierarchical ranking and arranging of the data of experience and the forces of his internal nature. A very frequent humanist action, then, is the hierarchical ordering of the items within the several distinguishable classes of data. The humanist sensibility loves to deal with apparent moral dilemmas and puzzles whose solutions are based upon an apprehension of the proper hierarchical premises. It enjoys considering questions such as these: is Garrick a good actor but a bad man? should Adam have chosen God or Eve? is the just or the expedient action to be preferred? In Chapter II of his *Autobiography* Gibbon exercises his hierarchical sensibility even over the question of the comparative desirability of childhood and age, and in the process of his reasoning, feels it necessary to reassert the very old-fashioned image of the chain of being. He is doubting the validity of Gray's picture of the joys of youth in *Ode on a Distant Prospect of Eton College:*

> I would ask the warmest and most active hero of the playfield whether he can seriously compare his childish with his manly enjoyments, whether he does not feel, as the most precious attribute of his existence, the vigorous maturity of sensual and spiritual powers which nature has reserved for the age of puberty. A state of happiness arising only from the want of foresight and reflection shall never provoke my envy. Such

degenerate taste would tend to shrink us in the scale of beings from a man to a child, a dog, and an oyster, till we had reached the confines of brute matter, which cannot suffer because it cannot feel.

The monistic tradition would reject entirely Gibbon's attempt to escape his childhood and to separate it from his maturity. In *Out of the Cradle Endlessly Rocking* it is Whitman's ambition to pass beyond such a distinction and to enact instead the wonder-working fusion of childhood and age. In *Ode: Intimations of Immortality* Wordsworth presents himself in the act of attempting to recover the "visionary gleam" vouchsafed the child. But Gibbon, inhabiting a moral world where distinction, separation, inequality, and hierarchy are almost self-evident ethical principles, would look upon the performances of both Whitman and Wordsworth as enactments of precisely the kind of "Dulness" exposed in *The Dunciad,* of which Thomas R. Edwards has observed: "The aim of Dulness is sameness, the utter absence of the differentiation that makes order possible. . . . In such a state intelligence has no place, for there are no qualitative differences to be discriminated. Dulness melts down and levels off the structural order of 'degree' that had been the imagination's dream since the beginnings of thought."

The distance between the dualistic and the monistic worlds is clearly apparent in the difference between the general theory of metaphor preferred respectively by "ancients" and "moderns." To the humanist, metaphor, which operates like rapid or almost instantaneous simile, does not actually assert that "a *is* b"; instead it suggests that "a is *like* b." Tenor and vehicle are never thought to interfuse; regardless of closeness of resemblance, the two terms in a comparison remain ultimately distinct. This distrust of the "reality" of metaphor underlies Johnson's point when he tells Boswell: "I do not approve of figurative expressions in addressing the Supreme Being; and I never use them. Taylor gives a very good advice: 'Never lie in your prayers. . . .' " But within the monistic rhetorical world all the way from Shelley to Wallace Stevens the metaphor is so far from being a "lie" that instead it becomes the avenue, and often the sole avenue, to reality: the two terms of a figure actually fuse and thus generate a more "real" third thing.

Johnson's conception of the ultimate frivolity of metaphor suggests his prodigious understanding of the permanent distinctions between form and matter, mind and body; and this understanding prompts his humane perception of the necessary distance between a man's ethical principles and his ethical practice. He is sometimes horrified by the kind of crude, mechanical assumptions on this question that he encounters. On one occasion he is moved to reprimand "one who said in his presence" that "he had no notion of people being in earnest in their good professions, whose practice was not suitable to them." Johnson explodes: "Sir, are you so grossly ignorant of human nature as not to know that a man may be very sincere in good principles, without having good practice?" In this vigorous Johnsonian rejoinder we perceive the truth of Mrs. Thrale's comment on his dualism: "all he did was gentle, if all he said was rough."

To the humanist, inconsistency is necessarily man's lot: to expect consistency from him is to deny by implication the paradoxical dualism that makes him man. Pope reveals his appreciation of this fact about man's nature when, in the *Essay on Man,* he reasons so that he makes the corrupt passions of man ironically productive of all his virtues. Indeed, the major paradoxical theme of the poem is

> Man's low passions, [and] their glorious ends.
> (iv, 376)

But Pope's attitude towards this subject is complacent when compared with Johnson's. Johnson seems more empirically aware than Pope that, as Imlac says in Chapter XVIII of *Rasselas,* "teachers of morality . . . discourse like angels, but . . . live like men." And Johnson's perception of the gulf between principles and practice is pleasantly complicated by an overriding irony and sympathy. So it is in the relation between Chapters XVII and XVIII of *Rasselas.* The first of these chapters depicts Rasselas's disgust and boredom with the pleasures of "[Egyptian] young men of spirit and gaiety," whose dissipations he finds "gross and sensual" because in them "the mind had no part." In the next chapter, however, determined now to live according to the promptings of his judgment, Rasselas is presented with the spectacle of the local Stoic who utters high principles of self-restraint and intellectual control until his daughter suddenly dies, whereupon he becomes a man like anyone else and breaks down completely. This Stoic is simply a bodying forth of Johnson's conviction that "no man has power of acting equal to that of thinking" (*Rambler* 77).

Johnson's honest and intimate acquaintance with himself—with, for example, his repeated experience of procrastination and violated resolutions—prevents his feeling anything but sympathy for others whose practices diverge grossly from their principles. It goes without saying that one of the sources of the sympathy which emanates from the pages of the *Life of Savage* is Johnson's intimate identification of himself with the character of his subject, whose principles "were . . . treasured up in his mind rather for shew than use, and operated very little upon his conduct, however elegantly he might sometimes explain, or however forcibly he might inculcate them." This sympathy with the paradoxical state of man also colours Johnson's interpretation of the character of Pope. In the *Life of Pope* he assures us that despite Pope's indulgence in sceptical levities and indecencies, "it does not appear that his principles were ever corrupted, or that he ever lost his belief of Revelation." Pope indeed becomes pleasantly emblematic of Everyman when Johnson explains why it took him so long to translate the *Iliad;* wise after his experience with the *Dictionary,* Johnson comments that "the distance is commonly very great between actual performances and speculative possibility." This is to say that a satisfactory monistic synthesis is not within the power of genuinely human creatures, at least in this state, although circumstances may be different elsewhere; as Johnson says, "The happiness of Heaven will be, that pleasure and virtue will be perfectly consistent." But in the sublunary sphere the distance between desire and performance is wide, so wide, in fact, that Johnson feels it necessary to give this advice, in the *Life of Sir Thomas Browne,* to those who would know man: "The opinions of every man must be learned from himself: concerning his practice, it is safest to trust the evidence of others."

But all humanists affirm the inconsistency of man: Johnson is simply more deeply immersed in the matter than others. Typical of the whole tradition is Swift's observation in his *Thoughts on Various Subjects:* "If a Man would register all his Opinions on Love, Politicks, Religion, Learning, and the like; beginning from his Youth, and so go on to old Age: What a Bundle of Inconsistencies and Contradictions would appear at last?" The arch-sin of Pride, indeed, is roughly equivalent to the assumption that human actions can be consistent. And so is the archenemy social science. Boswell is fond of exploiting the humanist premise of the inconsistency of man as a pretext for a gratifying self-wonder. He records in his journal in 1762: "What a curious, inconsistent thing is the mind of man! In the midst of divine service I was laying plans for having women, and yet I had the most sincere feelings of religion."

In the hands of Reynolds, the conviction of the ludicrous and pathetic inconsistency of man generates a characteristic and little-known humanist document, his fragmentary essay on Shakespeare. "Arts have little to do with reason," Reynolds observes. And from this Burkean premise he sets out like Johnson to justify Shakespeare's practice of "mixing tragedy and comedy." Like Burke and Johnson again, he conceives of his task as in part a skirmish with the "mechanical" French mind, and like them he turns away from systems and theories to inquire into "the natural and unsophisticated feelings of mankind." What the French critics have overlooked is simply that man is not a rational creature:

Theoretical systems . . . go on a supposition that by their precepts and order they can give a different disposition and quality
to the mind than nature had thought proper to give, that a man
ought totally to keep separate his intellectual from his sensual
desires. All this is fine in theory, but—

Man being what he is, an inconsistent being, a professed lover
of art and nature, of order, of regularity, and of variety, and
who therefore cannot long continue his attention without some
recreation; hence it is that the poet relieves the mind of the reader
[by variety].

Typical of English humanist criticism from Ben Jonson to T. S. Eliot is
the recourse to the actual, experienced operations of the human mind as a
basis for literary theory; and typical of the Augustan humanist tradition is
Reynolds's sanction of the "mingled drama" by means of an honest—if
compulsively dualistic—look at human realities:

Man is both a consistent and an inconsistent being, a lover of
art when it imitates nature and of nature when it imitates art,
of uniformity and of variety, a creature of habit that loves nov-
elty. The principles of art must conform to this capricious being.
. . .

Critics seem to consider man as too uniformly wise, and in
their rules make no account for the playful part of the mind.
Their rules are formed for another race of beings than what man
really is.

Because the mind works whimsically and inconsistently, and because men
are normally as pathetically abstracted and bemused as the inhabitants of
Swift's Laputa, "The theatre," says Reynolds, "acts as a flapper and rouses
in us for the time a fictitious feeling of interest and pleasing anxiety." It is
empirically if not theoretically true that, given the inconsistency of the
mind, tragicomedy will accord more with that mind's desires than "purer"
and less varied forms.

"We have," says Johnson, "less reason to be surprised or offended
when we find others differ from us in opinion, because we very often differ
from ourselves" (*Adventurer* 107). Of all the Augustan humanists Johnson
remains for us as for his contemporaries the prime exemplar of a splendid
human inconsistency. He has become a pattern for imitation and almost,
indeed, a humanist saint. Reynolds noticed that "From passion, from the
prevalence of his disposition for the minute, he was continually acting
contrary to his reason, to his own principles." And to Boswell his incon-

sistency was so interesting because it was so eminently typical of general human nature: "The heterogeneous composition of human nature was remarkably exemplified in Johnson. His liberality in giving his money to persons in distress was extraordinary. Yet there lurked about him a propensity to paltry saving." Johnson's last days, when he seems to be just exactly as certain of his imminent salvation as he is of his imminent damnation, remind us of those of Abraham Cowley, who uttered near the end this humanist prayer: "O Lord, I believe: help my unbelief. O Lord, I repent: pardon the weakness of my repentance." The uneasy partnership between the angelic and the brutal in Johnson's person—that extraordinary spirit in that outrageous body!—seems to project the whole humanist scheme of dualism and inconsistency. And a vignette that embodies all that we have been considering is Miss Reynolds's unforgettable portrayal of Johnson, the proud, sarcastical, puffing, heavy bear, lumbering noisily through the City very late at night and gently folding pennies into the hands of the abandoned children asleep in the streets.

What makes the human situation the more pitiful is that man is actually so limited and frail and tiny, especially when viewed next to the heroic images he is pleased to entertain of himself. As Sir Lewis Namier is reputed to have said, "Conservatism is primarily based on the proper recognition of human limitation." From the beginning the Augustan conservatives conduct their warfare with the eighteenth-century progressives by insisting on the ineradicable limitations of man. Locke's whole account of the mind stems from his premise that it is much more finite, limited, and frail than had been sometimes thought in the earlier seventeenth century. In the *Theory of Moral Sentiments* Adam Smith hits upon the transformation in the theory of man that has taken place within a couple of centuries; as he perceives, "Humanity does not desire to be great, but to be loved." And it desires to be loved because it is secretly conscious of the extent of its "private infirmities," as Swift calls them in one of his richest comments on the ethical use of the classics. Speaking as if without his customary mask in the "Digression on Madness" in *A Tale of a Tub,* he says: "the Brain, in its natural Position and State of Serenity, disposeth its Owner to pass his Life in the common Forms, without any Thought of subduing Multitudes to his own *Power,* his *Reasons* or his *Visions;* and the more he shapes his Understanding by the Pattern of Human Learning, the less he is inclined to form Parties after his particular Notions; because that instructs him in his private Infirmities, as well as in the stubborn Ignorance of the People." Here Swift, relying on the assumption of the uniformity of human nature, indicates that a primary use of ancient literature ("Human Learning") is to keep man reminded of his limitations and of the irony of his ambitions. Which is to say that the modern perversion of evangelicism, all the way from Puritans to Jacobins, is to be ascribed in part to the modern neglect of classical literature. If the modern Soame Jenyns had been more deeply read in the ancient literature of human limitation, Johnson suggests, he might have imbibed some salutary caution; as it is, says Johnson, Jenyns "decides too easily upon questions out of reach of human determination, with too little consideration of mortal weakness, and with too much vivacity for the necessary caution." After exposing Jenyns's attempts to reason accurately about the chain of being, Johnson concludes: "To these meditations humanity is unequal."

Johnson implies the whole humanist theory of composition—moderns would want to call it "creation"—in *Rambler* 169, where he argues that a thoroughgoing sense of human weakness is a foremost ingredient of literary genius. The main reason, he says, why the writings of the ancients seem preferable to those of the moderns is not so much that the ancients thought of all the good subjects first or that their language was more polished and subtle, but rather that "Their sense of human weakness confined them commonly to one study, which their knowledge of the extent of every science engaged them to prosecute with indefatigable diligence." That is, suspicious of themselves because of their general awareness of human limitations, they judged and revised assiduously, just like Milton and Pope: "much time, and many rasures, were considered as indispensable requisites; and that no other method of attaining lasting praise has been yet discovered, may be conjectured from the blotted manuscripts of Milton now remaining, and from the tardy emission of Pope's compositions. . . ."

Sometimes Johnson like Swift turns to the overtly physical to enforce the idea of the limitations of human nature. In *Idler* 32, for example, he writes that Alexander,

> in the pride of conquests, and intoxication of flattery, . . . declared that he only perceived himself to be a man by the necessity of sleep. Whether he considered sleep as necessary to his mind or body, it was indeed a sufficient evidence of human infirmity; the body which required such frequency of renovation, gave but faint promises of immortality; and the mind which, from time to time, sunk gladly into insensibility, made no very near approaches to the felicity of the supreme and self-sufficient nature.

And Socrates, wiser than Alexander, "by long observation upon himself and others, discovered the weakness of the strongest, and the dimness of the most enlightened intellect" (*Adventurer* 58). The liability of Gibbon's early Christians to delusion and self-deception suggests the threat to the frail human imagination that attends an excessive will to behold wonders. As it does throughout Chapters XV and XVI of the *Decline and Fall*, Gibbon's word "extraordinary" means here nothing short of "incredible" or "impossible": "The primitive Christians perpetually trod on mystic ground, and their minds were exercised by the habits of believing the most extraordinary events. They felt, or they fancied, that on every side they were incessantly assaulted by demons. . . ." Gibbon's "perpetually" and "incessantly" operate like Swift's "infallibly" to expose the total preposterousness of these proceedings. What is sacred to Gibbon is the sense of human limitation: the blasphemy is whatever calls it into question.

A similar sense of the sacredness of human limitations is the staple of Burke's whole career in rhetoric and polemic. As he points out in *Thoughts on French Affairs*, it was the mad pride of Louis XVI that helped dethrone him. In constraining and humbling his nobility and clergy, Louis revealed that "he could not bear the inconveniences which are attached to everything human"; he could not bear "those limits which Nature prescribes to desire and imagination. . . ." What Louis XVI forgot is precisely what Johnson, with his customary dualistic vision, sets before us in *Rambler* 178: "Providence has fixed the limits of human enjoyment by immovable boundaries, and has set different gratifications at such a distance from each other, that no art or power can bring them together. This great law it is the business of every rational being to understand, that life may not pass away in an attempt to make contradictions consistent, to combine opposite qualities, and to unite things which the nature of their being must always keep asunder."

The theme of human limitations is admirably "incorporated" by Swift in the image of the frailty of Gulliver's body. Indeed, it is remarkable what happens physically to poor Gulliver during his four voyages. He does far more suffering than acting. Even though as a surgeon he is more likely than most to dwell obsessively on his own physical injuries, and even though his commitment to the ideals of the Royal Society impels him to deliver his narrative with a comically detailed circumstantiality, he records a really startling number of hurts. In the voyage to Lilliput, for example, his hair is painfully pulled, and his hands and face are blistered by needlelike arrows. During his stay among the people of Brobdingnag he is battered so badly that he appears almost accident-prone: his flesh is punctured by wheatbeards; twice his sides are painfully crushed; he is shaken up and bruised in a box; his nose and forehead are grievously stung by flies as big as larks; he suffers painful contusions from a shower of gigantic hailstones; he "breaks" his shin on a snailshell; and he is pummelled about the head and body by a linnet's wings. And during his fourth voyage he is brought again into dire physical jeopardy: his final series of physical ordeals begins as his hand is painfully squeezed by a horse. Finally, as he leaves Houyhnhnmland, Swift contrives that Gulliver shall suffer a wholly gratuitous arrow wound on the inside of his left knee ("I shall carry the Mark to my Grave"). Looking back on the whole extent of Gulliver's experiences before his final return to England, we are hardly surprised that his intellectuals at the end have come unhinged: for years his body has been beaten, dropped, squeezed, lacerated, and punctured. When all is said, the experiences which transform him from a fairly bright young surgeon into a raging megalomaniac have been almost as largely physical as intellectual and psychological. So powerfully does Swift reveal Gulliver's purely mental difficulties at the end of the fourth voyage that we may tend to forget that Gulliver has also been made to undergo the sorest physical trials. During the four voyages he has been hurt so badly that, although he is normally a taciturn, unemotional, "Roman" sort of person, he has been reduced to weeping three times; so severely has he been injured at various times that at least twenty-four of his total travelling days he has spent recuperating in bed.

In addition to these actual injuries which Gulliver endures, he also experiences a number of narrow escapes, potential injuries, and pathetic fears of physical hurt. In Lilliput the vulnerability of his eyes is insisted upon: an arrow barely misses his left eye, and only his spectacles prevent the loss of both his eyes as he works to capture the Blefuscan fleet. Furthermore, one of the Lilliputian punishments decreed for Quinbus Flestrin is that his eyes be put out. And during the Brobdingnagian trip Gulliver's experience is one of an almost continuous narrow escape from serious injury. He almost falls from the hand of the farmer and off the edge of the table. Stumbling over a crust, he falls flat on his face and barely escapes injury. After being held in a child's mouth, he is dropped, and he is saved only by being miraculously caught in a woman's apron. He is tossed into a bowl of cream, knocked down but not badly hurt by a shower of falling apples, and clutched dangerously between a spaniel's teeth. He is lucky to escape serious injury during a nasty tumble into a mole hill, whereupon he "coined some Lye not worth remembering, to excuse my self for spoiling my Cloaths." And during the sojourn at Laputa, he is afraid of some "hurt" befalling him in his encounter with the magician.

But Gulliver, who acts like a sort of physically vulnerable *Ur*-Boswell on the Grand Tour, is not the only one in the book who suffers or who fears injury: the creatures he is thrown among also endure catastrophes of pain and damage, often curiously particularized by Swift. Thus in Lilliput, two or three of the ropedancers break their limbs in falls. A horse, slipping partway through Gulliver's handkerchief, strains a shoulder. The grandfather of the Lilliputian monarch, it is reported, as a result of breaking his egg upon the larger end suffered a cut finger. In the same way, the fourth voyage seems busy with apparently gratuitous details of injury and pain: for example, Gulliver carefully tells us that an elderly Houyhnhnm "of Quality" alighted from his Yahoo-drawn sledge "with his Hindfeet forward, having by Accident got a Hurt in his Left Forefoot."

Nor are all the manifold injuries in *Gulliver's Travels* confined to the bodies of Gulliver and his hosts. Gulliver's clothing and personal property suffer constant damage, and when they are not actually being damaged, Gulliver is worrying that at any moment they may be hurt. We are not surprised that a shipwrecked mariner suffers damage to his clothing and personal effects, but we are surprised that Gulliver constantly goes out of his way to call attention to the damages and losses he suffers: his scimitar, his hat, his breeches—all are damaged in Lilliput, and the damage is punctiliously recounted. In Brobdingnag the familiar process of damage and deterioration begins all over again: a fall into a bowl of milk utterly spoils Gulliver's suit; his stockings and breeches are soiled when he is thrust into a marrow bone; and his suit—what's left of it—is further ruined by being daubed with frog slime and "bemired" with cow dung. In the third voyage our attention is invited to the fact that his hat has again worn out, and in the fourth voyage we are told yet again by Gulliver that his clothes are "in a declining Condition."

Gulliver's clothes and personal effects, in fact, at times seem to be Gulliver himself: this is the apparent state of things which fascinates the Houyhnhnm before whom Gulliver undresses; and this ironic suggestion of an equation between Gulliver and his clothing, reminding us of the ironic "clothes philosophy" of Section II of *A Tale of a Tub,* Swift exploits to suggest that damage to Gulliver's frail garments is the equivalent of damage to the frail Gulliver. The vulnerability of Gulliver's clothing, that is, is a symbol three degrees removed from what it appears to signify: damage to the clothes is symbolic of damage to the body; and damage to the body is symbolic of damage to Gulliver's complacent self-esteem.

These little incidents of injury and destruction are pervasive in *Gulliver's Travels,* as we are reminded by the recurrence—very striking once we are attuned to it—of words like "hurt," "injury," "damage," "accident," "mischief," "misfortune," and "spoiled." When we focus on what is happening physically in *Gulliver's Travels,* we sense the oblique presence of this motif of frailty and vulnerability even in passages which really address themselves to something quite different. For example: "His Majesty [the Emperor of Blefuscu] presented me . . . with his Picture at full length, which I immediately put into one of my Gloves, to keep it from being hurt." It is as if Swift were determined not to let us forget that there is a pathetic fragility in all his fictional objects, whether animate or inanimate.

And Swift seems to have provided within his text a key to these pervasive reminders of the vulnerability of man and the fragility of his personal effects. In the second voyage, we are told in a voice which sounds perhaps more Swiftian than Gulliverian of a "little old Treatise" treasured now only by elderly women and the more credulous vulgar, a copy of which Glumdalclitch has been given by her governess. The burden of this mysterious little book, we are told, is precisely the theme of the physical frailty of man: the book shows "how diminutive, contemptible, and helpless an Animal . . . [is] Man in his own Nature." Like Johnson's version of Juvenal in *London,* the book emphasizes man's liability to accident and injury; it argues that "the very Laws of Nature absolutely required we should have been made in the Beginning, of a Size more large and robust, not so liable to Destruction from every little Accident of a Tile falling from an House, or a Stone cast from the Hand of a Boy, or of being drowned in a little Brook." Here Swift appears to avail himself of the myth of the Decay of Nature as a fictional surrogate for the Christian myth of the Fall. Although, as Miss Kathleen Williams reminds us, Godfrey Goodman's *The Fall of Man, or the Corruption of Nature* (1616) is perhaps the kind of "little old Treatise" Swift has in mind [*Jonathan Swift and the Age of Compromise* (Lawrence, Kansas, 1958)], I think we shall not go far wrong if we associate—even though we do not identify—Glumdalclitch's conservative little book with the Bible itself. The theme that Swift realizes by means of the image of Gulliver's physical frailty appears quintessentially humanistic: the theme is the inadequacy of an unassisted self-esteem in redeeming man from his essential frailties of mind and spirit. Swift's conception of Gulliver is close to Pope's feeling for the China jar which is Belinda. And Pope's sense of human frailty in the *Essay on Man* reminds us of Gulliver's fear for his eyes in Lilliput and for his body in Brobdingnag: addressing "Presumptuous Man," Pope taxes him with being "so weak, so little, and so blind." In one of its most significant moods the Augustan humanist mind conceives of man thus as a little delicate cage of bones and skin constantly at the mercy of accidental damage or destruction.

Johnson's sense of man's littleness is such that, if Swift had not already written it, he might himself have been tempted to sketch such a comedy of man diminished as Gulliver enacts in his second voyage. Boswell reports:

> I mentioned that I was afraid to put into my journal too many little incidents. JOHNSON. "There is nothing, Sir, too little for so little a creature as man. It is by studying little things that we attain the great art of having as little misery and as much happiness as possible."

What Gulliver appears not to learn during his stay with the Brobdingnagians Johnson, in *Idler* 88, indicates that he has mastered completely: "a little more than nothing is as much as can be expected from [man], who with respect to the multitudes about him is himself little more than nothing." We think of the preposterousness of poor, foolish Gulliver who imagines that he is doing a great thing in performing on the spinet before the King and Queen of Brobdingnag, pounding on the keys with "two round Sticks about the Bigness of common Cudgels." Says Gulliver: "I ran sideling . . . that way and this, as fast as I could, banging the proper Keys with my two Sticks, and made a shift to play a Jigg to the great Satisfaction of both their Majesties." We may be forgiven if we impute their Majesties' "Satisfaction" more to their sense of the ridiculous than to their sense of wonder. Writing Boswell in 1777, Johnson speaks as an educated and redeemed Gulliver when he refers to the *Lives of the Poets* this way: "I am engaged to write little Lives, and little Prefaces, to a little edition of the English Poets." In short, man's ethical obligation is to learn "how to become little without becoming mean . . ." (*Rambler* 152).

Reynolds suggests in the *Fifth Discourse* how the assumption of the littleness of man is the very basis of the practice of heroic painting, and by implication, epic poetry: one of Raphael's weaknesses when he is measured against Michelangelo, Reynolds argues, is that his "figures are not so much disjoined [as Michelangelo's] from our own diminutive race of beings. . . ." That is, the whole humanist conception of history-painting depends on a tacit agreement between artist and viewer that man in his natural state is very tiny: history-painting thus has the task and the opportunity not of "representing" man but of depicting him "enlarged" and ennobled by his heroic choices. This is to say that the very existence and appeal of history-painting presupposes a paradoxical view of man, a view which sees him as naturally limited, frail, and tiny, and yet capable of growing to heroism and dignity by willing to imitate images of the noble.

It may be worth noticing here the similarity between the humanistic theory of the heroic figure in history-painting and the humanistic theory of space in classical architecture. "Reason" and "logic," deceptive as usual, suggest that, placed within a very large and open architectural space like a cathedral nave or a palace gallery, man will feel proportionately diminished and little. But here as elsewhere reason and logic are wrong. Experience indicates that exactly the opposite is true: instead of making man feel smaller, large enclosed spaces make him feel larger, and high ceilings make him feel not shorter, as we might expect, but taller. Classical architecture, focusing like all humanistic aesthetic theory on the given nature of man, exploits the paradoxical capacity of the human imagination to enlarge its vision of itself. It is a curious characteristic of the human imagination that, presented with a very large enclosed space, it somehow operates in such a way as to regard itself as worthy of filling it. The designers of classical temples, theatres, and baths, and of cathedrals and palaces, create ample enclosed space partly, of course, as an index of conspicuous exhibition; but partly too to take advantage of the imagination's power to "enlarge" itself in the presence of the large. Anyone may make the experiment himself: he may stand in the livingroom of a small, low-ceilinged suburban house or in a low-ceilinged bus terminal and then betake himself to something like the central hall of Pennsylvania Station in New York and inquire of himself where he feels the most internal dignity. Sensing that architecture is built *for him* and as a comment *on him,* man will feel flattered and dignified under a high ceiling and insulted and diminished under a low one. It is significant that modern society is rapidly ridding itself of its high ceilings as if to make the point that man's native smallness is unredeemable by art or illusion. Just as the image of the heroic has largely vanished from contemporary literature, so in architecture we are tending to express the same sort of disbelief in heroic redemption which we have already asserted by creating a "consumer" world. The death of both history-painting and humanistic—that is, heroic—architecture seems thus to reflect a modern erosion of belief in the human paradox, that is, in the vision of man as at once tiny and at the same time capable of dignity.

For despite man's limitations, the humanist holds that he is the only creature capable of dignity, and his being *capax dignitatis* is the ultimate element of the paradox which is his nature. To Locke it is man's capacity for abstraction—for apprehending something like Johnsonian "general nature"—that constitutes his "excellency": "this, I think, I may be positive in," he asserts in the *Essay,* "that the power of abstracting is not at all in [animals]; and that the having of general ideas is that which puts a perfect distinction betwixt man and brutes, and is an excellency which the faculties of brutes do by no means attain to" (II, xi). This "having of general ideas" is what enables man, as Burke insists, to be largely a creature of his own construction, that is, to take an active role in the formation of his self-image. By the exercise of his power of perceiving "general nature" man gradually liberates himself from slavery to matter, place, and time, and frees himself to enter history—and thus real life—imaginatively. As Johnson concludes in the *Journey to the Western Islands* after a visit to the sacred island of Icolmkill: "Whatever withdraws us from the power of our senses; whatever makes the past, the distant, or the future predominate over the present, advances us in the dignity of thinking beings." And one thing totally inconsistent with human dignity is mechanism of any sort. It is on the free exercise of the will that human dignity depends. "Reason loses her dignity," as Johnson says, "in proportion as she has oftener yielded to temptation" (*Adventurer* 108).

It is this idea of the potential dignity of man, for all his depravity and littleness, that generates a feeling of pathos and tenderness in the humanist, a tenderness born from the perception of the gulf between man as he is and man as he has it in his power to become. Are we wrong to sense, in Swift's account of Gulliver's physical humiliations, a pathos mingling with the wit? Or in Pope's brisk ratiocinations an inexpressible underlying sympathy for man's touching blunders and self-deceptions? It is surely Johnson's exquisite sympathy for the state of man in his "blunders and puzzles" that impels much of his fury at Soame Jenyns. Outraged by Jenyns's suggestion that the problem of evil can be eased by positing a higher race of beings who torment us for their malignant pleasure, Johnson exposes Jenyns's argument by carrying it both to the point of absurdity and—more important—to the point of pathos:

> Many a merry bout have these frolic beings at the vicissitudes of an ague, and good sport it is to see a man tumble with an epilepsy, and revive and tumble again, and all this he knows not why. As they are wiser and more powerful than we, they have more exquisite diversions, for we have no way of procuring any sport so brisk and so lasting as the paroxysms of the gout and stone which undoubtedly must make high mirth, especially if the play be a little diversified with the blunders and puzzles of the blind and deaf.

There is no response to Johnson's quiet, simple, monosyllabic "and all this he knows not why" except Johnson's own: "It is not to be endured." This kind of protective tenderness towards the idea of man, showing itself through all the irony and the satire and the polemic, is a sign that we are close to the living heart of the humanist paradox. "When [Johnson] would try to repeat the celebrated . . . *Dies Irae*," Mrs. Thrale recalls, "he could never pass the stanza ending thus, *Tantus labor non sit cassus*, without bursting into a flood of tears." There are tears and tears in the eighteenth century, but Johnson's are memorable for being not at all sentimental. They are not Shaftesburian. They are drawn not by namby-pamby lambs and linnets but by the conception of man's conscious precarious location between the fact of mortal dissolution and the hope—always pathetic, for hope deceives—that all God's labour of incarnation and immolation has not been in vain:

> Quaerens me sedisti lassus.
> Redemisti crucem passus:
> Tantus labor non sit cassus.

The frail but noble hope, that is, that so much labour has not been lost, and that such a creature as man shall not in the end find nothing for his efforts at dignity and redemption but a broken promise and an unregarded grave.

The Role of the Horses in "A Voyage to the Houyhnhnms"

Conrad Suits

It is no longer the fashion in critical circles to believe that Swift was insane when he wrote the fourth book of *Gulliver's Travels*. Thanks to the acute insight of a number of our contemporaries, we are now invited to see that Gulliver himself was the mad party. As a consequence we are to regard Gulliver as ridiculous, a figure of fun. This conclusion derives from the premise, if Swift were not mad, Gulliver must have been, because only a madman could have held such a low opinion of human beings as that developed in the fourth book. A number of present-day commentators on Swift would then, in a word, have someone mad, for such deep-dyed misanthropy is the same thing as madness. Basing an argument on an alternative proposition can, however, be dangerous. In the present instance the critics have overlooked a third possibility, namely, that their own brains have undergone an unlucky shake, that in them fancy has got astride of reason and that, consequently, common understanding, as well as common sense, has been kicked out of doors. It will be one of the purposes of this paper to suggest that Gulliver was not mad and therefore not a comic figure; rather that he made valid inferences about human nature from the evidence before him and so was as sane as his creator, or as you or I for that matter. I do not make this attempt on the principle that an ounce of my own wit is worth a ton of anyone else's but on the grounds of the evidence and of what I conceive to be the nature of satire, neither of which considerations has anything novel about it.

From *University of Toronto Quarterly* 34, no. 2 (January 1965). © 1965 by University of Toronto Press.

No one has suggested that Gulliver is a madman upon his arrival in Houyhnhnmland. It is evident that when he encounters the horses for the first time he quite naturally assumes that they are simply of a superior breed and that the *human* inhabitants of the country consequently must be proportionately superior to any other human beings. Gulliver has not been in this strange land for an hour when he is placed side by side with a Yahoo and is struck with the physical similarity between himself and the "abominable animal":

> My horror and astonishment are not to be described, when I observed in this abominable animal a perfect human figure: the face of it indeed was flat and broad, the nose depressed, the lips large, and the mouth wide. But these differences are common to all savage nations. . . . The forefeet of the Yahoo differed from my hands in nothing else but the length of the nails, the coarseness and brownness of the palms, and the hairiness on the backs. There was the same resemblance between our feet, with the same differences, *which I knew very well*, though the horses did not, because of my shoes and stockings; the same in every part of our bodies, except as to hairiness and colour. . . .
>
> (IV, i; italics mine)

The differences between them are trifling. It is true, to be sure, that the master Houyhnhnm, although he concludes that Gulliver "must be a perfect Yahoo," is perplexed by the physical differences between Gulliver and his own Yahoos:

> he said it was plain I must be a perfect Yahoo; but that I differed very much from the rest of my species, in the softness and whiteness and smoothness of my skin, my want of hair in several parts of my body, the shape and shortness of my claws behind and before, and my affectation of walking continually on my two hinder feet.
>
> (IV, iii)

Furthermore, the report is spread abroad "of a wonderful Yahoo, that could speak like a Houyhnhnm, and seemed in his words and actions to discover some glimmerings of reason" (IV, iii). The point is that the Houyhnhnms themselves, not Gulliver, first observe these distinctions, so that surely it is too early to say that Gulliver's wits have been upset by his "exaggerated devotion" to the Houyhnhnms.

It is still possible, of course, that Gulliver has succumbed to madness, unassisted by any misapplied devotion to the horses. By the end of the third chapter, however, he has not yet arrived at this unhappy state:

> I expressed my uneasiness at his giving me so often the appellation of Yahoo, an odious animal for which I had so utter a hatred and contempt. . . upon my arrival hither I was as much astonished to see the Houyhnhnms act like rational beings, as he or his friends could be in finding some marks of reason in a creature *he was pleased to call a Yahoo, to which I owned my resemblance in every part, but could not account for their degenerate and brutal nature.*
>
> (IV, iii; italics mine)

Gulliver resents being called a Yahoo, as any normal human being would; yet he confesses to a resemblance which is forced upon him. To be sure, he is aware of physical differences which distinguish him from the Yahoos. The horses are too. Yet these very differences are turned against him. The master horse takes away with the left hand—or hoof—what he gives with the right. He concedes, as Gulliver reports, that "I differed indeed from other Yahoos, being much more cleanly, and not altogether so deformed, but in point of real advantage he thought I differed for the worse" (IV, iv). The master horse continues, speaking of Gulliver:

> That my nails were of no use either to my fore or hinder-feet; as to my fore-feet, he could not properly call them by that name, for he never observed me to walk upon them; that they were too soft to bear the ground; that I generally went with them uncovered, neither was the covering I sometimes wore on them of the same shape or so strong as that on my feet behind. That I could not walk with any security, for if either of my hinder-feet slipped, I must inevitably fall. He then began to find fault with other parts of my body, the flatness of my face, the prominence of my nose, my eyes placed directly in front, so that I could not look on either side without turning my head; that I was not able to feed myself without lifting one of my fore-feet to my mouth; and therefore nature had placed those joints to answer that necessity. He knew not what could be the use of those several clefts and divisions in my feet behind; that these were too soft to bear the hardness and sharpness of stones with-

> out a covering made from the skin of some other brute; that my
> whole body wanted a fence against heat and cold, which I was
> forced to put on and off every day with tediousness and trouble.
>
> (IV, iv)

Gulliver does not deny the justness of these observations, nor can any human being when he keeps in mind that the master horse is speaking of *real* advantages rather than imaginary ones. So one might conclude from this, if Gulliver is mad, so is everyone else.

Even such a supposedly distinctive mark of human excellence as a sophisticated speech is in reality a black mark against humankind. As the master horse again points out,

> the use of speech was to make us understand one another, and
> to receive information of facts; now if any one *said the thing which
> was not,* these ends were defeated; because I cannot be said to
> understand him; and I am so far from receiving information,
> that he leaves me worse than in ignorance, for I am led to believe
> a thing black when it is white, and short when it is long. And
> these were all the notions he had concerning *that faculty of lying
> so perfectly well understood among human creatures.*
>
> (IV, iv; latter italics mine)

Gulliver knows, as we all know, that speech exists, presumably, to "make us understand one another, and to receive information of facts." Yet we all know that, oddly enough, lying is common. Is this evidence of madness?

The remarks of the master horse upon the use of speech are, of course, the beginning of a series of attacks on what appear to be at least human perversions of reason. At this point (chapters v ff.) one can hardly avoid recalling the famous "Digression on Madness" in the *Tale of a Tub* as an early illustration of a powerful Swiftian technique. To consider but one example, in the "Digression," the reader is treated to a description of one "student" who is "tearing his straw in piece-meal, swearing and blaspheming, biting his grate, foaming at the mouth, and emptying his piss-pot in the spectators' faces. . . ." The comparison is then made with a military man: "Let the right worshipful the commissioners of inspection give him a regiment of dragoons, and send him into Flanders with the rest." The conclusion the reader is invited to make is not that the occupant of this apartment should be given a military command—that is patently absurd—but that military commanders should be in Bedlam. In *Gulliver's Travels,* as in the early work, the narrator describes what he sees or has seen; makes or invites comparisons; and invites conclusions on the basis of his comparisons. So when the supposedly demented Gulliver reports to the master horse "the usual causes or motives that made one country go to war with another," a long list of perfectly inadequate reasons (chapter v) follows, and the master horse, in his commentary upon European manners (chapter vii), sees a similarity between European occasions for fighting and those of the familiar Yahoos:

> the dissensions of those brutes in his country were owing to the same cause with ours. . . . For (said he) you throw among five Yahoos as much food as would be sufficient for fifty, they will, instead of eating peaceably, fall together by the ears, each single one impatient to have all to itself. . . . At other times the like battles have been fought between the Yahoos of several neighbourhoods without any visible cause; those of one district watching all opportunities to surprise the next before they are prepared. But if they find their project hath miscarried, they return home, and, for want of enemies, engage in what I [Gulliver] call a civil war among themselves.
>
> (IV, vii)

The master horse makes a series of such comparisons but leaves it to Gulliver to determine how far various descriptions of the character of the Yahoos might be applicable to the character of Europeans. As for Gulliver, "it was easy to apply the character he gave of the Yahoos to myself and my countrymen. . . ." He sees that the Yahoos fight for the same ridiculous reasons, or lack of them, as "civilized" men do, although the Yahoos "seldom were able to kill one another, for want of such convenient instruments of death as we had invented." Gulliver concludes:

> When I thought of my family, my friends, my countrymen, or human race in general, I considered them as they really were, Yahoos in shape and disposition, perhaps a little more civilized, and qualified with the gift of speech, but making no other use of reason than to improve and multiply those vices whereof their brethren in this country had only the share that nature allotted them.
>
> (IV, x)

Now the question is, whether Gulliver's conclusion is the conclusion of a madman. Unless I am mistaken, there is some small grain of satire in *Gulliver's Travels,* and so one must consider not whether the resemblances which Gulliver sees—or is helped to see—are exactly true and true in every case but whether the resemblances he sees are *sufficiently* accurate to justify his making identifications. Do the "shining stones of several colours" and the Yahoos' senseless passion for them resemble precious stones and human avarice or do they not? Does the favourite of the leading Yahoo, in his nature, in his conduct, and in his fate, resemble the favourite of a European court in his nature, in his conduct, and in his fate, or does he not? Does the conduct of a Yahoo who is "young and fat" and wanting for nothing resemble the spleen in the "lazy, the luxurious, and the rich" among humans, or does it not? Does the behaviour of female Yahoos toward a female stranger resemble the common behaviour of women toward a new arrival of their own sex or does it not? To say that such comparisons are exaggerated and that therefore whoever accepted them as justified was somehow out of his senses is to misapprehend rather completely the nature of satire. No one, to my knowledge, has maintained that George Orwell was mad when he compared the Bolsheviks with pigs in *Animal Farm,* or that Milton was insane when he referred to the prelates of the Church of England as a "grim wolf with privy paw." By such reasoning *all* satire would be the work of madmen.

Nonetheless, one virtuoso would have it that "Gulliver's account to his Houyhnhnm master in chapters v and vi of a European society made up of wholly vicious people, particularly doctors, lawyers, rulers, and statesmen, is clearly the result of his eyes being blinded and his understanding perverted . . . by the perfection of the Houyhnhnms . . . it is clear that Swift did not present chapters v and vi as an accurate picture of European society." In refutation of the thesis that Gulliver was a "humourist," as this critic puts it, and consequently that his mind is disturbed, one need simply recall the numerous conversations which Gulliver held with the enlightened King of Brobdingnag. In these talks Gulliver describes European society as an interested party and tries to place it in the best possible light. Yet, no reader unless he is a modern critic can question the accuracy of the Giant King's famous conclusion:

> by what I have gathered from your own Relation, and the Answers I have with much Pains wringed and extorted from you; I cannot but conclude the Bulk of your Natives, to be the most pernicious Race of little odious Vermin that Nature ever suffered to crawl upon the Surface of the Earth.

In brief, the King of Brobdingnag and the master horse are brothers under the skin so far as their opinions of the human race are concerned. In fact, they differ only in their forms. If then the conclusions of the Giant King are sane conclusions and if the conclusions of the master horse are substantially those of the giant's, what reason is there to suppose that Gulliver has suddenly gone mad when he adopts the conclusions of the horses?

Again, are we to imagine that Gulliver was out of his mind when he described the bizarre types of Book III—the *really* crazy mathematicians, musicians, projectors, and the rest? These are, it need hardly be said, types of Swift's contemporaries which Gulliver presents in a most unflattering light. In sum, the first three quarters of *Gulliver's Travels* is an exposure of human folly and vice which even the most hysterical apologists for mankind have swallowed without difficulty. Why then should they choke at Book IV, in which Swift continues the attack? Or, in other words, why should Gulliver be branded as insane when he simply arrives at conclusions about his own kind which any intelligent reader will have made long before?

The prime purpose of the foregoing discussion was to attempt the rehabilitation of Lemuel Gulliver. He was not mad. His conclusions that civilized Europeans are really Yahoos in body and mind, with the added attraction that they are even worse, are valid in terms of the book. Without going so far as saying that Gulliver is Swift, one still may conclude that Gulliver's conclusions are Swift's conclusions. So unless we would have Swift mad too, perhaps we should agree that Gulliver knew what he was talking about.

II

A number of recent commentators have decided that the horses, allegedly admirable, are in fact not so. On the basis of what proof they have to offer of this assertion, they make a number of conclusions among which are first, that Gulliver's admiration of them is evidence of his madness; second, that Swift is attacking the kind of pride in man "which convinces him that he can live by the light of his unaided reason"; third, that man is superior to both Houyhnhnms and Yahoos in being potentially salvageable; fourth, that the horses represent an impossible ideal. It is evident that if it can be shown that the horses were in fact to be admired, the first three of the above inferences can be leveled at a stroke. And this is what will be attempted in this section of the paper.

To begin, what are the horses like? They are handy with the needle; they can build houses; they raise crops; but above all, they are completely rational and are guided by reason in all branches of equine affairs. But what is this much-vaunted reason? It is variously defined, but a definition which was common to Swift's generation and corresponds to the reason of the horses, as we shall see, is this: it is a faculty which makes right judgments instantaneously and without regard to interest. The laws of reason "are always and everywhere the same, and like the axioms of mathematics they have only to be presented in order to be acknowledged as just and right by all men." This kind of reason is not characterized by intricate logical processes which are subject to error and useful for purposes of deception. As Locke asserts: "Reason is easier to be understood, than the fancies and intricate contrivances of men, following contrary and hidden interests put into words."

When the master Houyhnhnm says "nature and reason were sufficient guide for a reasonable animal . . . in showing us what we ought to do, and what to avoid" he is repeating what Locke had already said:

> The state of nature has a law of nature to govern it, which obliges everyone; and reason, which is that law, teaches all mankind, who will but consult it, that being all equal and independent, no one ought to harm another in his life, health, liberty, or possessions.

In other words, the laws of reason are not only self-evident but beneficent as well. This being the case, the master Houyhnhnm, being a rational animal, cannot understand how anyone could be ruined by the law: ". . . he was at a loss how it should come to pass, that the law which was intended for every man's preservation, should be any man's ruin" (IV, v). The explanation is of course that human reason is perverted, that men follow "contrary and hidden interests put into words." Men substitute a sham for the real thing because their passions [read "vices"] prohibit its operation. Gulliver speaks as if in evidence of Locke's assertion: "I said there was a society of men among us, bred up from their youth in the art of proving by words multiplied for the purpose, that white is black, and black is white, according as they are paid" (IV, v).

If the noble Houyhnhnms are in reality absurd, or at least deficient, in being completely rational animals, and if this is Swift's whole point, their absurdity or deficiency, one would think, ought to be evident. One present-day commentator finds them cold, lacking in pity and benevolence, self-satisfied, and arrogant. Are they indeed so? When Gulliver arrives in Houyhnhnmland, the first two horses he meets stroke him with their hooves, but one of them "squeezed it [Gulliver's hand] so hard between his hoof and pastern, that I was forced to roar; after which they both touched me with all possible tenderness" (IV, i). When Gulliver is on the road to the master horse's house his guide allows him to rest when he grows tired. Later, the master horse "very graciously consented" to keep the secret of Gulliver's clothes. When Gulliver is brought into the company of his master's guests (other horses of course) they are required to treat him "with civility." Our critic's charitable feelings are offended most of all by the heartless banishment of Gulliver. She, like Gulliver, thinks "it might consist with reason to have been less rigorous." The fact of the matter is however that the master horse showed possibly more compassion than was becoming in a completely rational being. He hesitates to tell Gulliver of the decision of the council. He was "at a loss how to begin what he had to speak." The master horse admitted that "for his own part he could have been content to keep me in his service as long as I lived." Even though it is plain to the Houyhnhnm that Gulliver is a menace (he needed only to be "exhorted" after all by his fellow horses), yet he shows compassion for him not only in words but in deeds: he allows him two months in which to prepare a boat, for he does not wish him to drown. This may seem an iron kind of benevolence, but in the circumstances, it would have consisted with reason to have exterminated Gulliver, Yahoo—more or less—that he was.

Apparently this same critic refuses to accept as fact that "friendship and benevolence are the two principal virtues among the Houyhnhnms, and these not confined to particular objects, but universal to the whole race. . . . They will have it that nature teaches them to love the whole species. . . ." (IV, viii). There is really no point in disputing this because it is as much a "fact" as the horses' ability to speak. Nor does it seem entirely irrelevant to point out that just such a benevolence is supposedly at the heart of Christian teaching and that hospitality towards strangers was an obligation among the ancients. The horses were indeed lacking in the kind of restricted benevolence displayed by doting parents for their own possibly ugly, sullen brats; but which is to be more admired, a benevolence in which "reason only . . . maketh a distinction of persons, where there is a superior degree of virtue" or the kind which operates only when it sees its own likeness reproduced, and for no other conceivable cause?

Is the practice of eugenics, a rational practice, admirable or no? Is it admirable to produce defective human beings or whole ones? Is the absence of "jealousy, fondness, quarreling, or discontent" in marriage admirable because of the operation of a general benevolence dictated by reason, or is it better that husbands and wives should plague each other and replace a transitory fondness with a snarling possessiveness? Is it admirable that the education of women should be so strictly limited that they are "good for nothing but bringing children into the world" and "to trust the care of our children to such useless animals . . . yet a greater instance of brutality" or is it not? Is it admirable to accept death calmly when there is no avoiding it anyway, or is it admirable to moan and wail to no purpose?

If it is granted, on the basis of a contrast between the ways of the Houyhnhnms and the well-known ways of mankind, that the ways of the former are to be admired, it does not follow that Gulliver is mentally disturbed for admiring them; nor does it follow that Swift is attacking the notion that the light of the unaided reason is a sufficient guide for human conduct, for the very simple reason that the only alternative in sight is in itself absurd. I refer, of course, to the ways of men and Yahoos. Nor, again, does it follow that man is superior to the horses because he may be saved. In fact there seems to be no connection whatever between any kind of judgment on the horses and man's ultimate destination, if any. One of the striking facts about *Gulliver's Travels* is that there is almost no mention of religion in it. It would seem that if Swift were bent on pointing out salvation as a peculiar property of mankind, he would have done so. Instead, he treats abstruse theological issues as absurd and mentions no other kind. Those critics who make such an inference are simply leaping into a void, supplying the links between horses and the Kingdom of Heaven out of such airy materials as they discover in their own predispositions.

III

It has been said that the horses represent an impossible ideal, and thus indicate not only Gulliver's madness in admiring them, but "the bankruptcy of the 'natural' man" as well. No one would deny that the horses represent an impossible ideal but not impossible in the sense of ridiculous, as I have tried to show. The ideal is *unattainable* but still to be admired. But if the ideal is out of reach, what is the point in offering it up to mankind? In other words, if human beings cannot imitate the horses, what are the horses there for? What is their role in the book?

To begin an answer to such questions, why are the Houyhnhnms *what* they are; that is, why are they horses? They are horses rather than some other animal, perhaps for various reasons, but the most obvious reason is that Swift wished to make the inversion of the normal master-servant relationship. This would have been impossible were his rational creatures dogs, let us say, or foxes, or skunks.

Why should Swift want to make such an inversion? What purpose could such a procedure serve? Presumably it has something to do with what Swift was bent on saying. Need one be reminded that Aristotle, long ago, defined man as a rational animal, and this, his rationality, distinguished him as no other consideration could from the other animals? What then is the implication in the sole fact of making the inversion of the normal master-servant relationship? It is, most clearly, to deprive man of his vaunted rationality, because the rational animal must be the master. Does this mean then that horses are rational animals? Or that one is to take seriously the ordinary non-horselike characteristics ascribed to the Houyhnhnms? Obviously not. The whole point of inverting the normal man-animal relation is not to elevate animals at the cost of humanity as Montaigne might have done but to deflate man's notion of himself by stripping him of his proudest possession.

By way of making this clearer, if need be, allow me to analyse briefly the objections which a recent critic has made (and this is irony indeed) to the alleged pride of the horses themselves. When the master horse finds fault with Gulliver's body, this critic argues, he is displaying a pride or arrogance of his own. But wherein lies the defect of the horses' criticism? Man prides himself on his upright carriage—he does not walk around on all fours; yet why is such a posture superior to going on all fours? In brief, this is not evidence of a fault (pride or arrogance) in the horses but simply evidence that human notions about the inevitable superiority of their own shapes are groundless. *Human beings* are arrogant, not the horses.

In fact this critic is falling into the very conceit that Swift is attacking, man's notion of the "Human Form Divine," to borrow Mr. Quintana's expression; that is, the vanity that humans are somehow "nobler" in their anatomies than animals are. Are we to suppose that when we read about the hideous complexions of the Brobdingnagians that Swift is bent on finding fault with *giants?*

This is further evidence that the horses are not to be taken as models of a superior kind of existence. In the first place, such creatures obviously do not exist. In the second place, no one would be likely to identify himself, or wish to identify himself, with a horse. The whole point of the existence of the horses is to show not that men should be like horses but that men are not what they like to think they are: rational beings.

IV

The following conclusions appear to be justified from the foregoing considerations. Human beings, except for minor differences, look like and behave like Yahoos. They differ primarily in having a trace of reason, which they use for bad ends (they pervert it), and thus are worse than the Yahoos.

Human beings like to think of themselves as rational creatures, but if they really were rational creatures, they would think and behave as the horses do. But they do not. By thus attributing rationality to a nonhuman species Swift does not succeed in convincing us of the superiority of horses, in this respect, to human beings (it is evident that such a race of horses is entirely imaginary) but simply that man is not rational. Rationality is desirable, however, even though unattainable. By making the horses, a nonhuman animal, rational, Swift has produced a double insult, or double attack, upon mankind in its physical being and in its mental being and has, on the one hand, obliged humans to identify themselves with disgusting animals, and on the other hand, has precluded the possibility of humans identifying themselves with horses.

V

Another critic, less inclined to fill old bottles with new wine than some, has argued that Swift is one with Gulliver through nine chapters of Book IV but parts company with him in the last three, leaving Gulliver alone in his dementia. Our unfortunate traveller, so runs the argument, after his exposure to the ways of the horses, is incapable of distinguishing between the truly Yahoo-like features of human beings and their more praiseworthy traits. Not to mention Gulliver's own blameless family, Pedro de Mendez, albeit a man, is clearly a decent fellow, yet Gulliver can scarcely tolerate him.

Is this surprising? After his experiences, it is only natural that Gulliver should see Mendez as a Yahoo. Gulliver's response to his own kind is no more to be wondered at than the response of the man returning to Plato's cave after a vision of Reality, as R. S. Crane has suggested, or St. Paul's condition after his heavenly illumination, to borrow from George Sherburn. Nor is Gulliver so mad that he is unaware of the Portuguese captain's good qualities. He simply cannot reconcile himself to his body. He *smells* like a Yahoo. The association between physical qualities and moral ones, even though unfair to Mendez, is understandable in the light of Gulliver's recent experiences. Indeed, the presence of a "good Yahoo" is essential to Swift's artistry. What better means could Swift have employed than to have Gulliver swooning and stuffing his nose with tobacco leaves in order to express his loathing of the human race? The very extremity of Gulliver's conduct emphasizes the hopeless distance between even the best human beings and rational creatures.

If one wishes to argue, not unreasonably, that Pedro de Mendez is an exception to the general repulsiveness of mankind, he can find support in Swift's own comments upon Book IV. For example, in a letter to the Reverend Thomas Sheridan, dated September 11, 1725, he advises: "Therefore sit down and be quiet, and mind your business as you should do, and contract your friendships, and expect no more from man than such an animal is capable of, and you will every day find my description of Yahoos more resembling." The admonition "contract your friendships" implies that there are some decent persons in the world—who would deny it? Similarly, Swift has remarked, "Oh! if the world had but a dozen Arbuthnots in it, I would burn my *Travels*." But what are a few sound apples in a barrelful of rotten ones?

If Swift's revelatory comment on the human race is indeed to be found at the end of Book IV, then one should look at the end of Book IV— chapters x and xi are not the end. In chapter xii Gulliver is clearly impugning the motives of colonial powers in an unquestionably Swiftian way. In so doing, he is accepting what he was unwilling to accept in earlier voyages, in which he is plainly *naïf*. Gulliver's final comment, beyond any reasonable doubt, has Swift's trademark upon it. Here is Swift's technique and, I submit, an explicit statement of what *Gulliver's Travels* is about:

> My reconcilement to the Yahoo-kind in general might not be so difficult, if they would be content with those vices and follies only which nature hath entitled them to. I am not in the least provoked at the sight of a lawyer, a pick-pocket, a colonel, a fool, a lord, a gamester, a politician, a whore-master, a physician, an evidence, a suborner, an attorney, a traitor, or the like; this is all according to the due course of things: but when I behold a lump of deformity and diseases both in body and mind, smitten with *pride*, it immediately breaks all the measures of my patience; neither shall I be ever able to comprehend how such an animal and such a vice could tally together . . . and therefore I here entreat those who have any tincture of this absurd vice, that they will not presume to come in my sight.

Gulliver does regard himself as somewhat foolish but not because he has been unjust to mankind. He confesses his foolishness in imagining that the tale of his adventures would have any improving influence upon the human race. His *last* word—speaking of last words—occurs at the end of

"A Letter from Captain Gulliver to his Cousin Sympson": "I have now done with all such visionary schemes for ever." If such a conclusion is in any sense a retraction on Swift's part or anything but one lash the more, then I am a sorrel nag.

Swiftean Picaresque: *Gulliver's Travels*

Ronald Paulson

So far the center of interest in Swift's satire has been a symbol of the perversion of values, turning this way and that to offer exposition of all its various facets. *A Tale of a Tub* comes no closer to a narrative in time and space than the scattered references to the Grub Street Hack's goings and comings and his increasing concern with his book and its purchasers as he nears the end of his writing and publication time approaches. The Horatian dialectic, seen in the story of the brothers, is reflected in the Hack's attempt to reconcile the value terms of morality and art (such as "universal benefit of mankind") with the assumptions of the moderns; but the relationship set up remains a static one, a sort of constantly reiterated tableau.

When he turned to narrative in *Gulliver's Travels* (1726), Swift utilized the fiction of the picaresque novel. Some of the time Gulliver is simply an observer, traveling and recording, becoming more or less of a gull by the extent to which he accepts what he sees. But these parts are largely limited to a chapter or so in each voyage and to much of the third voyage. More often he is a touchstone: by his enormous size and equal magnanimity he sets off the puzzled, treacherous, belligerent, or presumptuous reactions of the Lilliputians. At the center of Swift's action is the relationship between the traveler and the strange people he meets.

For example, among the Brobdingnagians, where Gulliver is specifically a servant with contrasting "masters," the brutality of the giant farmer is brought out by his treatment of the tiny, helpless Gulliver; and the

From *The Fictions of Satire*. © 1967 by The Johns Hopkins University Press.

pettiness and human pride of Gulliver are shown by his posturing before his second master, the kind King. The relationship shifts as Gulliver goes from master to master. The Emperor of Lilliput is very like Lazaro's first master, the blind beggar, and similarly vulnerable, and Gulliver is like Lazaro, the complacent servant, adjusting to his surroundings, revealing his master's villainy by praising or even imitating it. But the relationship is made overwhelmingly ironic by the servant's being a mile high. Like the picaro, who assumes the values of his masters, Gulliver ends by assuming the values of the people he visits. It follows that his complaisance turns him (as it does Lazaro) into a fool who makes possible his master's knavery. In the case of his good masters, Gulliver imitates that aspect which is least appropriate to him; returning from Brobdingnag he acts like a giant, and returning from Houyhnhnmland he acts like a horse. There are other nobler aspects he could imitate—and in this respect his is a more complex situation than the picaro's. By the end of the voyage to Brobdingnag the emphasis has shifted from the master's tyranny to the servant's willingness to be tyrannized, and this situation no doubt explains something of Gulliver's relationship to his Houyhnhnm master. The relationship between master and servant, then, is Swift's central irony, explored in a slightly different way in each voyage.

Swift's cast of characters owes something to the satiric fiction we have traced in his other satires. In all but the third voyage, which reverts to the old and simple form of the satiric anatomy or survey, the protagonist is given a master, various outside threats to his safety, and a friend. The master represents the structure of order, whether good or bad, which protects Gulliver from the forces of enmity and disorder—unruly soldiers, an enemy like Skyresh Bolgolam, rats, dwarves, nasty children, wasps, and Yahoos. These figures, who like Bolgolam are "pleased, without any Provocation, to be my mortal Enemy," are completely negative. In fact, by placing in parallel functions the Bolgolams and the rats and monkeys who attack Gulliver in Brobdingnag, Swift suggests that such obvious threats are probably amoral rather than immoral. The friend is the unnamed man who warns him of the Lilliputians' plans to destroy him, or Glumdalclitch in Brobdingnag, or the Sorrel Nag in Houyhnhnmland. (Sometimes the friendship proves ironic, as in Reldresel, who argues for the kindness of blinding Gulliver instead of killing him.)

While the forces of evil are hardly even supplied with motives for their natural viciousness, the master is guided by an awareness of his own position or advantage—fear that Gulliver will go over to the Blefuscudians, or the desire to make money, or the fear that Gulliver may cause the Yahoos to revolt. So from Gulliver's point of view we have once again the structure of Swift's first-person satires: the undisguisedly evil on one side (Gulliver is never deceived by Bolgolam or the jealous dwarf) and the obviously good on the other. In the middle is the ambiguous figure who puts a good face on his selfish actions: the emperor who uses Gulliver to carry out his policies, and whose cruelty is marked under fine phrases. Even the King of Brobdingnag and the Houyhnhnm master, though not intended as evil creatures, are masters and follow the pattern. They cannot see others except in relation to themselves; anything beyond their experience baffles them. The King, though wise, is simply so large that he regards Gulliver with an undue detachment, in effect imprisoning him like a bird in a gilded cage and hoping to find a mate so that this curious species can be propagated; and the Houyhnhnm master, though surpassingly wise, cannot see Gulliver as more than a Yahoo of superior intelligence (and so, dangerous). To both of them he remains a *lusus naturae*. When the Houyhnhnm master explains why Gulliver must be sent out to sea to certain death, he sounds very much like the Emperor of Lilliput justifying the proposed murder of Gulliver, just as Gulliver, when he tries to justify his master's decree, demonstrates an irony as cutting as in his earlier attempt to justify the Emperor's sentence.

But the Brobdingnagian and Houyhnhnm masters are present less as comments on themselves than as comments on Gulliver. Gulliver's function changes with the second voyage, and he becomes himself the object of satire, assuming the role of the middleman who attempts to rationalize his miserable situation into a state to be proud of. Even in Lilliput he finds on one side of him the ideals of liberty and duty to one's country, on the other enslavement, and entirely to his own disadvantage, attaches the name of liberty to the fact of his slavery, justifying his degradation by means of the rhetoric of his masters. He is the man who puts a good face on his own unsatisfactory situation by seeing it as his "masters the Moderns" do. He shows his descent from the Grub Street Hack as well as Martinus Scriblerus (as whom he originated) in his automatic reactions as a correct modern— collecting specimens in Lilliput and weighing hailstones, keeping a cabinet of curiosities, and wishing to dissect a louse in Brobdingnag; showing his pride in England as well as in the latest "modern" inventions for improving warfare.

Like any searcher for a Utopia, Gulliver sets out voyaging to escape the restraints of his homeland. The first page gives us this impression through words suggesting confinement: his father's "small Estate," applying himself "close" to his studies, the cost being "too great for a narrow Fortune," his being "bound Apprentice" to a surgeon, and receiving "small

Sums of Money." Opposed to these references and the emphasis on specific numbers of years, pounds, and the like, is the indefinite "long Voyages." After his first voyages, he settles in London but soon sets out again in order to escape the corruptions of business without which one cannot succeed in England: "for my Conscience would not suffer me to imitate the bad practice of too many among my Brethren"; and a subsequent business has begun to fail. The sea seems to represent release for him; and so it is the first of a series of ironies on this theme when, running into the ultimate in freedom, the violent storm at sea that sets him free even from the confinement of his boat, he wakes up and attempting to rise, is "not able to stir: For as I happened to lie on my Back, I found my Arms and Legs were strongly fastened on each Side to the Ground." Even his hairs are bound to the earth, and he is in a kingdom far more constricting than his homeland.

The allegorical message (emphasized in Hogarth's print, *The Punishment of Lemuel Gulliver,* published in December 1726) is this: England in seeking freedom (the individualistic freedom for which the Whigs stood) has found itself in the most constricting kind of world—one of people six inches high who treat the good old Englishman as a slave in spite of the obvious discrepancy in their sizes. And the foolish, "gullible" Englishman gratefully accepts this slavery: the privilege of turning over on his side to make water, of living chained in the equivalent of a dog's house, and of kissing the hand of a mite. (One need only recall the figure of Arbuthnot's John Bull, and disguise the allegory considerably—since Arbuthnot was on the winning side when he wrote, and Swift was now on the losing side. The character of John Bull was not unlike Gulliver's—both were ordinary bluff Englishmen, somewhat dense, as their names equally imply.) The situation of the majority cowed by a minuscule, single, actually powerless figure is a usual Swiftean image for the enemy, which he employed about the same time in the image of William Wood. Here numbers are on the Lilliputians' side, but obviously the tail is again wagging the dog if they can order Gulliver around. So on the political level, Swift is ridiculing the folly of the great lethargic mass that allows itself ("in the most submissive Manner") to be exploited by fear or custom or something of the sort when there is no reason to do so.

On the level of human action, however, Gulliver is a foolish, subservient man, easily enchained by plausible knaves and apparent authority. The repetition of the word "liberty" (the refrain of the first voyage) points to the relationship: Gulliver's humble petitions for his "liberty," the Emperor's refusal and limited grant, and "the Liberty of walking backwards and forwards in a Semicircle." Once he is physically released, his liberty is even more restricted without the physical fears. Chapter III begins with the humiliating relationship between the Emperor and his advisers, the ropedancers and the stick jumpers; and it goes on to the equally humiliating, though less reasonable, relationship between the Emperor and Gulliver. Gulliver's eager building of a tilt field with his handkerchief is described, as well as his service as the Emperor's arch of triumph and his humble reception of the "charger" which grants him his "liberty."

The unambiguous self-enslavement of Voyage I becomes in Brobdingnag a less obvious but more sinister one; for here the little Gulliver, whose pride grows as he shrinks in size (a kind of compensation for one's littleness, as it was in the *Tale* for one's transcience), fancies himself free when he is obviously kept as a kind of toy or pet locked in a box; whereas in Lilliput, although he was physically free, he allowed himself to be convinced that he was a servant or captive. Here, more than anywhere else in his travels, Gulliver thinks of himself in terms of his "masters," and his progress can be measured by them. One is a tyrant, one is benevolent— and yet Gulliver's behavior is the same with both. Fear of reprisals, as with the farmer's child, causes him to be obsequious among these huge people, as respect for abstract authority did in Voyage I. But once among the royal family, his servility is based on his growing pride; and the ignominy of being shown off by his first master changes to an anxiety to show off before the King. As soon as he is presented to the Queen he slips into courtier's jargon, and he is soon telling how during meals he sits at the King's "left Hand before one of the Salt-sellers." He is only pleased when the Queen is "diverted" by him, as when the dwarf releases flies under his nose, or when she is "agreeably entertained with my Skill and Agility" at rowing a boat or with his laborious performance at the piano ("the most violent Exercise I ever underwent"). He is constantly referred to as a "Sight," "Spectacle," "Show," or "Curiosity"; and even Glumdalclitch, "although she loved me to Excess, yet was arch enough to inform the Queen, whenever I committed any Folly that she thought would be diverting to her Majesty." Even his explanation of the "State of Europe" is a performance and a show as he stands on the top of a cabinet "which brought me almost to a Level with his Face." The resemblance between these shows and the involuntary shows on the farmer's table, with admission charged, completely escapes Gulliver.

The prison box he lives in is thus not a reflection on the Brobdingnagians but on his own pretensions. He designed it himself, is safe in it and happy, and does not see it as a prison until the King suggests that if he could get a woman of Gulliver's size he would like to see the pigmy race propagated. "But," says Gulliver, more out of pride than self-aware-ness, "I think I should rather have died than undergone the Disgrace of leaving a Posterity to be kept in Cages like tame Canary Birds." Even when his first cry upon being picked up by a rescue ship is "to be delivered out of the Dungeon I was in," he sees no connection between the dungeon his box has become floating in the water and the one it was in the Brobding-nagian court. He sees no humor in the reference to Phaeton's fall made by Captain Wilcocks, who cannot understand what was the "enormous Crime, for which I was punished at the Command of some Prince, by exposing me in that Chest."

Much the same situation is portrayed in the fourth voyage. Gulliver's eagerness to become a Houyhnhnm and deny any connection with Yahoos follows from his eagerness to become a show for the Brobdingnagian royal family. The Houyhnhnm master persuades his friends to treat Gulliver "with Civility," because "this would put me [Gulliver] into good Humour, and make me more diverting." Whether we regard the Houyhnhnms and Yahoos as opposite extremes of the human and inhuman, or of human attributes—reason and passion—or of good and evil, the point of Gulliver's role as a whole is to become a middleman who attempts to attach the reason of a Houyhnhnm to the pride and body of a Yahoo.

Therefore, if Gulliver derives in a sense from the corruptible picaro he also derives from the Swiftean middleman, the villain of the other satires examined. However, as the derivation from the picaro implies, if this figure is much lower than Houyhnhnm, he is also not so debased as a Yahoo. He is much more normative than Swift's earlier villains, and this has been brought about by the shifting of emphasis from the wickedness of Gulliver's imitation of his masters to the consequences of his imitation: imprisonment, insecurity, betrayal, and even madness. There is also a much greater ad-mixture of truth and well-meaning in Gulliver's imitations, as well as a more idealistic motive that drives him to emulation in all but the second voyage.

Something of his character, particularly in the fourth voyage, can be explained by reference to another classical source for the dupe of which Swift was so fond. The *Nigrinus* of Lucian, though it derives from Horace's Satire II.3 (concerning Damasippus), produces a more ambiguous and dis-turbing satirist-satirized situation. Like Horace, Lucian presents a man, A, repeating ecstatically what another man, B, has lectured to him. There may be considerable truth in B's words, which are largely satiric, but they are somehow inapplicable to A, or to people in general, and A's enthusiasm is excessive and his understanding incomplete. The listener, C, ironically agrees to A's account, but by his questions brings out the absurdity of A's position.

In Lucian's fiction a friend reproaches "Lucian" for his haughty airs now that he has returned from a journey—he will no longer have anything to do with his old friends. "Lucian" explains that it all came from seeing Nigrinus, the platonic philosopher, who has revealed to him the real ugliness of the apparently pleasant life he has been living. "Lucian" had gone to Rome to see an oculist about his failing eyesight and instead found Nigrinus, who improved his spiritual vision, turning him into a misanthropic satirist. The consequence, he shows, is halfway between drunkenness and frenzy. In the course of "Lucian's" account Nigrinus is compared to an intoxicating drink, a beacon far out in the ocean upon which he fixes his gaze, an archer who impales Lucian's heart, and (his interlocutor finally adds) a mad dog whose bite Lucian is now communicating. It all suggests that we should approach Nigrinus warily. He has unhinged "Lucian": "I was seized with a violent attack of giddiness; I was bathed in perspiration, and when I attempted to speak, I broke down; my voice failed, my tongue stammered, and at last I was reduced to tears." This is the effect of such philosophy on an ordinary man. Nigrinus states an ideal—but a philosophical ideal which, if taken seriously, would make man simply withdraw from life. His attacks on Roman corruption, which closely follow those of Juvenal, are to be accepted as true. But Nigrinus's platonism causes him to withdraw from all human contacts: "From my high seat in this vast theatre," he says, "I look down on the scene beneath me; a scene calculated to afford much entertainment. . . ." Like Horace, Lucian catches three different groups in his satiric net: he uses Nigrinus as a way to castigate the vices in Rome and to present an ideal; but Nigrinus is also a philosopher, and in a human context his solution is an absurd extreme; finally, "Lucian" himself will have to come down to earth again before he will be a better man for his experience. Yet, we are left with the possible interpretation that Lucian *is* presenting Nigrinus's view as the ideal, and the joke is in the discrepancy between this ideal and his own, or any human's, ability to follow it.

In Houyhnhnmland Gulliver, like Lucian, encounters someone who shows him a truth he had never before suspected and it virtually unhinges him, turning him into a railing satirist. At first sight this appears to be a new role for Gulliver; the external revelation is a contradiction to his beliefs in the superiority of people who look like him. But, as soon becomes apparent, Gulliver adjusts the new revelation to his own case, pitting himself *and* the Houyhnhnms against humans; he does not change himself, if anything ending a less desirable man. Like Lucian with his nose in the air,

Gulliver refuses to live with Yahoos like his wife and children and spends his time in the stable.

Gulliver demonstrates how the Swiftean villain, by some shifts of emphasis, becomes a character who, if not in fact a hero, can be regarded as essentially ordinary, an Everyman. Much of his effect depends upon the fact that Swift has moved from a static portrait showing this figure at his worst to a narrative in which the decent but fallible man finds his way through a world of frightful or deceiving experiences such as extremes of size and of reason and passion. The acts of folly, though climactic, do not completely cancel out the many neutral or even virtuous acts.

Gulliver is not intended as the hero of a *bildungsroman:* he makes no self-discovery, comes to no awareness of himself, except to the parody of awareness he suffers in Houyhnhnmland. He is closer to the Horatian "you," the test figure who guides the reader between polar errors. But the direction of the satire is less toward a proposed (or implied) code of conduct than toward the eighteenth-century preoccupation with the definition of man. *Gulliver's Travels* is less closely related to Pope's Horatian satires than to his *Essay on Man.*

Satiric structures appear at their simplest in the third voyage, in which the Laputans, Struldbruggs, and the rest, like Lazarillo de Tormes's fifth master, are merely observed by Gulliver. The skeleton is not covered, the rhetoric is naked, and the fiction is the relation between an observer and an object: sometimes the observer is normative, sometimes ironically ingenuous, sometimes gulled by appearances. The relationship at its most complex produces simple error followed by disillusion and revaluation wrought by contact with the ghosts of Glubbdubdrib and the Struldbruggs. Book III is the traditional satiric anatomy of misdirected reason, at its most typical in the survey of the Academy of Lagado in which a tour of the Royal Society is equated with one of Bedlam. The trips up to the floating island, down to the ghosts of Glubbdubdrib, and horizontally to other odd places are unvarnished descendants of the Lucianic dialogues, equally concise and brilliant but largely unintegrated. The voyage does make some sense on two levels other than the rhetorical: on the metaphysical it extends Swift's study of man from body to mind, and on the representational it begins to prepare us for Gulliver's breakdown in Houyhnhnmland (developing the disillusionment begun in the King of Brobdingnag's "odious little vermin" speech). But like the rhetoric these are naked, and roughly indicated (almost a sketch) as compared with the full rendering of the other three voyages. (Though parts of the voyage were written as late as 1724, other parts clearly contain vestiges of Martinus Scriblerus's travels and whatever else did not fit in the other voyages.)

The first two and the fourth of Gulliver's voyages also began as Lucianic devices for getting new perspectives on man but embodied them in close-fitting fictions. Lilliput and Brobdingnag are vantage points from which to see man's true situation and humble his pride; through a telescope or a microscope, or from a far higher or lower physical position, man could be seen with more detachment or in more minute detail. Lucian's and Rabelais' aim with the same device was to shake up the reader's accepted values; Swift's is the same but applied first to his protagonist Gulliver and second to the reader who identifies with him. While Rabelais (if not Lucian) intended his reader to emerge with a sense of growth, discovery, and confidence in himself, Swift hopes he will emerge humbled and chastened. Pascal, who had also suggested the use of these vantage points, summed up the effect:

> If a man will look at himself as I suggest, the sight will terrify him; and, seeing himself suspended in the material form given him by Nature, between the two abysses of Infinity and Nothingness, he will tremble beholding these marvels, and I think that, as his curiosity turns to awe, he will rather gaze in silence than dare to question them.

This is the general rhetorical aim of the devices in *Gulliver's Travels,* though many variations are rung. The fourth voyage simply substitutes shape and other opposing qualities for size, probably originating, as R. S. Crane has shown, with Swift's inversion of the traditional equations of *homo* with *rationale* and *equus* with *irrationale* (and, for that matter, *hinnibile*) to be found in Latin logic books. Another of Crane's illuminating insights into the fourth voyage is that Gulliver is used there in the same way as the man in Plato's myth of the cave who is forcibly taken out and brought face to face with reality:

> he will suffer sharp pains; the glare will distress him, and he will be unable to see the realities of which in his former state he had seen the shadows; and then conceive some one saying to him, that what he saw before was an illusion, but that now, when he is approaching nearer to being and his eye is turned toward more real existence, he has a clearer vision,—what will be his reply?

These satiric devices have in common the polarization of Gulliver and what he sees—Lilliputian, Brobdingnagian, and Houyhnhnm. In the general sweep of his narrative Swift uses the extremes of size and shape as part of a dynamic structure which advances from one alternative to another, gradually questioning and defining the poles of Gulliver and his alter egos. Like

the earlier narrative satires we have examined, Swift's is constructed on a
series of parallels established through echoes and allusions. For example,
when Gulliver expresses nausea at the Queen of Brobdingnag's
"craunch[ing] the Wing of a Lark, Bones and all, between her Teeth, although it were nine Times as large as that of a full grown Turkey," the
reader recalls his earlier remark that his Lilliputian servants "were astonished
to see me eat it [a sirloin] Bones and all, as in our Country we do the Leg
of a Lark. Their Geese and Turkeys I usually eat at a Mouthful . . ." or,
yet earlier, that the great pieces of meat the Lilliputians prepare for him are
"smaller than the Wings of a Lark." Gulliver's drawing his sword and
amazing the Lilliputians with the sun glancing off it is echoed in the Brobdingnagian horsemen who do the same, with the same effect on Gulliver.
The contrast shows how different the little man among the big is from the
big among the little. There is, of course, dramatic irony, as in the Brobdingnagian king's desire to find Gulliver a woman his size "by whom I
might propagate the Breed" in the light of Gulliver's similiar desire when
he was preparing to leave Blefuscu. Thus the rat who ate some of his
Lilliputian sheep on the return voyage becomes the rat who tries to eat
Gulliver in Brobdingnag, and the doghouse and chain in Lilliput becomes
Gulliver's box in Brobdingnag. The effect of such parallelism and contrast
in a satire like *A Tale of a Tub* was to give a thematic unity to a work that
represented a radical disunity on the level of action (the speaker's conscious
argument). In *Gulliver's Travels* the effect is to create a series of parallel
experiences.

If each contrast has an immediate point to make about man, together
they serve as alternatives of action that suggest the direction the reader
should or should not take—and that test the protagonist and reveal his
growth or lack of growth. For instance, Gulliver's fear, when he is at the
mercy of a Brobdingnagian field hand, that "human Creatures are . . .
more Savage and cruel in Proportion to their Bulk" is contrasted with the
reader's memory of his gentle treatment of the Lilliputians. The reader,
feeling apprehension with Gulliver, should still remember and recognize
that size limits viewpoint, and that in fact the *smaller* the man the crueller
he is likely to be. But once placed as part of a temporal and causal continuum
between voyages, the scene makes the reader also aware that Gulliver, as
the same character who visited Lilliput, sees no connection between this
situation and his own gigantic benevolence toward the Lilliputians—he has
not learned from his experience.

The parallels run through all four voyages (though less noticeable in
the third), beginning with the basic situation of each voyage: Gulliver arrives

in a new country, slips into the assumptions of the natives, is threatened with catastrophe, and escapes and returns to his own country. From one to the other there is a progress not so much from good to evil as from safety to danger, or from experiences that Gulliver can take in his stride to those with which he cannot finally cope. The progression is reflected in the disasters that place Gulliver in each strange land. These advance from natural disaster that wrecks his ship to shipmates that run for their lives and leave Gulliver among the Brobdingnagians (we can hardly blame the sailors, however, for leaving him in their fright, particularly since he had no business going ashore; the sailors went to get water, he to gather scientific specimens); then from the pirates who capture him and the wicked Dutchman who prevails upon them to cast him adrift, to the final evil of his own crew mutinying and marooning him on a remote island. While these events trace a downward plunge in human experience characteristic of the satiric world view, they also influence Gulliver's changing attitudes as he moves from the harmless land of pigmies to the dangerous land of giants, from the mad or evil lands of the third voyage to the shocking experience of the Yahoos.

The system of parallels also sets up expectations of other parallels that help to clarify some of the more obscure parts of the fourth voyage. In the first two countries Gulliver is examined by philosophers and concluded to be a *lusus naturae,* and so when the Houyhnhnms cannot decide whether Gulliver is a Yahoo or a unique creature we tend to accept this as another case of man's inability to grasp what does not fit his picture of himself, as well as a sign of how difficult it is to define a human being. In each country before Houyhnhnmland (with some exceptions within the third voyage) Gulliver adjusts to the viewpoint and customs of his hosts. In Lilliput he is soon bragging of his title of nardac and, when he hears that the Emperor intends to kill him, he can barely shake himself free of the assumption that he is a loyal subject; so in Brobdingnag he begins "to imagine himself dwindled many Degrees below [his] usual Size," as in Houyhnhnmland he sees himself through the Houyhnhnms' eyes as a Yahoo in a suit. When he returns from Brobdingnag, however, he has come to see himself as a Brobdingnagian, regarding the sailors who rescue him as "the most little contemptible Creatures I had ever beheld" (recalling the king's opinion that Europeans are "little odious vermin"), and when he walks along a road in England he is "afraid of trampling on every Traveller" and calls "loud to have them stand out of the Way." Thus when he sees things from the viewpoint of the Houyhnhnms in the fourth voyage, he also ends by looking upon the sailors who rescue him as the Houyhnhnms look upon Yahoos, and later can get no closer than a table's length from his wife and children, spending his time in the barn with the horses.

It will be noticed, however, that most of the parallels that appear in the fourth voyage go back to the second voyage rather than to the first. The monkey who takes Gulliver for a relative in Brobdingnag becomes the female Yahoo who takes him for a Yahoo of the other sex in Houyhnhnmland, and the normative Captain Wilcocks who rescues Gulliver from Brobdingnag certainly suggests that we are to take Captain Mendoza, who rescues him from Houyhnhnmland, as similarly normative. One set of parallels concerning relative sizes connects the first and second voyage, and another, concerning Gulliver's pride, which only begins to emerge in Brobdingnag, ties together the second and fourth.

With the scene in which the King of Brobdingnag and his philosophers with difficulty decide that Gulliver is a *lusus naturae,* Swift enters upon the theme of human definition that has been latent though implicit in both the contrast of sizes and the centrality of Gulliver-Everyman. Pascal concluded from his beneficial shock of showing man "the two abysses of Infinity and Nothingness": "For, I ask, what is man in Nature? A cypher compared with the Infinite, an All compared with Nothing, a mean between zero and all." Thus Swift asks, is it still a man if it is only six inches high, or six miles high? Or if it has the body of a horse or of an ape? The question of when is a man free is merely a part of this larger question. Gulliver is clearly no *lusus naturae;* but he is, on the one hand, the individual lowering himself to the role of a slave, an animal, a show; on the other hand, by this very process, he demonstrates how unsuitable human pride is to man's real circumstances. Having cast away all liberty and independence, of action and thought, Gulliver increasingly exults in his own integrity, courage, and nobility. His prison box is in fact his reality—or the human reality, like Pascal's image of life as a condemned cell. The vermin speech of the king, though it applies to the people of Europe Gulliver has described to him, acts as a correlative to Gulliver's own unconscious decline. That man can build this prison into a myth of pride is the subject of Swift's satire; but much besides is involved in the image of the helpless Gulliver in his box or on his little show platform.

Regarded as generalized Man, Gulliver in Lilliput is at his best the large heroic spirit who defends his country and holds no grudges even when betrayed by that country, though he escapes from it; at his less than best he is a fool, a gull who accepts the standards of the Lilliputians and allows himself to be exploited, rationalizing his exploitation with terms like liberty and duty; at his worst he is the man who, acquiring a Lilliputian sensibility, exploits his size and desires to take back these little people to European laboratories and museums. At the end of his stay among the pigmies he has become himself a pigmy and a master. Thus he represents the various things that can befall man as a larger-than-life creature: he *can* be good, generous, and heroic; but he can also accept the standards of the mites, or, on the other hand, regard them as less than human.

Then, in his next voyage, Gulliver begins as the scientist he was at the end of his first voyage. He has set out this time because of his "insatiable Desire of seeing foreign Countries," and he insists on going ashore with the party seeking water on Brobdingnag: "that I might see the Country, and make what Discoveries I could." In short, he is off in search of specimens, and instead of another Lilliput (for which he is now presumably prepared, with bottles and pins) he finds a people for whom he is himself a specimen.

But if the sudden reversal from telescope to microscope image uses Gulliver to define a new aspect of man, it also catches the Brobdingnagians, who themselves figure in the overall human definition. They are part of a natural progression such as Pascal suggests: Gulliver exhibits the Lilliputian cattle, is himself exhibited by the Brobdingnagians, shows himself off to the Brobdingnagian royal family (a way of seeming important), and finally shows the teeth and other Brobdingnagian rarities to Europeans. Even the huge Brobdingnagians, as the ancient book shows, have no reason for pride.

If we take the famous and climactic scene in which the King utters his condemnation of contemporary Europeans, we can see how Swift's fiction supports, extends, and yet qualifies the satiric and metaphysical strategies to which we have referred. As a rhetorical device the King is of course a satiric perspective—a way of seeing the politics and wars in Europe from a position that will render the Europeans indeed "the most pernicious Race of little odious Vermin that Nature ever suffered to crawl upon the Surface of the Earth." But he is also part of a fiction, which causes the reader to recognize two simultaneous facts about his speech: that people in Europe *are* awful; and that from his point of view, people in Europe are awful. What he says is true, but at the same time he is a mile high and setting straight the mite who has been entertaining him and bragging too much. The first clearly carries the satiric impact; the second, a version of the satirist-satirized fiction, complicates the whole satiric situation but also qualifies the impact of the King's speech. Facing each other in this scene are Gulliver, in his pettiness and pride, and the giant, too-detached King. As the King is a telescope for seeing in perspective the wars and follies of Europe that appear in closeup heroic, so Gulliver is a magnifying glass that reveals the ugly reality of the apparent beauty of Brobdingnagian ladies.

Satirically—or rhetorically—the King's point of view is a good corrective for shortsighted men, as Gulliver's is in some instances for the farsighted Brobdingnagians. But we have by no means exhausted the fiction, which goes on to place the King himself one chapter later when Gulliver reads the old treatise which describes the Brobdingnagians in very similar terms to those used by the King on the Europeans: "how diminutive, contemptible, and helpless an Animal was Man in his own Nature." This is a treatise, Gulliver learns, that is now "in little esteem, excepting among the Women and the Vulgar." Gulliver, as usual, sees no connection; but the reader sees the King and his point of view as they look to super-Brobdingnagians—those giants of former days to whom the King might appear the same *lusus naturae* Gulliver is to him.

If the King is placed in relation to the nature of man, he is also placed in relation to his immediate environment. His point of view is not only an effect of his stature but must be taken also as a psychological reaction to the appalling praise Gulliver has been bestowing on obviously wicked and foolish behavior; the King is inextricably part of a relationship with the mite who is trying to impress the giant. Nor can Gulliver's speech be disentangled from the traveler's long-repressed chauvinism, the courtier's desire to be useful ("I hoped I might live to do his Majesty some signal Service"), the pigmy's need to overcompensate for his size, and Gulliver's particular tendency to find common cause with his masters. Some of these qualities are indicated as he speaks; others come from his placement in relation to his past. Gulliver standing on his platform addressing the King on the state of Europe has to be placed satirically and psychologically in relation to his exhibiting the Lilliputian livestock, his being taken for a specimen himself and exhibited in Brobdingnag, and his later performances for the royal family. In the same way, Gulliver's attempt in Chapter 7 to argue the King into using gunpowder to overcome all his enemies asks to be placed in relation to his earlier magnanimity toward the conquered Blefuscudians against the wishes of the Emperor of Lilliput, one of the few instances when he refuses to fall in with the assumptions of a master.

Where the satire and the ramifications of the fiction part is hard to say, but as causes are indicated, and the situation particularized, the traveler's chauvinism may come to be read as homesickness and the pigmy's desire to shine as insecurity—qualities less easily satirized. This juncture of the representational and rhetorical-metaphysical structures, I believe, explains much of the effect of *Gulliver's Travels,* especially in the great scenes like the one just discussed and Gulliver's self-recognition as a Yahoo. The representation at every point extends the satire and complicates the image of evil but not without qualifying in some sense the central condemnation.

My own feeling is that Swift understood the effect—up to this point at least—and was willing to sacrifice the absoluteness of the King's powerful speech to the larger realization that the King is only right in one sense about one aspect of man; and that his and Gulliver's speeches themselves represent other aspects.

Swift is trying to suggest, ultimately, what man is, not just what he is not, and the Brobdingnagian-human, Houyhnhnm-Yahoo contrasts are the approximations through which he seeks his definition. Moreover, his metaphoric parallels show man not only what he is, but why he is that way. The reasons for man's slavery to material forces, as opposed to spiritual, are shown to lie in his foolish fear of authority and in his equally foolish pride in himself, depending on the circumstances. In a way, *Gulliver's Travels* is simply a satire of consequences: slavery results from uxoriousness or pride; the simpler third voyage points this up, showing that a misdirection of reason leads to abstraction, loss of wives, impractical inventions, and rundown estates. In the fourth voyage we are shown that filth and squalor result from overreliance on the body and, as a final warning, that withdrawal from the human, even cruelty, result from overreliance on the otherwise good reason. The third voyage, in a reversion to an older type of satire, dwells on consequences; however, the other voyages spend much of their time on *causes,* showing with almost Defoe-like relish *how* and *why* a man becomes an object or a proud slave, a satirist or a misanthrope.

Gulliver's reaction to the Houyhnhnms and Yahoos has been so carefully prepared for that the reader is left with a strong awareness of the causes of his behavior. On the one hand he has been shown succumbing to foreign customs, seeing things through his host's (or master's) eyes in each country; on the other, he has been presented with an increasingly unpleasant and disillusioning set of experiences, climaxing in the revelations of the King of Brobdingnag and the magicians of Glubbdubdrib and, more personally for Gulliver, in the mutiny of his own crew. Everything has led him to think worse and worse of man. A third chain of causes can be traced to his increasing feeling of inferiority and, as compensation, his pride. Perhaps his self-exile from his wife and family also contributes. All of these details are, of course, perfectly consistent with Swift's primary intention, which is satiric. But when the system of parallels is embodied in the man himself instead of in what he observes (in the analogues of himself), they give Gulliver a past—perhaps even more of one than Robinson Crusoe. Crusoe exists in each moment of time as a man in a particular problem and with a particular past, which has been given us in detail. But his past bears on the present only as (if we can believe him) sin leads to consequences, and the reader may not be inclined to accept this interpretation of causality; while Gulliver's past contributes directly to the crucial moment of his confrontation with the Yahoos.

The multiple functioning of a satiric device finds its *locus classicus* in Gulliver's fourth voyage, which critics continue to argue about because they think it must be taken in only one way: either Gulliver is being satirized or he is not, either the Houyhnhnms are the ideal or they are not; whereas, not only does Swift use Gulliver in different ways at different times, he often uses him in two different ways at once. Gulliver is both satirist and satirized, the norm and the object of satire, and however factitiously, he appears to change in time. Each change is a new function; at best it is a kind of conversion, from subservience to princes and ministers to distrust, from fatuous admiration of all things European to skepticism and disillusionment, and from horrified awareness when his crew maroon him to stupid acceptance when the Houyhnhnms cast him adrift. But Gulliver conveys a sense of time, and the satire directed at him is qualified by the impression we have of the causes of his foolish actions and his gradual collapse.

Even the sheer fact of living with a first-person speaker through 300 pages, or 290 pages more than *The Modest Proposal,* contributes to the general effect of the satire. This effect has been commented on by Ian Watt, who believes that Swift has placed "a general representative of man collectively considered" (Gulliver as Everyman) in a situation where he becomes "man individually considered, with a particular wife and a particular problem," in short, a particular John, Peter, or Thomas. As Swift wrote in the famous letter to Pope, when he turns to these particular men from "that animal called man," his hatred changes to love; "and our feelings change," Watt writes, "if not from hate to love, as in Swift's letter, at least from amused detachment to a much closer emotional involvement." While Watt accepts the effect as an accident, I believe, as I suggested earlier, that in part at least it served the important rhetorical function of submerging and implicating the reader.

When Gulliver realizes in Chapter 2 of the fourth voyage that he himself physically resembles the abominable Yahoo— that his body alone does not make him a human being—Swift obviously intends his reader to feel a powerful shock. This is one of the great moments in satire, and it has produced howls of outrage or thoughtful revaluation from readers. The effect depends on the reader's seeing at that moment through Gulliver's eyes. It is characteristic of Swift's method that he does not stop at this point but proceeds to demonstrate that Gulliver's (and our own) reaction is subject to satiric scrutiny. The satire catches all of us who forget that we are, after all, related to a Yahoo and those of us who, accepting this, try to repudiate the Yahoo in ourselves altogether.

Gulliver is the definitive embodiment of Swift's reader, his true audience, who can tell the difference between humanity and inhumanity, but whose complaisance, whose ability to adjust to the values of knaves, draws it into reading with the false audience. Swift draws the reader into Gulliver's own character (or into sympathy with it) so that he can experience Gulliver's feeling of revulsion in his famous discovery, and his subsequent hatred of humans, before being turned about to see that he (and Gulliver) were seeing life in oversimplified terms. But implicating the reader can have two effects—as Fielding was to recognize fifteen years later when he satirized Richardson's *Pamela*. It can catch the reader in a folly and shake him into moral awareness, or it can turn satiric entanglement into empathy, which is the effect Watt experiences in the fourth voyage.

The effect is also to shift the reader's attention away from an idea and onto a character; he becomes more aware of Gulliver talking (of how he speaks and why) than of what he says. The Yahoos and Houyhnhnms are at times less real than the perception of them and the mind that does the perceiving. Swift has used a satirist-satirized fiction in *Gulliver's Travels* which, very different from the version in his earlier satires, draws him in the direction of the satirist-observer, away from the image of evil; it has involved him in problems of definition, and focused his interest in the operations of the perceiving mind on a complex satiric device that represents more hero than villain. Perhaps the crucial point about Gulliver's behavior in Houyhnhnmland is whether the reader focuses on the internal or the external as the subject. That we can do both not only shows Swift as an efficient satirist, less concerned with consistency than with thorough exploitation of his material, but also that he is at the crossroads of the old and new epistemologies. Reality for him is still in the Yahoos and the Houyhnhnms, and in the consequences suffered by Gulliver and his family, but it is also in the interior drama of the observer's mind.

Swift seems to have considered the most effective satire (both as persuasion and as representation) to be one in which the satirist himself is missing or transformed beyond recognition; one that does not draw attention to itself as a satire and is, in fact, a complete rendering of the satiric object. As the satirist disappears, interest in him is displaced to the satiric object, and then first, to a greater interest in his ethos, in attempts to understand the how and why of him (with Swift, who regards his mind as the center of danger, the operation of his mind becomes a main concern), and second, to a greater attention to verisimilitude, a desire to make the satiric object (which includes the form in which it expresses itself, its project, and so forth) more convincing.

Given this general trend, Swift's procedure has been to create a middleman as his villain—partly because he expresses Swift's idea of present-day evil; but also because he serves to catch larger and smaller fish as well, often including the reader. In *Gulliver's Travels,* then, Swift uses these characteristics of his middleman but applies them to his voyager, Gulliver. The Grub Street Hack's isolation and defeat, his gullibility, his use of other's theories to justify his own shortcomings, his pride and feeling of sufficiency—all are transferred to the relatively normative figure, the obtuse but developing protagonist, becoming in many cases sources of sympathy.

In one sense, we shall see [elsewhere], this transference facilitated a change from the gullible but normative character to the hero-satirist, with many of the same characteristics (thus the villain, William Wood, and the hero, the Drapier, are equally isolated and ignored by their would-be supporters). But it also produced a series of relationships whose complexity is evident from the attention that has been given to them by readers, scholars, and critics to this day. Contemporaries, however, learned little from Swift. It is ironic that the eighteenth century, which brought to perfection the ironic persona, the dramatized satire, should in general have thought (like the Elizabethans) of satire as a tone, usually invective. Swift's influence was doubtless felt more as a creator of satirists, from Bickerstaff to Gulliver in Houyhnhnmland to the "Dean" himself, than as a creator of complexly ironic fictions. The main influence Swift exerted on Fielding, for instance, was through the less inverted of his fictions, and Fielding seems to have been typical in regarding him primarily as a rhetorician, the outraged satirist—or ironist—standing behind every one of his satires. Therefore, when the run-of-the-mill writer attempted satire, he introduced a satirist attacking a satiric object.

Travel and Translation: Textuality in *Gulliver's Travels*

Grant Holly

I take it as axiomatic that intertextuality, acknowledged and unacknowledged, is always at work in our readings of "individual" texts, and, therefore, I can say without embarrassment that in part, at least, this essay, itself a part of a larger study on the nature of interpretation, grows out of a reading of Freud's theory of repression. What is so important in Freud's theory, which is logically, if not chronologically, the source of most modern theories of interpretation, is the way it both suggests and represses the identification of the interpretive act with repression itself. For Freud repression is not merely the process which confines or conceals material which interpretation attempts to recover, though that is what the apparent psychological imperialism of his project taken as a whole seems to suggest ("Where id was, ego shall be"). It is also a process of creation, elaboration, explanation, and interpretation. What is repressed, in other words (and this is true both in terms of the being of the reader and the being of the text), is the dominance of signifying over the signified. This repression is perpetuated in all analytics which seek to discover the meaning or meanings of the text.

The essay on *Gulliver's Travels* which follows is divided into two parts. The first attempts to show the way in which Swift's text makes signifying its subject, by implying a vast textuality which incorporates the reader and which, therefore, he can participate in but is no longer free to comment on. As a way of avoiding the hypostasizing of signifying as the signified

From *Criticism* 21, no. 2 (Spring 1979). © 1979 by Wayne State University Press.

of the text, the second part of the essay attempts to indicate the problematic of differencing along which signifying plays without fear of falling into sense or significance.

I. The World and the Book

> It must—and the paradox is ever-changing yet inescapable—say, for the first time, what has already been said, and repeat tirelessly what was, nevertheless, never said. . . . Commentary averts the chance element of discourse by giving it its due; it gives us the opportunity to say something other than the text itself, but on the condition that it is the text which is uttered and, in some ways, finalized. . . . The novelty lies no longer in what is said, but in its reappearance.
> —Michel Foucault, "Discourse on Language"

Gulliver's Travels elaborates a problematic of redundancy: a problematic which predicates the impossibility of escaping resemblances and the necessity of repetition. In spite of the apparent strangeness of his adventures, it is impossible for there to be generated in Gulliver's narrative a story which is not like other stories, just as it is impossible for Gulliver to make a voyage which does not take him home—both in terms of its ultimate destination and the standards according to which he views his discoveries—or for him to encounter a creature which does not resemble man. Gulliver can never really voyage because he can never exceed the limits of what he already knows.

Though this is not the usual statement of the case, it is in fact consonant with the critical approaches to the Travels which are usually taken. Most criticism, whether historical or interpretive, is committed to dealing with the text in terms of its signified, to attempting to recover the original clarity and wholeness of that signified before it fell into writing and was broken by articulations. The text qua text, the text as signifying material, cunningly eludes the analyst, who reads it merely as an arrow that points to a signified of transcendental importance, or gazes through its "transparency" to regions beyond. Paradoxically, however, the code of analysis will not admit either the "transcendental" or the "beyond" into the parameters of its commentary. Analysis is pinioned by the opposing intentions of eluding the text and being faithful to it; and while in the service of the former, it seeks to be original and innovative, it must, according to the constraints of the latter, labor like Borges's Pierre Menard to repeat in its own time and place the object of its commentary—to say, for the first time, what has already been said.

One consequence of this situation is that literary analysis turns out to be a ritual and compulsive (rather than analytic) activity, for in terms both of the text upon which it comments and the audience to which it speaks (fellow critics), it must invent a predetermined harmony. The true innovativeness of criticism resides in its ability to feign surprise at the discovery in the text of the very principles which animate its own discourse. Another consequence is that while analysis masquerades as a different kind of discourse from the texts it talks about, it is in fact an extension of those texts.

Satire is especially seductive in this regard, because it seems to posit the unspoken view of an author, a truth or truths beyond the instabilities of signifying, temptingly obscured by the text, fetchingly draped in fable; as well as suggesting that the elements of the narrative are substitutes, perhaps part of a systematic code, which stands for things for which there are in fact no substitutes.

The flexible text of the Scriblerian tradition, however, with its true beginnings which are false beginnings, its pseudonymous editors, publishers, friends of the author, its personae, its annotations, its systematic way in other words, of blurring the distinctions between outside and inside, the world and the book, attacks the illusions of the authoritative text, a signified which can escape the signifying process, and a commentary which is part of a different discourse from the work it comments on. These latter ideas are the very foundations of criticism, and one suspects, its *raison d'être,* for they permit us to assert our *superiority* to the work, to proclaim our *understanding* of what it is *about,* and thus to locate ourselves beyond the flux of its signifying in the "real world" to which it refers.

On the other hand, the boundaries which separate the world of *Gulliver's Travels* from the world to which it refers turn out to be self-effacing: both in terms of the story and the manuscript tradition. The task essential to essays on *Gulliver's Travels* of repeating in their own time and place what has been repeated in the text—the original conception or fact which existed before writing in the mind of the author, or in the world in which he lived, and which, coincidentally, happens to conform to the essayist's understanding—is disconcertingly the same task undertaken by Gulliver himself. Wherever he goes and whatever he sees, his experiences are communicated as a ratio of what is already familiar to him. The Lilliputians are twelve times smaller than man, while the Brobdingnagians are twelve times larger, Glubbdubdrib is about one-third the size of the Isle of Wight, Brobdingnag has a liquor which tastes like a "small Cider," flies the size of "a Dunstable Lark" and wasps which are "as large as Partridges" and sound like the

"Drone of Bagpipes" (III, iii). The examples are countless. Gulliver is always linked to the familiar by a chain of similes. For him and his reader alike, the *Travels* takes place in an atmosphere of metaphor which makes everything comparable to something else. Similarly, though it is well known that Swift complained of the liberties that Mott, the bookseller, took with his work, it is equally well known that Swift took pains to occult his own relationship to the *Travels*. Mott told Pope that the manuscript was "dropped at his house in the dark, from a hackney coach," and the instructions that went along with it encouraged the publisher to make whatever alterations his skill and judgment in determining the tastes of readers deemed necessary. When Faulkner asked Swift for a correct version, the copy to which he was sent turned out to be nonexistent. Indeed, though there exist corrected versions of the *Travels,* they differ from one another and are apparently not the origin of Faulkner's 1735 edition (generally considered authoritative), the source of which remains obscure.

This strategy, not unusual for Swift, of disguising the ownership of his work, is not merely part of the history of the book, i.e., the history of its coming into being as an object quite apart from the possibilities of signifying it opens, it is the very stuff of its natural history, i. e., the principle of its elaboration through displacement, substitution, translation, the flow of textuality on which the potentially quiescent book is perpetually carried towards other shores. In Gulliver's letter to his cousin, dated 1727 but conjectured to have been composed for the 1735 edition where it first appears, Gulliver complains about the addition, to the first edition, of remarks about Queen Anne which he says he never made, but admits they are an accurate representation of his views. Additions to the work, in other words, seem to be in keeping with it. When he complains shortly thereafter that his cousin has "either omitted some material Circumstances or minced or changed them in a Manner that I do hardly know mine own Work," it may mean that the text has been altered beyond recognition from its original fixed significance, but it can also mean that the boundaries between the original and interpolations are indistinguishable, thus obliterating the uniqueness of the original—making it just another version. The manuscript, he goes on to say, has been destroyed. He has supplied corrections, but he is uncertain of them. Since the one which he mentions, that "Brobdingnag" ought to appear "Brobdingrag," has been completely ignored by the editor, and since Gulliver regards language as moving steadily towards the unintelligible ("as I remember upon each Return to mine own Country, their old Dialect was so altered that I could Hardly understand the new," A Letter from Gulliver to his Cousin Sympson), we have no reason to believe that there can be an authoritative text or a definitive reading: like the changing dialect, the text may be in a state of perpetual metamorphosis.

In *Gulliver's Travels* the narrative gestures towards itself as signifying material in the repeated occurrence of emblems of the text—instances within the narrative which replace the signified or transform it into the image of another text—from which we can infer that the way out of the narrative is barred by the proliferation of substitutions, translations, and comparisons which constitute an endless and inescapable textuality. The alternations of reduction and expansion which characterize the first two books of the *Travels,* for example, are emblematic of the interchangeability of the world and the book. Gulliver, the student of medicine, navigation, languages, of "the best Authors, ancient and modern; being always provided with a great Number of Books," (I, i)—finds himself besieged by beings the size of illustrations. Like the reader of the *Travels* compelled to replicate his approach to it in his reading, Gulliver is a prisoner of his own world reduced to the dimensions of the book. This, however, is not the only permutation of the situation. Gulliver, the gigantic form whose limbs are virtually beyond the ken of the Lilliputians, whose body they swarm over like ciphers on a page, is himself the emblem of that textuality into which the reader, like the Lilliputians, descends, and where all that he encounters reflects the textuality that engenders it, producing, like the Lilliputians' account of the contents of Gulliver's pockets, a potentially endless round of circumlocutions. The voyage to Brobdingnag emphasizes this process by reversing it: the text expands to the size of the world and Gulliver enters it, literally, inhabiting the miniature world of their toys, walking through the pages of a book in order to read it, pacing a map of the kingdom even as he paced the island of Lilliput. What was once construed as the world, is now, in a larger context, shown to be a text, a transformation by contextualization that implicates the reader and his world as well.

As opposed to the interpretations of *Gulliver's Travels* which see it formulating its significance at a high pitch of meaningfulness above language and beyond the characterizations of its text, I suggest that we regard its "meanings" as part of the strategy of self-perpetuation of a signifying urge, more powerful than "meaning," but being no more than it is, on the surface, ready to efface itself to create the illusion of an independent purpose, a beyond which can be voyaged into, an otherness which can be discovered. Gulliver's experience, indeed his very being, betrays this signifying urge. For him, expression is constantly beneath the semantic and comprehensible. As a perpetual foreigner, even on his returns home, Gulliver is always addressed in an alien "jabber," to use his own word. As an oddity wherever he goes, Gulliver's significance is constantly being read not only in what he says, but in what he is, in the ambiguous signs of his size and shape. In Lilliput, his significance is understood in terms of his bodily functions, in the impact of his great hands and feet, and in the continued signifying of decay which would be brought about by his death. In Houyhnhnmland he is read according to his physical shape and the affectation of clothing—a system of signs which indicates the limits of the body. In Book III, Gulliver takes the place of the reader, confronting in the Academy of Lagado and the series of adventures that follow, analogues to the episode to which we have just alluded: the project for the decipherment of feces, or the perpetual translation of speech brought about by the endless physical and mental decay of the Struldbruggs, for example. Throughout, his own attempt to communicate and the responses of those he meets take place on the level of cries and gestures, on the mute and strident level of physiology, of a speech which is ingrained beyond any hope of interpretation. The spectrum of this speech ranges from the undefinable roars of the Yahoos to the inarticulatable speech of the Houyhnhnms—ranges, in other words, along a continuum of ambiguous noise which Gulliver perpetuates (since it is incomprehensible) in his "understanding" as we do in ours.

Let us say then that the true subject of *Gulliver's Travels* is the legendary discourse which animates the narrative. This legend manifests itself in two ways. In the first it is seen by Gulliver and the reader as an ever-receding spirituality, a ghostly presence which flies before the material onslaught of the events which constitute Gulliver's life or the signifiers which confront the reader, in precisely the same way that the purposes of Gulliver's voyages elude his efforts to achieve them, and Gulliver's account of his travels fails to eliminate the reader's questions concerning (the significance of) what took place. This is the teleological aspect of the legend, the aspect which awaits the reader, veiled in the darkness of the unsaid, and towards which the narrative gazes for the solution of questions of meaning and purpose. Insofar as the narrative is seen as pursuing this legend, it is being read metonymically, i. e., as a series of parts building towards completion.

But there is implicit in this manifestation of the legend another aspect, one which reverses the priorities and expectations of the first. The sign of this second manifestation of the legend is the analogical relationship which joins what are generally considered to be distinct categories: the world and events (out there) on the one hand, and the text and signifiers on the other. What are for Gulliver "the events" which make up his "life" are for the reader merely signifiers which enable him to read. On the other hand, Gulliver, forced to encounter his "experiences" as a foreigner, is constantly "living his life" on the level of signifiers, i. e., as a reader, while the "reader," whose work the narrative is, whose "reading" is a making because his effort is needed to *transform* the text, though he may discuss the narrative as a record of events, as the sign of a transcendental signified, experiences it as an event in itself. The narrative, from this point of view, is its own legend, the long signature of narrativity.

It is this aspect of the narrative that elaborates a problematic of redundancy, for in it narrativity, which is a kind of signifying, is itself revealed as the signified. And the tendency towards the expressed, towards, that is, a revelation of purpose or meaning, is repeatedly included in the larger strategy of exploiting the means of expression.

Consider, for example, the initial paragraph of the first chapter of Part One, "A Voyage to Lilliput":

> My Father had a small Estate in *Nottinghamshire;* I was the Third of five Sons. He sent me to *Emanuel-College in Cambridge,* at Fourteen Years old, where I resided three Years, and applied my self close to my Studies: But the Charge of maintaining me (although I had a very scanty Allowance) being too great for a narrow Fortune; I was bound Apprentice to Mr. *James Bates,* an eminent Surgeon in *London,* with whom I continued four Years; and my Father now and then sending me small Sums of Money, I laid them out in learning Navigation, and other Parts of the Mathematicks, useful to those who intend to travel, as I always believed it would be some time or other my Fortune to do. When I left Mr. *Bates,* I went down to my Father; where, by the Assistance of him and my uncle *John,* and some other Relations, I got Forty Pounds, and a Promise of Thirty Pounds a Year to maintain me at *Leyden:* There I studied Physick two Years and seven Months, knowing it would be useful in long Voyages.

The overall tone of the paragraph is one of explanation. In telling us that his father's estate is "small" and that he is the third of five sons, Gulliver alludes to circumstances of economic and social constraint which will presumably contribute to an explanation of why something happened, of how he got to be where he is, etc. However, what follows is a series of statements, each of which perpetuates the tone of explanation because it is eliminated as an explanation by the succeeding statement. Gulliver's career at college might well be what the first sentence explained; or the details of that career: Emanuel College, Cambridge, his being fourteen years old, the three years residency and his dedication to his studies, might contribute directly to an explanation. Neither of these alternatives is the case, however. "But" seems to negate what has immediately preceded it. The phrase which it initiates reinvokes the issue of economic and social constraint and could serve, it is true, as an explanation for Gulliver's being "bound Apprentice" (though not for why he is apprenticed to a physician, or to "Mr. James Bates"). Further, his being apprenticed to a physician named Mr. James Bates might be part of an explanation, but at this point, these explanations, and potential explanations, are themselves undermined. Gulliver chooses to spend his allowance on the study of navigation, and he reveals that he has, all along, intended to travel.

The force of this revelation transforms everything that has preceded it. Clearly, the paragraph builds up to the word "travel." It is presumably the outcome which the information that preceded it explains. Yet none of this information really bears directly and in itself on Gulliver becoming a traveler. The explanation of this outcome is, interestingly enough, attributed simultaneously to the most internal and the most external of sources: "Belief," "always" held, and therefore, the implication is, more profound than any reasons which might be found to justify it, and "Fortune," which is always mysterious and beyond the reach of explanation. The intimate and the vast, each in its own way, appeals to our sense of the inadequacy of language, and to a signified outside the influence of the sign. (*What I really mean* in terms of the ego's private sense of the inexpressible value of what he says, and *What I really mean* in terms of the significance of the ego's life taken as a whole). If "Fortune" is the explanation, the cause of which "travel" is the inevitable result, then what precedes Gulliver's revelation is less an explanation than it is a demonstration: in this case a demonstration of the way in which fortune is signified by a series of irrelevant explanations; and, in any case, if we use this paragraph as a paradigm for the whole text, of the way in which the text will seem to require something not textual, some transcendental signified, to explain its significance. This view is represented by all those critics who see Swift's satire as saying one thing by saying something else, or who think of the narrative in terms of what view, philosophy, politics, etc., it criticizes or advocates.

However, this view cannot be sustained if we pursue our analysis. "Fortune" does not suffice as an explanation, because what it explains is by its very nature unfinished, or more properly, in transit. Indeed, strictly defined, "travel" is pure process, neither here nor there, but a perpetual on-the-way. Far from permitting the cessation of the series of postponements that preceded it, "travel" seems to perpetuate them in an image. It is, in other words, a redundancy. Moreover, it is not "travel," alone, that we are given here, but Gulliver's intention to travel. In this context, I submit, to intend to travel is rather like meditating on the possibility of staring fixedly out the window: the one is the iconic equivalent of the other. The phenomenon of intention (which is part of the tone of explanation) seems to suspend the occurrence of the event, i. e., "life" or "travel" for Gulliver and the signified for the reader, and offers in its place a series of preparations. In so doing, it creates the illusion that the narrative develops according to the role of metonymic contingency, i. e., what is said is one of the potential outcomes of what has been said, and, in its turn, predicates a congeries of possibilities, one of which is what will be said. And in a sense this is true. However, in this passage, the past, present and future of narrative are also ways of saying the same thing.

To make this point it is worth considering these aspects of the narrative one at a time. 1) The future is clearly the direction in which the paragraph points, and the realm which contains the anticipated and, therefore, apparently unexperienced "travel." 2) The past, just as clearly, has been a time taken up by postponements and preparations. Here, however, the situation becomes more complex. Since travel is itself oriented towards the future, and since travel is the process which postpones "being here" from one place to another and marks the period of preparation which separates departure from arrival, there is the clear sense that what has been postponed or prepared for is embedded in the postponement and in the preparation—that the future, in other words, is embedded in the past. This somewhat abstract statement of the case applies to the series of nonevents (nonarrivals) which constitute the paragraph up to the mention of travel. At that point, as we have already noted, the redundancy is doubled by the merger of travel and intention. After travel is mentioned, Gulliver proceeds to relate a series of unacknowledged trips. He *leaves* Mr. Bates, *goes* to his father, and is suddenly (without any account of his journey) in Leyden, and all this is merely preparation for travel. Once we have been sensitized to this proliferation of equivalences, we cannot help but notice that the study of "Physic" [for] "two Years and seven Months" is itself a long voyage. The predominant force in the paragraph has become metaphor. 3) Throughout Gulliver's repetition (narration) of his past, he suppresses the present moment implicit in that past when actual travelling took place. This present is repeated in the reader's present, for the process of reading is analogous to the process of travelling, especially in that the reader suppresses this process (signifying) in expectation of an explanation (signified), just as Gulliver has suppressed his actual travelling in expectation of taking a trip.

II. THE MIRROR AND THE MAP

*Satyr is a sort of Glass, wherin Beholders do generally
discover every body's Face but their Own.*
                          —*The Battle of the Books*

At last I beheld several Animals standing in a Field.
                          —*Gulliver's Travels*

The definition of satire which opens the "Author's Preface to 'The Battle of the Books' " is certainly an epigram on the extent of human pride and the reluctance with which men engage in self-criticism—among the main themes drawn from Swift's satires by modern readers—but it is both more than that and a remark of a different order. This extraordinary statement, which encourages us to think of a book as a mirror and a reader both as the characters within and author of the text, marshals the machinery of repetition as part of a strategy of displacement and alteration. What is it that the beholder sees but fails to recognize in the glass but his own beholding, i. e., the process by which the text as an empty signifying is given a face by his reading.

The word "translation" implies a journey which is a journey home: the return to what was already, if only potentially, there—an assertion of the mirror symmetry of things. At the same time, however, translation begins a never-ending process—the ever-renewed recognition of discrepancies which lead to an endless round of compensatory circumlocutions. So, for example, the Lilliputian explorers who descend into Gulliver's pockets to catalogue their contents must translate what they find into familiar terms. The process destroys the validity of names but offers no alternative to them. Things disappear beneath a cloud of words which grows with the proddings of analysis, until we must suspect that the significance of names is their gesture towards the system which produces them, a gesture which is acted out in their endless proliferation into other names.

For the returning Gulliver, home is not what it used to be. A new child, a race of Lilliputian sheep and a collection of Brobdingnagian ephemera (which translate the hairs of the king's beard into a comb, and a corn from the maid of honor's foot into a cup), the uncontrollable desire to warn the natives of his homeland to beware lest he crush them, or to prance and neigh with the horses, his final inability to tolerate the smell of the place, and the perception that even the words which were once familiar to him have undergone an apparent transformation of significance which obscures the outlines of meaning in general, all contribute to the sense of an ineluctable metamorphosis—entropy disturbing the order of the features in the face of identity. Gulliver returns from the looking-glass world, the world which is like his *own,* to find that nothing is the same, that his world is merely *like* the one he has left. In this sea of likenesses, there is no point of reference, no world beyond the text, only a series of maps and the idea of mapping.

Indeed what the *Travels* reflects is the process of mapping. The letter from "Richard Sympson" entitled "The Publisher to the Reader" which is part of the 1726 edition, admits the "bold" editing of "innumerable Passages relative to the Winds and Tides, as well as Variations and Bearings in the several Voyages. . . . Likewise the accounts of Longitudes and Latitudes . . . to fit the Work as much as possible to the general Capacity of Readers." Of course this is part of the satire on nautical language—that there could be so much struck out and still so much left behind, indicates the extravagancies of this sort of jargon. On the other hand, the work's first claim to verisimilitude is through the integrity of these kinds of references, and through the mapping that they would permit. The implication is that it is not what the geologists call "real-world structures" but mapping itself, the system, or mode of dispersal, which can create the illusion of a world, which the text maps. This is not to say that the contemporary reader, at least, would expect to be able to find the flying island or Lilliput by paying careful attention to the text, and to doubt its veracity if he could not. To do so would be regarded as incredibly naïve. However, the way satire is typically regarded makes it the map of some distinct but nevertheless substantial continent *or* archipelago of meaning. By analogy, reading does not carry us beyond the text but situates us within it. What *Gulliver's Travels* satirizes can be said to be the illusion of a world beyond the map, of a signified beyond the flux of signifying. What it reveals is that the notion of a world beyond the map and of a text which can be confined in a book are themselves part of a discourse, which speaks the world, and which, in every utterance about the world, is being mapped.

We can chart four ways in which *Gulliver's Travels* reflects mapping, each of which characterizes not only what takes place in the narrative, but also our reading of it. First, there is the project of mapping by innuendo which we are encouraged to engage in because of the general ambience of satire. This charting of the invisible by what is visible on the mirror's surface is like the work of the Lilliputian tailors who fashion a suit of clothes for Gulliver based on calculations derived from the measurement of his thumb, and seems to be emblematic of the way this section should be read: asking the reader to work from smaller to larger, drawing a picture of his own world from Gulliver's account of the Lilliputians'. However, the "larger" of the Brobdingnagian adventure which follows, and the caricature of the work of the Lilliputian tailors by the mathematics of Laputa in Book III, suggests that once begun, mapping leads only to a series of versions.

Here we see the close relationship of the mirror and the map, both of which in their purest sense attempt to replicate the world—the former at a glance, the latter by the patient elaboration of a representational network so refined that nothing will be able to escape it. This is the fantasy that Josiah Royce engaged in his *The World and the Individual* (1899):

> Let us imagine that a portion of the soil of England has been leveled off perfectly and that on it a cartographer traces a map of England. The job is perfect; there is no detail of the soil of England, no matter how minute, that is not registered on the map; everything there has its correspondence. This map, in such a case, should contain the map of a map, which should contain a map of the map of the map, and so on to infinity.

Just as mirrors map the beholder, dispersing his image according to the rules of their surface, so maps mirror the techniques of beholding, arranging everything for the convenience of reading. In Brobdingnag, Gulliver cannot "forbear smiling":

> when the Queen used to place me upon her Hand towards a Looking-Glass, by which both our persons appeared before me in full View together; and there could be nothing more ridiculous than the Comparison: So that I began to imagine myself dwindled many Degrees below my usual Size.
>
> (II, iii)

Gulliver is hardly freed by his self-awareness, however. To break the mirror's spell and redefine the normal, he still must map the Brobdingnagians onto his own world. This problem is the same for the reader who must deal with the lies of the narrative like the Houyhnhnms—asserting the existence of that which he denies—thus making the preposterous the border of truth.

The second form of mapping is the rhetorical mapping which we have already discussed in our analysis of the first paragraph of Book I. It consists of the accumulation of details with the apparent intention of outlining a purpose or, in the case of the navigational information, a place. Since the details fail finally to be resolved into any pattern or outline, we must conclude that it is the role reading plays in completing the rhetorical gestalt which is being mapped.

The third form of mapping is embodied in the graphics of *Gulliver's Travels:* in the size and shape of the book, the kinds of type, the table of contents, the layout of books and chapters, headnotes, engraved scenes and designs, and, of course, the maps and diagrams. These are aspects of the work on which Swift probably had no direct influence. Nevertheless, they have every right to be considered in an analysis of the *Travels* since, as I have argued, *Gulliver's Travels* is about techniques of portraying significant structures. The work naturally includes the crafts which support its bid for our attention and belief—at whatever level. When we open *Gulliver's Travels,* for example, we are confronted by a "portrait" of its protagonist which sits on a pedestal on which appears CAPT. LEMUEL GULLIVER with the epithet from Horace, *Splendide Mendax,* in script beneath. The oval which frames the portrait is a shape common to both portraits and mirrors, thus underlining the mimetic aspirations of this kind of painting. But the image is not a portrait, pure and simple, for two reasons, both of which indicate the decay of the signified and the predominance of signifying. In the first place, it is the engraving of a portrait, which implies that it is a representation of a representation, a double translation which, though it still achieves the illusion of a three-dimensional object in a two-dimensional space, presents itself much more openly as a mapping, the product of the conventional cuts and striations of a style of engraving.

In the second place, the image cannot be considered a portrait in the usual sense because there is no such person as "Lemuel Gulliver." The frontispiece is marked with the portrait of a skull: it merely exemplifies a mode of signifying—advertises or catalogues a style of engraving which, since in this context it is tied to no thing to be engraved, can be regarded as pure fabrication. Following this thought one step further, we can see that the signified of this mode of signifying can be nothing other than the literal "Gulliver," the name inscribed on the pedestal below, which is itself a mode of signifying, unattached to any particular signified but undergoing a continuous process of translation, beginning with the epithet from Horace (which itself requires translation) and leading into the text beyond. As we look at the whole design, what we see is the sign of engraving balanced on the engraving of a sign. What is reflected in the mirror's frame is technique, reading and writing—the discourse that maps the body and according to which the body is read (Gulliver as physician and navigator). While on the blank face of the pedestal, the reflection of Gulliver as pure language, a signifier floating over a signifier, over a double which is another, maps the characteristics of the face above—the heavy black of the eyebrows over the flexible, wiry lines of the other features. Both parts of the frontispiece merge on the level of the interchange of line. The circle of the frame and the rectangles of the background seem to establish the abstract of this linearity, forming in the process the indecipherable hieroglyph of its signature, while within these limits the different realms of picture and language are joined in the larger problematic of differentiation which engenders signifying.

Finally there is the mapping of so-called human characteristics on fantastic creatures. Against the critical commonplace that the *Travels* defines "man" by a process of triangulation, as the unspoken signified implied by the extremes of the text, I offer the view that it indicates "man" at every point. The extremes which separate the Lilliputians and Brobdingnagians, Houyhnhnms and Yahoos, and the way, for example, the imagining of the Houyhnhnm race involves contorting their bodies into a sitting position and their using the pastern and hoof in the manner of the opposing thumb and forefinger, prove the elasticity of the concept "human." "Man" is the reflection of a discursive order, whatever constitutes the subject of reading and writing. The text prepares us for this view by making the human difficult to recognize on what we would have thought were its own terms. The work stretches the limits of the human so that the distinction between man and animal disappears. Great animals become mere mouthfuls for the voracious appetite of Gulliver in Lilliput. In Brobdingnag he is reduced to contesting his existence with insects. The natives take him for a kind of weasel, a monkey takes him for its young. By the time he is embraced by the Yahoo female in the fourth book, the idea of human has been so identified with the animal that it is possible for the animal to be identified with the human. "I fell into a beaten Road, where I saw many Tracks of human Feet, and some Cows, but most of Horses," says Gulliver, marooned in Houyhnhnmland. "At last I beheld several Animals in a Field . . ." (IV, i). Here we see the absolute separation of signifier and signified—for as Gulliver's adventure in Book IV goes on to demonstrate, any of the signs over which he puzzles on the roadway can be the signifiers of a creature with human characteristics.

Rather than thinking of *Gulliver's Travels* as the sign of some signified, however complex, I suggest we think of it as a demonstration of the way the signified grows out of the signifier, think of it as a sign of signifying. From this point of view, the text loses its purposiveness and progresses by means of associations which in themselves indicate a compulsive signifying.

As the third book opens, we find Gulliver, acting out elements of his name, living the life of a gull: surrounded by sea, he rests upon a rocky island, reposes in nests made of dry seaweed, dines on eggs. Islands and eggs reflecting one another in their roundness and reifying the circularity which connects Gulliver's life with his name, proliferate into more islands, a series of them explored by Gulliver, until island and egg merge in the flying island. There the predominance of the sign is perpetuated in the geometrical designs which emblazon the clothing of the inhabitants (an indecipherable writing, like the [nearly legible] marks which fill the illustration of the automatic writing machine), by the immersion of the Laputans in the self-contained languages of mathematics and music, and the repetition of circularity which marks the relationship of master and servant, the island and the land beneath, tyrant and tyrannized, body and mind—indeed a host of gull and egg questions around which the book turns—until we realize that Gulliver's return home is no more than the inevitable folding back of the text upon itself.

When Gulliver tells us that in Brobdingnag, "After much Debate, they concluded unanimously that I was only *Replum Scalcath,* which is interpreted literally *Lusus Naturae* . . ." (II, iii), a modern editor demonstrates the potency of this literalness by glossing *Lusus Naturae* as a "a freak of nature"—now the literal translation of a literal translation. It almost goes without saying that the literal phrase "a freak of nature" is not transparent enough *not* to require glossing itself, and that the gloss would require its own gloss and so on until the resources of the lexicon had been exhausted. The literal cannot be regarded as the most basic level, the very type of the signified. It is instead the stuff of signifying, the proliferation of letters, of which meaning is a transient by-product. In this regard, Gulliver is a character in the literal sense, a man of letters. The hard and soft sounds of his name map the gateways of articulation, give us a sense of the texture through which the paths of significance must be broken. Where he goes and what he sees seem to grow out of his name: Lemuel Gulliver, Lilliput, Brobdingnag, Glumdalclitch, Lagado, Glubbdubdrib, Luggnagg, Struldbruggs. . . . Throughout there is the rhythm of dactyls and anapests, like the clatter of horses' hoofs, nagging evidence of a level of marking and articulation more persistent than sense.

"The Houyhnhnms," we are told, "have no Letters," but they are nothing but letters, the very principle of the unintelligible signifying temporarily repressed by a conventional pronunciation. "The whining of a horse, perhaps best pronounced, *Whin-num,*" ventures an editor, indicating my pronunciation and perhaps yours as well, but we should not let this habit obscure the indecipherability of the marks. "When I offered to slacken my Pace, he would cry, Hhuun, Hhuun; I guessed his Meaning and gave him to understand, as well I could, that I was weary, and not able to walk faster; upon which he would stand awhile to let me rest" (IV, i). I am not arguing that "the English Orthography" (IV, i) is inadequate for recording the cries of horses (because that might imply that there was some accurate orthography), nor would I say nay to the reader who says he knows the equine sound to which Gulliver refers with "hhuun." On the contrary, I want to suggest the aptness of this orthography which, in the face of an unspeakable language, develops an unpronounceable script. As the history of criticism of the *Travels* shows, the meaning of Houyhnhnm words, either in themselves or in Gulliver's translation of them (and we must not forget that much of the narrative is a translation) is highly debatable. In the same way, whatever pronunciation we choose for the Houyhnhnm words represses a host of others. It is this repression which I have tried to indicate in this essay. This has been a difficult task since I believe there is nothing to repress: the *something* for which we might look, the signified of the text, the meaning of the text, is itself the invention of repression. What is repressed is a signifying that has no meaning other than what it is (for it is our being): the hydraulics of life and death which, like the coursing of blood through our veins, we learn not to hear.

The Displaced Person

Patrick Reilly

Gulliver travels to find himself. As much as *Oedipus* or *Der zerbrochene Krug* the action is a search for identity, its ultimate question as shocking as that posed by the twentieth-century death camps: not "where is God?" but, much more appallingly, "where is man?" In pursuit of this mystery, Swift employs throughout certain recurring images and themes—giants and girls, sexuality and vermin—as aids to identification.

The opening voyage, addressing a personal dilemma as well as universal concerns, is the most autobiographical; in the figure of the baffled giant, Swift investigates his own captivity in Lilliput. One of the most bitter sensations known to man is the consciousness of failure affixed to a conviction of ability. When the man is not merely talented but a genius, the agony of bewilderment, of unjustified self-reproach, is commensurately greater, and the mystery of defeat, forever soliciting explanation, can become a mode of diabolic torment. That Swift saw himself as both genius and failure we need not doubt, for his own word is the evidence. "What a genius I had when I wrote that book!" The note of elated discovery and gratified pride in his own belated tribute to the *Tale* only enhances and authenticates the sense of accomplishment he experienced in the rereading; and the reception of the *Travels* as recorded by Johnson—"It was received with such avidity that the price of the first edition was raised before the second could be made; it was read by the high and the low, the learned and illiterate. Criticism was for a while lost in wonder"—must surely have

From *Jonathan Swift: The Brave Desponder*. © 1982 by Patrick Reilly. Manchester University Press, 1982.

ratified in him the conviction of his old power. He had, in addition, other spectacular triumphs. The purpose of *The Conduct of the Allies,* says Johnson, was to persuade the nation to a peace, and never had pamphlet more success. In *The Drapier's Letters* he had, single-handed, defeated a government attempt to exploit Ireland—and, for Swift, saving the Irish was a labour that might have confounded Hercules himself.

The ordinary man shakes his head in perplexity on hearing such a life described as failure; what, he wonders, would Swift have accepted as success? Yet genius remains inconsolable; if there is one indisputable fact about Swift, it is his bitter, invincible conviction of defeat. We might pardonably exaggerate by describing him as a man programmed for defeat, and the great fish which he just missed catching as a boy was indeed, as he told Pope, to haunt his whole life as prophetic admonition, symbol of all those near things that darkened his career. The man whose pantheon of heroes was an assembly of spectacular failures—Brutus, Junius, Socrates, Epaminondas, Cato, More—was acutely sensitive to the obstacles cumbering the path of heroic virtue in a spiteful, petty, levelling world. He caustically supplies the one infallible test of a true genius: all the dunces are inveterately leagued against him. He provides the recipe to those seeking advancement through the power of the word:

> Write worse then if you can—be wise—
> Believe me 'tis the way to rise.

The pain of personal failure, the sense of wasted endeavour, of words marshalled to no creative purpose—doses prescribed for the dead, appeals to animals incapable of amendment, the charmer's skill squandered on deaf adders—all this hangs heavy over Swift's work, is indeed, paradoxically, the source of its greatness. No other writer of genius has so much made the foolish futility of words the master theme of his achievement, and it is this that partially justifies Leavis's pronouncement about great powers exhibited consistently in negation and rejection.

Failure is less tantalising when the great man falls through some excess or shortcoming, the tragedy of *hamartia* as defined by Hamlet, "the stamps of one defect" that pulls ruin upon a whole array of virtues. This helps to assuage whatever dismay we feel at Antony bested by Octavius or Coriolanus broken by the tribunes. Great men undoubtedly, but the reconciling pity is that greatness should be so lamentably vitiated. The reconciling element disappears, however, when heroism perishes with no *hamartia* to dull the edge of pain. The defeat of goodness is for Swift as nerve-jangling as Aristotle predicted, and we need only read Swift on More's fate at the hands of "Henry the Beast" to appreciate how unappeasably angry he could become at the spectacle of unmerited suffering—the greatest Englishman of all time murdered by the worst.

Swift reechoes the perplexed anguish of the Psalmist: how long, O God? Why does God forget his servant, hide in the seasons of distress? Why do the good fail, the wicked flourish? Why is the genius doomed to die like a poisoned rat in a Dublin hole while mediocrities monopolize power? Nor is it simply his own personal debacle that torments him. His friend Bolingbroke provides yet another confirmatory instance of the same perverse law that condemns great ability to impotence. In his poem "On the Death of Dr Swift" there is a footnote telling us that Bolingbroke "is reckoned the most universal genius in Europe," but that Walpole, dreading his gifts, has conspired with George I to keep him in the political doldrums. The mystery remains: how has an intellectual giant like Bolingbroke been outmanoeuvred and outsmarted by a commonplace rascal like Walpole? What is this strange moral equivalent of Gresham's Law which continually awards victory to Lilliputians, while the colossus, superior gifts notwithstanding, is lucky to escape with eyesight and life?

There is plausible internal evidence that Swift uses Lilliput to explore certain crises in his own life or in the lives of his friends; the giant's "eminent service" in extinguishing the blaze in the royal apartments which so offends the Empress that she declines ever again to enter the polluted palace, is an allegory of Queen Anne's outraged resolve never to advance the author of the *Tale*—or, alternatively, of the royal ingratitude towards Bolingbroke who had put the nation in his debt by concluding the Peace of Utrecht. Both book and treaty are giant achievements, maligned by pygmy malice. Gulliver, lodged in the profaned temple, desecrated some years before by an unnatural murder, recalls Swift's revulsion at the execution of Charles I, always for him, as his sermon on the royal martyr shows, the nadir of revolutionary evil. But, detailed interpretation apart, there is clearly something in the image of the bemused giant, curiously impotent despite enormous power, that holds intense personal interest for Swift. Not that Gulliver *is* Swift; on the contrary, he is in his role as wide-eyed ingénu laughably different from his sharp, knowing creator. The ropedancing and the crawling under sticks which so fascinate him as ceremonies unknown to the rest of the world are sickeningly familiar to Swift as the contemptible cantrips of power-seekers everywhere. But, however unlike in other ways, Gulliver as giant among pygmies is an apposite metaphor of Swift in his society, just as Gulliver's unavailing efforts to live decently and usefully, placing his great powers at the public service but forever frustrated by the envy of little men, is a thinly disguised rendition of his creator's unhappy fate.

Gulliver visits fantastic countries without ever leaving the real world.

The veracity he is so touchy about is never really in doubt and his appeal to his long sojourn among the honest horses as verification of his story, is superfluous. Escapist is thoroughly inapplicable to a book which entraps us while pretending to visit exotic regions. Johnson's outrageous dismissal of the *Travels*—a mere matter of thinking of big men and little men with everything else at once falling into place—is unpardonable; what about flying islands and crazy academies, hideous immortals and sorcerers' realms, rational horses and Yahoos? Yet this perverse judgement is relevant to the first two voyages and can help us identify their salient characteristics: the only thing fantastic in Lilliput or Brobdingnag is Gulliver himself, so that it *is* finally nothing more remarkable than a question of relationships between big and little men.

These worlds are perfectly credible, totally recognizable—naturally enough, since they are both our own, diminished and magnified in powers of twelve. Gulliver impatiently waves away the printer's plea for changing the original text; how can he be prosecuted for what has happened so long ago and far away?—thus betraying these travels into remote nations as investigations of contemporary England. Kinship is established when Gulliver spots his first Lilliputian, a human creature not six inches high, with a bow and arrow in his hands and a quiver at his back, while he himself lies pinioned, sword at his side, pistols in his pocket. Unsurprisingly, Lilliput has the same dismal record of war and massacre as England—six feet or six inches, it is the same bellicose, destructive animals. Far from "remote," Lilliput's problems in warfare, political careerism, religious intolerance, are those of Europe. Not the country nor its customs and concerns but Gulliver's status within it—this creates the elements of fantasy and fairy tale, establishes it as the children's classic. Giants are a norm in fairy tale and "A Voyage to Lilliput" presents a metamorphosis as startling as any in Ovid or Kafka.

Gulliver changes. Shipwrecked an ordinary man on a Pacific beach, he loses consciousness and is reborn nine hours later a giant. Lest we miss the gestation symbolism, he tells us afterwards his stay in the new universe was just over nine months. How seems the world to someone who awakes to a twelvefold increase in stature? Swift supplies a comic analogue to Marlowe's Faustus, an examination of the benefits and perils of being suddenly raised far above ordinary mortals. Its picquancy is a function of Swift's own Olympian self-awareness linked to his sense of restriction and confinement, a fettered giant in his irksome Dublin exile. The dream of power is as old as the dream of immortality and the latest import from American comic books via television in the awesome figure of the Incredible Hulk, who uses his prodigious strength to right wrongs and foil villains, is testimony to the dream's staying-power, in however debased a form. The ordinary man fancies that, given giant power or eternal life, all things are possible, but just as in Part Three Swift destroys the dream of immortality by depicting it as a Struldbrugg nightmare, so in Part One he explodes equally naïve expectations by showing that the giant Gulliver fares no better in Lilliput than his intellectual counterparts, Jonathan Swift and Henry St. John, do in eighteenth-century England. "A Voyage to Lilliput" scrutinises the fate of the giant in society by presenting him in certain representative guises: as Polyphemus, Hercules, Samson, and also as intellectual titan, bringer of new truth to ordinary men.

Irony is present from the start in the simultaneous recreation of Gulliver as giant and prisoner. His first impulse to resist as a match for their greatest army is followed by a prudential decision to submit, the linguistic problem circumvented by calling upon the sun as witness of the promise. The Lilliputians evince a similar capacity for prudential morality. They don't try to kill him while he sleeps, sensibly, since the aroused giant would have burst his bonds and caused a bloodbath. The initial relationship between giant and little people is a perfect *exemplum* of Swift's lifelong thesis that decency and commonsense, morality and reason, are ideal bedfellows, that men go to heaven with half the pains of the hellward journey.

The irony of Gulliver's dual status—giant and captive—is, however, soon matched in the ambivalent Lilliputian response. He is, clearly, a notable acquisition; when he eats and drinks, they exhibit an ecstatic proprietary pride in the doer of these wonders. When, freed from the ropes but securely chained, he at last stands erect, they gasp with delighted astonishment. Their attitude to him is rather like Magwitch's to Pip: my gentleman, our giant. But pride competes with other considerations. Like a modern nuclear reactor, Gulliver is both promise and threat, at once source of power and fear, and however gentle and obedient, he poses serious problems for his hosts' technology. What if he breaks loose, runs amok, causes famine or plague? Even if they manage to kill him, will not the stench of the monstrous carcass produce disastrous environmental pollution? Can they afford so costly a luxury with the consequent strain upon their tiny resources?—he needs six hundred domestics and armies of craftsmen of all kinds from joiners to tailors, he consumes daily enough food to keep 1728 Lilliputians alive, the removal of his excreta requires a squad of labourers with wheelbarrows working a full shift.

His everyday acts are potential catastrophes: a man who extinguishes conflagrations simply by urinating might be welcome in London in 1666 or Chicago in 1871, but always there is the fear that he might just as easily drown the government as save the city. His mere presence is a peril in town or country. He must stick to the highways and stay out of the fields where a stroll would mean total devastation. Visiting the metropolis, he has to wear a short coat for fear of destroying buildings and there is a two hours' curfew to avoid a massacre of citizens. What if he sleepwalks? or sneezes? It's like living with a petrochemical complex on the doorstep. Every time he relieves himself, the health authorities face a major crisis in pollution disposal, the modern equivalent of a giant oil tanker wrecked daily on your coast. When he eats and drinks the spectacle is magnificent, but pride in his prowess and aesthetic delight are tempered by a frightened glance at the ravaged foodstore or the ledgers of a desperate exchequer. And yet the Lilliputians clearly find it a comfort to have a giant on their side and the high risks of his maintenance nag less when he puts on a fearsome display of the latest European weaponry; waving his scimitar or firing his pistols, he appeals to the same emotions, brings the same comforting reassurance, as do the newest NATO missiles or the massive Warsaw Pact armaments rolling through Red Square.

From the start he decides to be a "good" giant, earn his parole by contradicting the stereotype of the wicked ogre. His first conscious impersonation is of a mock Polyphemus. When the hooligans who stone him are delivered to him by the military for punishment, he puts them in his pocket and takes one out, like the Cyclops with the companions of Ulysses, as though he were about to eat him. The officers' dismay gives way to rejoicing when instead he uses his terrible knife to cut the culprits' bonds before gently setting them free—the ogre is really a genial giant, forever obliging and anxious not to disturb. He passes with full marks this clemency test and in a remarkable demonstration of power and magnanimity completely fulfills Isabella's injunction to the great ones of the world:

> O, 'tis excellent
> To have a giant's strength, but it is tyrannous
> To use it like a giant.

The policy of being a model prisoner seems to pay off when the Emperor, hearing of the incident, decides to give Gulliver a chance to prove himself "a useful servant." He becomes a kind of court entertainer or circus strongman, a Samson desperately eager to placate his captors by feats of strength and entertainments, using his handkerchief as exercise ground for the royal cavalry, straddling his legs to provide an imposing triumphal arch for the full military parade. Mildness reaches a charming apogee as the natives dance in his hand and the children play hide-and-seek in his hair—there could be no more striking proof that the passage from Polyphemus to lovable giant has been fully accomplished.

After such exemplary behaviour, it comes as no surprise when he at last obtains his freedom. With freedom, however, we have the first hint of something rotten in Lilliput. Gulliver is freed not as reward for good conduct but to frustrate an enemy invasion, and but for this emergency might have lain in chains for ever. Swift's own experience in securing the remission of firstfruits for the Church of Ireland taught him how sweet people seeking favours could be, how ungratefully curt after you had delivered. Gulliver, like Swift, delivers; he guarantees Lilliput against aggression by walking off with the enemy fleet, his spectacles a shield against arrows. Without the stir of one Lilliputian scientist, the nation acquires a new, stunningly invincible weapon that blows skyhigh the armaments parity with Blefuscu. But when the Lilliputian Emperor, insatiable for world empire, avid to become literally as well as panegyrically lord of the universe, spurns an advantageous peace, like the Whig hawks, and demands unconditional surrender, the reduction of Blefuscu to a colony, and universal dragooning into the Little Endian Church, the tool rebels, the weapon declines to be used: Gulliver, refusing to be an instrument for reducing a free people to servitude, withdraws his giant labour. The invasion threat over and Blefuscu, like Louis XIV at Utrecht, ready to treat, Gulliver declines to pulverise them into unconditional surrender. In response, forgetting all his debts to Gulliver, the Emperor begins plotting his death and the way is clear for Gulliver's two further impersonations of harassed, tormented titanism, Hercules and Samson.

Before this, however, we have the spectacle of Gulliver as intellectual giant, bringer of new, startling truth to little men and meeting the customary fate attending such giants ever since Plato's philosopher returned to the cave to enlighten its inhabitants about the world outside. The giant's flagrant capitulation to the petty follies of Lilliputian politics has already been noted. Certainly, Gulliver, in consequence of his ludicrous complaisancy, has only himself to blame if the little people treat him as a born Lilliputian with the full set of petty prejudices; but, at the same time, there is something absurdly egotistic in the easy assumption that whatever concerns a Lilliputian must also be of obsessive interest to a giant—a *drurr* may be crucial in Lilliput but Gulliver has to take it on trust. The very uncomplaisant god of "The Day of Judgement" surveys scornfully the petty wranglings of the odious vermin who dare to make him a party to their disputes before squashing them all underfoot.

It is therefore comically appropriate that smack in the middle of this display of egotism, Swift should insert a devastating critique of the Lilliputian reaction to Gulliver's news of the giant world. The little people credit only one world, that divided between their two great empires. They reject Gulliver's account of Europe on a priori grounds as incompatible with established truth, applying in the process pygmy reasoning and Lilliputian standards to the whole universe. Gulliver must have fallen out of the sky, from the moon or a star, since clearly a hundred such creatures would speedily eat the world to death—"world" is obviously a synonym for Lilliput. The logic is impeccable given the closed system of Lilliputian conditioning—and against the walls of this system Gulliver beats in vain in his attempt to persuade his hosts to a radical reappraisal of reality. There is no evidence in the text that he is exasperated by their resolve not to be enlightened, but this simply emphasizes the temperamental gulf between Swift and Gulliver, for similarly circumstanced the greatest single torment of Swift's life was his inability despite all his art and striving, to make people see.

If Gulliver as intellectual giant can be contemptuously ignored, Gulliver as good servant turned awkward is another matter, especially when his maintenance cost is remembered. Even a docile Gulliver comes dear; when refractory, the opportunity cost of his upkeep becomes totally unacceptable. Lilliputian vindictiveness gathers against the recalcitrant giant all the more readily when the budget is on the agenda. Gulliver's myopia is nowhere more humorously demonstrated than when, thinking he is honouring the royal host, he overeats scandalously, while the Treasurer Flimnap sourly looks on, thinking not only of his "faithless" wife but of the depleted exchequer. The Lilliputians by now want rid of him—what good is an intractable giant? But the dilemma is painful; exiled, he might cross to Blefuscu and take both fleets with him. The overriding priority is how safely to jettison this disobliging encumbrance, and in the context of the parallels already established between Lilliputian and European history, it is appropriate that the methods of elimination proposed should resemble closely the tragic ends of the two mightiest heroes in western mythology, Hercules and Samson.

It is fitting that the jealous treasurer should conceive a plan of strewing a poisonous juice on Gulliver's shirts to make him tear his flesh and die in torture: the shirt of Flimnap, Lilliputian replica of the shirt of Nessus, the device whereby Hercules, that other victim of love and jealousy, is untimely destroyed. The second, more merciful plan, proposed by Gulliver's friend, the Secretary Reldresal, looks back to Samson's treatment by the Philistines.

Blinding the giant is in every sense the ideal solution: it will confirm "all the world" in its appreciation of imperial mercy, it will suitably acknowledge the giant's former services before he turned nasty, and it will make him totally dependent on his captors for the rest of his life. Strong as ever, he will be able to "see" only through his master's eyes; he will be braver than ever, for dangers unseen cannot deter, and he need fear no longer for his eyes, the one concern that almost frustrated the removal of the enemy fleet. The Emperor's decision is a compromise between death and blinding; Gulliver is to be blinded, then gradually starved to death—boring operations can begin in distant parts of the kingdom to find areas suitable for disposing of the noxious carcass to prevent atmospheric pollution.

Gulliver, to whom this plan is leaked through the loyalty of a high-placed friend (Philby in Lilliput), can now only react. He is being forced to his dismay into the role of Samson, and the always unstable relationship of guest and host has now clearly declined into that of captive and captor, victim and executioner. Propaganda about royal mercy notwithstanding, he recoils from the role of docile, tractable giant, eyeless in Lilliput at the mill with slaves, but equally he rejects with horror the part of heroic, defiant Samson, pelting the tiny metropolis to pieces with stones, pulling the whole guilty empire crashing down upon his puny enemies. Far from hero, Gulliver is comic as he desperately cudgels his brain trying to see the lenity of the imperial sentence or shrinks from harming the Lilliputians in grateful remembrance of that exalted title of Nardac so graciously bestowed upon him in happier days.

Salvation comes to him, ironically, by way of inexperience, his character as ingénu, young, rash, foolishly precipitate, as Swift supplies a delightfully comic instance of the advantages that sometimes accrue from being a fool among knaves. He simply decides to leave Lilliput and let the little people live as they did before he arrived. With greater maturity, deeper knowledge, a fuller acquaintance with the ways of princes, he would have seen the Emperor's unbelievable mercy, have embraced joyfully so mild a chastisement as mere blinding. He avoids it because, young and blessedly ignorant, he is still headstrong enough to disregard expert advice. The radical critique of habituation posing as knowledge, the merely provisional, relative and contingent claiming to be absolute and immutable, first seen in the offhand dismissal of Gulliver's European "fantasies" by the little people, is now redirected towards Gulliver himself as target as he confesses shamefacedly, on the basis of subsequent experience, what a fool he was in saving his eyes. Such "knowledge" as he has since then acquired is, Swift implies, as damaging as exposure to the stench of a dead giant, as fatal as radiation sickness, in the manner in which it weakens and finally deadens the instinctive human response, the intuitive moral reaction, to straight evil; adaptation to certain modes of experience is the disease that destroys humanity.

The international crisis sparked off by the flight to Blefuscu, which attains comic heights with the Emperor of Lilliput demanding in egotistic abandon the instant return of the defector in chains, is only defused when Gulliver finds a boat from the giant world. What better solution to the impasse than Gulliver's unimpeded departure? The Emperor of Blefuscu observes the conventions by politely asking him to stay on as *his* servant, but is mightily relieved when the Man-Mountain just as politely declines. Both empires are at last free "from so insupportable an encumbrance" and can cheerfully return to the mutual massacre that Gulliver's intervention threatens to end; Golding's officer sails away from the island, in Swift's version, and leaves the boys to Beelzebub. The little world has no place for giants who will not abet its corruption; it will always prefer Barabbas to Christ, Flimnap to Gulliver, Walpole to St. John.

Gulliver's leaving the world of the little people is the last ironical juxtaposition of Swift's giant with his own situation. Gulliver sails easily away from Lilliput, captivity ended, an innocent in the evil political world yet miraculously endowed with the power to leave it behind. Swift, shipped off to his Dublin exile, is still the captive giant, cruelly aware of the stink of political life, yet powerless, despite all his great powers, to master, amend or even escape it. Gulliver is liberated from Lilliput, Swift remains as agonizingly imprisoned among *his* little people as ever.

Gulliver leaves Lilliput to seek himself, for he is not at home with the little people. Swift's restless search, using travel as a metaphor, contrasts sharply with Pascal's recommended quietism. Pascal knows what ails us: an inability to sit quiet in one little room. Only on reaching that littlest room of all, the grave, is the frenzied hunt after distraction ended, the last unalterable identity assumed—eternal prisoner or heir to paradise. Swift avoids such otherwordly speculation, his preferred categories being reason and animalism rather than heaven and hell. He always resists committing himself unequivocally to what man cannot know; "if the way to Heaven be through piety, truth, justice, and charity, she is there." The search for comfort concerning his dead mother includes, characteristically, a scintilla of scepticism, a hint of doubt, if only in its mode of formulation; a conclusion is implied rather than affirmed and he and we together are left to hope that it is unchallengeable. Swift will assert only the empirically indisputable and his kingdom is very much of this world, what happens to men here and now his concern. Discussing heaven, he chooses predictably the negative mode; we know, not what goes on there, but what doesn't— neither marriage nor giving in marriage. It is what men do on earth— ropedancing in Lilliput, amassing shining stones in Yahooland, marrying and giving in marriage in England—that obsesses Swift. Where Pascal is interested only in the identity disclosed in the grave, the *Travels* pursues identity in this life and does so by forbidding in advance any pretended distinction between an alleged human nature (*animal rationale*, God's image, etc.) and the deeds of men. "Th'art the deed's creature": our deeds possess and define us, we think them ours but we are theirs, and we discover ourselves in the mirror of everyday life rather than in some final judgement after death. And so, against Pascal's advice, Gulliver is sent on his travels to gather the data enabling a final assessment of human nature to be made. The present aim is to show the part played by Gulliver's girls in reaching this verdict, the importance of sexual evidence in the *Travels* in defining human nature, how indeed at certain points in the text the sexual test assumes crucial significance not only thematically but as a structural prin- ciple in the book's organisation.

Gulliver travels because Swift needs evidence; only with the dossier complete and the prosecution case invincible, is he allowed to give up the sea and write his memoirs. To ask therefore why Gulliver returns from Lilliput is like asking why Hamlet doesn't kill Claudius in the prayer scene — the short answer is that there are three voyages and two acts to go. But this, undeniable if trite, refers to the needs of the artist rather than the demands of the art. To leave matters as shockingly obvious as this is to convict the writer of ineptitude or literary bad manners. Genius is the synchronization of external requirement with internal necessity to that what has been willed seems also inevitable: what Shakespeare and Swift want is what Hamlet and Gulliver decide. They will be done on earth as it is in heaven; *en la sua voluntade e nostra pace:* the words would be as appropriate in the mouths of Hamlet and Gulliver as in that of God's submissive subject. The Creator's world is a masterpiece ruined by characters who insist on doing their own thing.

Swift's literary strategy is of course very different from Shakespeare's; his gift is enlisted under satire and he never refines himself out of existence— behind the persona we suspect always a real presence and the guarded scepticism that made him, in the matter of Irish coinage, distrust the ap- parently honest Maculla as much as the rascally Wood, is equally evident in his relations with his own literary creations. From the narrator of the *Tale* to Gulliver, the Drapier and Modest Proposer, his characters are always delegates, never representatives; they say and do only what he wants. If we accept Keats's definition of the poet as having no character or identity, a chameleon forever "filling some other body," delighting as much in an Iago as an Imogen, then we must deny the title to Swift. Hack, Gulliver, Drapier, Proposer, do not relate to Swift as Timon, Lear, Antony to Shakespeare. Swift never set characters free in his sense because he never trusted anyone to speak for him—any persona who had tried anticipating Burke's line with the electors of Bristol would soon have got short shrift. Nevertheless, Swift is as aware as Shakespeare of art's exigencies; Gulliver's return from Lilliput, as much as Hamlet's delay, is motivated internally and not just because Swift is hankering for Brobdingnag. No more than Hamlet does Gulliver know that he's a fiction, at his creator's beck and call; the relationship is rather that identified by Augustine when discussing man's free will and divine foreknowledge: God knows *and* man is free. The artist, like the Creator, foresees what the character will choose.

Gulliver *is* needed for Brobdingnag but the internal justification is that giants cannot live with ordinary people without becoming their conquerors, tools or victims. Gulliver is no conqueror—never once in Lilliput does he use his giant strength to hurt anyone or even retaliate when attacked. He is willing to be a tool, but not to the degree required by pygmy megalomania, so the only part left him is that of victim. Even his complaisancy, however, does not extend to suicide or passive martyrdom. He cannot remain permanently in Lilliput; sooner or later, he will be killed or forced to kill in preemptive strike against his enemies. He is a displaced person, nowhere more strikingly revealed than in his sexual position . Reproduction is one of the chief characteristics by which we identify living organisms and the life of the ordinary man includes among its essential elements sex as well as sleep and food. Saints and the Dean of St. Patrick's may have different needs and priorities, but high on the average human agenda is the instinct to mate and procreate—and Gulliver is indisputably the ordinary, everyday representative of eighteenth-century English humanity. Swift's book is founded upon the fact that so unimaginatively banal a man could never have invented such fantastic places, and he is so manifestly not Scheherazade that the surest testimony of their existence is his telling us so— he is as incapable of such marvellous lies as the Houyhnhnms themselves.

His ordinariness is evident in the circumstances of his marriage, when, taking advice, he decides to alter his condition. He marries because everybody does; it is normal, almost routine, and he is the last man to challenge the prevailing orthodoxy, preferring, in sexual as in other matters, the human average. But in Lilliput he is barred from sexuality, fated to everlasting celibacy. The superb sexual equipment which excites the admiration of the soldiers marching between the bestrid legs of the colossus is, paradoxically, useless; big may be beautiful, but in Lilliput only at the sacrifice of utility value, at least as an organ of reproduction. As a fire extinguisher, he is priceless, as an object of aesthetic admiration, unique, but this very uniqueness certifies him unfit for Lilliput. The eunuchs who, in Yeats's graphic description, crowd round Don Juan as he enters hell, enviously contemplating his mighty thigh, are presumably right to be envious, hell being what it is, or are very foolish eunuchs indeed, but sexual envy is certainly the last thing to direct towards Gulliver in Lilliput.

The Man-Mountain, taker of fleets, invincible in war, is simultaneously not really a man at all, being forbidden full human participation. That Swift intends this is plain from the superb comedy of Gulliver hotly protesting his innocence of adultery in Lilliput, indignantly spurning the slanderous allegations of liaison with a court lady. So proud at having been made a Nardac, he is commensurately furious at being labelled adulterer, completely failing to see that in his position the honour is just as absurdly misplaced as the libel. A major irony of the *Travels* is Gulliver's susceptibility to brainwashing, his smooth accommodation to new environments. Swift's Olympian view sets him above such relativistic follies; Gulliver may think he's a Lilliputian but Swift knows better, and nowhere is the delusion more hilariously exposed than in these solemn protestations of sexual innocence. Gulliver returns from Lilliput not just because another voyage impends but because he has no future with the little people. They are, as he points out at the end of the *Travels,* not even worth conquering, and their final irrelevance to man as an abiding home is dramatised most vividly in terms of total sexual disparity. If you can't sleep with them, you can't live with them: it is, after all, the truism from which biology begins.

In Brobdingnag the total reversal of situation leaves the underlying constant unaffected—voluntary permanent residence is still unacceptable and for the same reason. The giants, unlike the Lilliputians, can of course keep him prisoner. The little people are relieved to see him go, for the miniature balance of power is disastrously upset—Gulliver is both misfit and menace in Lilliput because he is greater than man. In Brobdingnag he is misfit because his insignificance makes him the prey of rats, dogs and monkeys. Trifles, literal and culinary, threaten his existence: drowning in the soup, stifling in the cream, falling from the table, being pecked to death by birds or stung to death by bees; even reading a book is both strenuous and hazardous, like the regimen of an Olympic athlete. Glumdalclitch frets over little Grildrig as though he were an incubator baby, forever at risk.

The forfeiture of manhood is again, though in a very different way, dramatised by exhibiting the stranger as complete sexual misfit. The contemptuous impudicity of the maids of honour torpedoes any claim to manhood he might make. His greatest uneasiness is that they use him with a total lack of ceremony, like a creature of complete inconsequence, stripping naked in his presence, uninhibitedly and insultingly, with no attempt at concealment.

It is a peeping Tom's dream and in Marlowe's *Faustus* Robin lasciviously loiters on thoughts of a life blessed with such magical powers as Gulliver possesses, but Gulliver, in his position of "privilege," far from being turned on, is disgusted and humiliated. The Brobdingnagian beauties, all blotches, moles and hairs, repel rather than tempt, are styptics to the erotic imagination as they urinate copiously and with blatant abandon in his presence—what a Brobdingnagian Strephon can only discover in foolhardy exploration is obligingly displayed to Gulliver's nauseated gaze. It is this casual, open indifference that he finds so humiliating, and his sense of shame is merely intensified when indifference modulates into deliberate stripteasing. It is, significantly, the handsomest of the girls, a lively sixteen-year-old, who takes the greatest liberties with the manikin, frolicsomely seating him, helpless and fuming, astride her nipple, "with many other tricks, wherein the reader will excuse me for not being over particular." But, as Swift well knows, the reader is not so easily fobbed off—his imagination has been triggered and he cannot help but be intrigued as to the kind of games they get up to in Brobdingnagian bedrooms.

The young lady is not some teenage erotomaniac; her conduct would doubtless be very different were a real man present and her first trick is in any case impossible with a male of her own species. Gulliver is, for her, simply not a man at all, just a little instrument for making fun or provoking sexual jokes (the more uproarious when set against his outraged expression), possessing finally no more dignity than a dildo. No wonder he persuades his nurses to contrive some excuse for not seeing that young lady any more, for nowhere else in Brobdingnag (and only once more in the whole of the *Travels*) is his sense of shame and degradation so forcibly impressed on him. Bad enough to be stroked condescendingly by the Giant King and called little Grildrig, so insulting to his humanity, but the obscene jests of the playful teenager strike at the very root of his manhood, emasculate him entirely. Helpless in the hands of the giantesses, writhing vainly against loathsome submission to the monstrously magnified flesh, Gulliver could serve as emblem to Spinoza's section of the *Ethics* dealing with the passions and entitled, significantly, "Of Human Bondage."

Gulliver naturally dreams of liberty amid such degradation. The Giant King, bent on keeping him, commands as overriding priority the acquisition of a female of Gulliver's race upon whom he can breed. Far from feeling grateful at this projected catering for his sexual needs, he sees this as the greatest insult of all and prefers death to "the disgrace of leaving a posterity to be kept in cages like canary birds, and perhaps in time sold about the kingdom to persons of quality for curiosities." He is now what the cattle of Lilliput were to him: a species of animal worth cultivating for its curiosity value but little else, and that the curiosity value may have a commercial spin-off leaves the intrinsic triviality unchanged. The envisaged sale of his descendants is the ultimate mortification; Gulliver shares the view, so superbly dramatized in the *Modest Proposal,* that the reduction of men to items of merchandise is the clinching denial of their humanity. The twin assumptions of the *Modest Proposal*—to be bought and sold is the sign of an object, to be kept for stud purposes the sign of an animal—are foreshadowed as Gulliver, anticipating the fate of the Irish poor, confronts both degradations in Brobdingnag, and the great bird that carries him out of the land of giants restores him to a society where his status as man will be renewed.

This claim to a unique human status is the central problem of the *Travels.* Swift was acutely aware of environment and custom in providing the standards by which we compare and judge: a great horse to a Welshman is a little one to a Fleming. The search for a basic human identity, some irrefutable constant infallibly certifying recognition, is pursued through all the voyages and it is intentionally mortifying that the only constants discovered are shameful. The relaxation of tension in the third voyage is attributable to Gulliver's ceasing to be an actor and becoming instead a detached observer. He surveys cynically the curious antics of Laputan ladies deceiving their starstruck husbands, a feat so easy that adultery becomes a yawn. He discovers that female perversity is the same the world over, a constant distinguishing all the daughters of Eve; he admits that the story of the great lady who deserts a loving, generous husband for an old deformed footman who beats her daily smacks more of Europe than Lagado— but "the caprices of womankind are not limited by any climate or nation, and . . . are much more uniform than can easily be imagined." Gulliver would doubtless have cited Emma Bovary, Anna Karenina and Connie Chatterley as further conformations of this judgement. But in Part Three sex is other people's problem, not Gulliver's.

In Lagado sexual vanity is exploited by a shrewd chancellor into an inland revenue dream; men pay taxes as sexual *conquistadores,* their own returns accepted as gospel truth. Women are assessed on their own declared beauty and skill in fashion, but "constancy, chastity, good sense and good nature were not rated, because they would not bear collecting." Glubb-dubdrib reveals the filth behind history, the great European houses riddled with bastardy and syphilis. The standard route to high title and fortune is sodomy, incest or the selling of a wife or daughter. Gulliver's role as observer of sexual problems is nowhere more evident than in his intro-duction to the Struldbruggs. The Luggnaggians are not so sadistic as to condemn married Struldbruggs to everlasting misery; the union of two immortals is unchallengeable ground for divorce, the spots on the foreheads clear proof of irreparable breakdown. Gulliver's delusions of bliss eternal vanish when he sees the immortals—the most mortifying sight I ever beheld, and the women more horrible than the men." Swift resumes the attack, begun in Brobdingnag, against the false, fleeting attractiveness of the female; the face that launched a thousand ships will seem shockingly different through a microscope or when Helen is a mass of wrinkles, and those romantics who talk glibly of loving for ever should wait till they see a Struldbrugg woman. Cumulatively, these unflattering observations throughout Part Three may signal the beginnings of a shift away from the affectionate husband of the first two parts, grieving over his lost wife and children, towards the alienated misogynist of the last voyage, returning from Houyhnhnmland with much the same view of woman as Young Goodman Brown brings back from the forest; but it seems more sensible to ascribe these general reflections to Gulliver's function within Part Three as observer rather than participant.

Certainly the satiric impact of Part Four derives from an opening in which Gulliver appears as loving husband and father. His home life, all those acid comments on women notwithstanding, is still normal—"I left my poor wife big with child." Conjugal rights and wedded love are clearly on a good footing and the narrator laments the decision to go seafaring again, leaving wife and children after five months of happiness, failing to learn the lesson of "knowing when I was well." What happens to transform him from loving husband to raging misogynist? As much as *Oedipus,* "A Voyage to the Houyhnhnms" charts a passage from unreflecting innocence to shocking awareness of pollution. Gulliver is initially as convinced as Oedipus that he is in no way related to the surrounding corruption. Disgust is his sole reaction, as stifled by the excremental onslaught he faces his Yahoo brethren. A more imaginative man might have afterwards recalled the problems his own animal nature had set the Lilliputians, but he expe-riences no hint of recollection or identity, no tremor of affinity, simply intense antipathy for the most revolting of all the creatures he has encountered. The Yahoo is for him completely other. It is the horses who first spot the resemblance; to his "everlasting mortification" they refer to him as Yahoo and later, when comparisons are made, he has to admit in his heart that the abominable creature beside him is "a perfect human figure." Only his clothes prevent the horses from making a total identification. Like a criminal overlooked in a lineup by a confused witness, he gains a temporary reprieve, but knowledge grows within and the rest of the book is an exercise in species identification, during which the evidence accumulates and drives him reluctantly towards admission of kinship. The long search for man's essence is almost over and the last, irrefutable proof of his Yahoo nature is the sexual test as irresistible criterion of species definition.

The evidence adduced is both negative and positive: the contrasting life-styles of Houyhnhnm and Yahoo, rational creature and brute; the methodology is that of the field scientist, anthropologist or ethologist—provisional, empirical, pragmatic. That a creature is truly rational should be as demonstrable from its sexual behaviour as from every other aspect of its life. The formal structure of the voyage is as logical as "To his Coy Mistress." The hypothesis of rationality is tested against Houyhnhnm practices and sustained. Their attitude to sex and marriage is clearly intended as exemplary, an intelligent combination of eugenics and population control, the rational power employed to tame the domain of libido. Procreation is the sole aim; once achieved, intercourse stops. They produce one offspring of each sex and only if a casualty occurs do "they meet again." They avoid the elaborate courtship and financial haggling inseparable from fashionable European marriage: "The young people meet and are joined, merely because it is the determination of their parents and friends; it is what they see done every day, and they look upon it as one of the necessary actions in a reasonable being."

There can be little doubt as to which side Swift would have favoured in the present debate within Britain's Indian community as to whether the traditional system of arranged marriage should prevail or give way to the western practice of individual choice determined by love. And the same justification urged by Indian conservatives in support of the ancient way is advanced by Swift in his eulogy of Houyhnhnm wedlock—marital violation is unknown among the horses, since the perfervid emotional atmosphere that spawns Medeas and Clytemnestras, Isoldes and Cleopatras, is simply not present. "The married pair pass their lives with the same friendship and mutual benevolence that they bear the others of the same species who come in their way; without jealousy, fondness, quarrelling, or discontent." It is the ban on fondness, the odd man out in a group of otherwise unopposedly bad qualities, that arrests attention as signifying a loss of control that disqualifies one as *animal rationale*. Female Houyhnhnms are properly educated—given, that is, the same education as males, so that they are not simply, as in Europe, viviparous animals. Taking all these as the characteristics of a rational species with regard to sexual activity, Swift challenges us to measure man against this proffered standard. The conclusion is negative: in every way man differs from the rational horses.

By contrast, Yahoo sexuality confirms the already frightening physical resemblance to man. With the aid of his Houyhnhnm tutor, Gulliver discovers the elementary biological truth that all members of a species look and behave alike in all important respects, that, even if similarities are not always immediately obvious, they soon become apparent once group characteristics are ascertained. He quickly perceives the blatant irrationalism of Yahoo sexuality. They are, he learns, uniquely disgusting in that the female will admit the male even after conception, an infamous brutality of which no other sensitive creature is guilty. They swing between "fondness" and "quarrelling," rampant copulation and a bitter intersexual strife found nowhere else in nature. Desire is unbridled and unregulated; the female will periodically lure the young male into the bushes while simultaneously counterfeiting fear, exuding at such times a "most offensive smell." Listening to the catalogue of their transgressions, Gulliver tremblingly awaits the revelation of the unnatural appetites of Europe, for surely here, as in all else, there is kinship too? But the horses know nothing of these perversions; men have, apparently, the edge in sophisticated depravity, "and these politer pleasures are entirely the production of art and reason on our side of the globe."

Throughout Swift's writing, from *The Mechanical Operation* onwards, there is a preoccupation, if not indeed fascination, with the dark irrationalism of sex. In Captain Creichton's memoirs there is the anecdote of the covenanting preacher who, on the run, hiding in a maidservant's bed while the soldiers seeking his life searched the house, nevertheless managed to get the girl pregnant; and Swift, clearly intrigued, recounts elsewhere a similar story of a nobleman, in the death cell to which treason had brought him, impregnating his wife shortly before his own execution. One easily imagines Swift shaking his head as he pondered these incongruities, divided between baffled amusement and scornful indignation. His sense of the rational is so patently offended by the discordance of a creature, for whom the grave yawns, pursuing sexual appetite, manifesting in so bizarre a fashion the irrational drives that rule him. Such incidents must have seemed to him too disturbingly akin to the situation of insects whose last living act is fertilising the female that devours them. Meditating on this, Swift fore-shadows his compatriot Beckett: "They give birth astride of a grave, the light gleams an instant, then it's night once more."

The sexual identity of man and Yahoo is undeniable. Against all the evidence there is only man's verbal denial, supporting it his everyday conduct. The insistence on praxis, so crucial to Swift's life and work—as he wrote to Bolingbroke, "I renounce your whole Philosophy, because it is not your Practise"—is nowhere better exemplified than in the final voyage. Gulliver clings to the myth of his differentiation, but the Yahoos know better; when they see his naked arms and breast, they claim him as their own. The exposed beauties of Brobdingnag were no more exposed than he nc .. For the first time we see him as family man, holding an infant in his arms, the reality of Yahoo fatherhood emphasized when all his attempted tender ministrations end in the child soiling him, an occupational hazard of every father since Adam nursed Cain. Gulliver as Yahoo father textually precedes Gulliver as Yahoo lover, but the illogicality is artistically appropriate for the latter role is the book's climactic terminus.

When, bathing stark naked in the river, Gulliver so inflames the young female Yahoo that she leaps hungrily upon him, we have the last piece of the jigsaw, the ultimate, undeniable proof of kinship. Only the sorrel nag's timely intervention saves him, forcing her to withdraw: "she quitted her grasp with the utmost reluctancy" and "stood gazing and howling all the time I was putting on my clothes." The comedy incapsulates the grief of unrequited love, with the young Yahoo as desolate as Troilus looking towards the Greek camp where the lost Criseyde now lies. For the Houyhnhnms it's a great joke, but for Gulliver it's the end of the line, finis to self-deception; he must be a real Yahoo "since the females had a natural propensity to me as one of their own species." *Quod erat demonstrandum.* Reproduction will out.

It is so easy, in sharp contrast to Lilliput and Brobdingnag, for a family man from England to go on being so in Yahooland. Gulliver, who as a young man had been an avid reader of travellers' tales, must have read stories about sexual intercourse between African women and male apes— read and rejected them as contrary to nature, since breeding across species was regarded as incredible. He knows (it is what so unnerves him in the bathing incident) that the necessary characteristic of a species is a readiness to breed together. Here is identity at last, self-recognition with no possibility of error. When the Yahoo girl leaps upon him, she is really saying, with an irony Nathan never intended, thou art the man. *Ecce homo.*

With grim comedy Swift reveals Gulliver struggling from the hold of his would-be lover, aware, to his intense mortification, that in the deepest sense he can never escape her again, for he is hers by right and by nature. Who can argue with the sex glands? It is the shame of Brobdingnag carried to its furthest pitch; there he was helpless only because of a secondary, relative attribute, his size, now the humiliation is both primary and essential. After the blind alleys of Lilliput and Brobdingnag, he has found his proper niche, is at last sexually in the right place, a sexual equal, a possible mate, a Yahoo; like Antony, though in horror rather than delight, he can finally say, "Here is my space." It follows that the horrified rejection of the female Yahoo adumbrates the future repulse of her sister, Mary Gulliver; the crushing disappointment of the amorous Yahoo is given its appropriately refined form in Mary's complaint of neglect in the epistle Pope wrote for her:

> Welcome, thrice welcome to thy native Place!
> —What, touch me not? what, shun a Wife's Embrace?
> Have I for this thy tedious Absence born,
> And wak'd and wis'd whole Nights for thy Return?

In her chagrin at the unaccountable retreat to the stables, Mary even descends to sexual innuendo: "What mean those visits to the Sorrel Mare?" But, however understandable in a discarded wife, there is no call for the reader to find more in the text than Swift has made clear: *not* hippomania, a new set of perversions, but an admission by man of Yahoo guilt. Gulliver's "native Place" looks decidedly unattractive in a context of Yahoo parallelism and the erstwhile lover of mankind has at last truly seen himself, in a lake in Houyhnhnmland.

And what, after all, *is* his "native Place," where has Gulliver's sixteen-year search for man taken him? To *animal rationale,* glory of creation?—or to a species of animal incapable of amendment, a vicious *lusus naturae?* Corresponding to these warring definitions are two opposed versions of man's origins. The *Travels,* predictably, displaces the ancient myth of Genesis, of the child of God, made in his image but driven for sin from the Garden, with a new, naturalistic account of human beginnings from which any hint of a special relationship with a Creator is rigorously excluded. Houyhnhnm tradition has it that the Yahoos are not indigenous but that many ages ago two of these brutes appeared together upon a mountain, whether produced by the heat of the sun upon corrupted mud and slime, or from the ooze and froth of the sea, was never known; so prolific were they in breeding that within a short time they had overrun and infested the whole nation. The divine injunction to increase and multiply, with its accompanying promise of the earth as fief, is set aside for a view of human increase as the noisome proliferation of vermin. This degraded report of our first parents looks forward to Wilberforce's interpretation of Darwin or man's advent as described in Golding's *The Inheritors,* rather than backwards to Milton's noble pair, descending in tragic dignity after their ejection from Eden to the challenge of the world below. True, it is the unchristian Houyhnhnm who speaks, but where in the *Travels* is the proof that he is mistaken, that man is not brute but *imago Dei?* Can we seriously doubt on the evidence of his sexual behaviour to which category he belongs?

The origin of Yahoo man as stated in this Houyhnhnm anti-Genesis is the climactic scandal of a scandalous book. From its day of publication, amid the chorus of delighted acclamation, sounded an adversary voice that spoke for outraged humanism. The artistry, on such a view, only made the offence the more unpardonable. It was a "bad" book and Bolingbroke, reacting to his friend's masterpiece as Lord Longford to an inspired pornographer, tells us why: it was "a bad design to depreciate human nature," and if the design had been executed with the highest genius, so much the worse for its perverted motivation. The root of the offence is easy to find. More than a century before the traumatic scandal of Darwin, the *Travels* declines to distinguish man from the rest of the animal universe but instead decisively relegates him to the brutes. "If the book be true . . . religion is a lie . . . and men and women are only better beasts." This was a typical nineteenth-century reaction to Robert Chambers' *The Vestiges of Creation,* a rudimentary dry run for Darwin's epochal work. When *The Origin of Species* appeared, its deliberately mild and unprovocative tone did not save it from the fury of those who found there an appalling interpretation of the world. The superintending providence of God over nature and with it the uniquely privileged position of the human race as centre and *raison d'être* of creation seemed totally discredited. Even the docile Darwin could not refrain, if only in a private letter, from mocking his indignant critics: "Here is a pleasant genealogy for mankind."

The "better beasts" and "pleasant genealogy" have already surfaced, however unscientifically, in the *Travels,* with the man–Yahoo identification and the Houyhnhnm version of human evolution. The dismissal of Genesis and special creation, of the revered distinction between human and animal, anticipates the central Darwinian idea of an underlying unity in the development of life and it is no consolation to mortified man to find himself deposed as perfection of nature by a creature so patently unreal as a rational horse. Either man is *animal rationale* or there is no such thing. The scandal of the *Travels* is its apparent espousal of the latter alternative. Man, priding himself as star of the show, is demoted to a contemptible extra. No wonder that *vous autres,* the star's idolators—a party to which Gulliver as lover of mankind also belonged before his last voyage—were offended; they were meant to be. Even those, like Bolingbroke, who had broken with orthodox religion, still upheld, perhaps the more fiercely, a secularised version of man as *imago Dei,* creation's masterpiece. The eighteenth-century backlash of Deists and rationalists against the black legend of human nature promulgated by Augustinian Christianity and its naturalistic fellow traveller, Hobbesian psychology, helped boost the benevolent view of man. The standard homiletic denunciations of man as sink of iniquity, routine in seventeenth-century Calvinism, were becoming increasingly repugnant to rational philosophers of the Bolingbroke kind. Swift, with his mission to vex, surely welcomed the anger that his book would incite in such quarters.

Not just the Lilliputians but we, too, watch with puzzled consternation as, from the opening pages, Gulliver's animal attributes, gargantuanly enlarged, are thrust provocatively upon our attention. Swift was no Darwin; he set out to antagonize in a deliberate display of exhibitionist coattrailing designed to enrage the champions of human dignity. When Gulliver, lying bound on the beach, urinates, it is for the little people the equivalent of Niagara, a fearful torrent whose noise and violence stun them—one of the few occasions, significantly, when we look *with* the Lilliputians rather than *at* them. Later, Gulliver's home, the morally polluted temple, becomes literally so when, caught in the Swiftian dilemma between urgency and shame, the chained giant creeps inside to excrete.

Why does Swift drag such detail before us, domiciling us to a landscape of torrential urine and giant excrement, an effluent society where the body's prodigious waste can threaten plague or douse conflagrations? It is almost as though Gulliver, after his nine-hour sleep on the beach of Lilliput, has reverted to monstrous infancy, his bowel and bladder movements a matter of public concern and discussion—we must wait for Leopold Bloom before the hero's excretory functions are again assumed to be of significant interest to the reader. Gulliver justifies the exhibitionism in his self-exculpatory insistence that only once was he guilty of such uncleanliness, for afterwards he always defecated *al fresco* to make the removal of the offensive matter quick and relatively easy. He adduces this as proof of his personal hygiene, in indignant rebuttal of what detractors have nastily insinuated since his book was published. But if self-vindication is a plausible explanation of Gulliver's indiscreet disclosures, if he is driven by a commendable anxiety to be distinguished from lunatics like Jack in the *Tale* with his disgusting slogan, "he which is filthy, let him be filthy still," this nevertheless leaves undecided why Swift determinedly trumpets such goings-on.

It only becomes intelligible (as other than a personal hang-up) on the assumption that Swift attacks human pride by rubbing our faces in the mess we make and pretend not to notice. He solicits outrage with these baited revelations, banking on being accused, like Gulliver in his letter to Sympson, "of degrading human nature," for how else will he be able to launch that stinging parenthesis—"for so they have still the confidence to style it"? Bolingbroke, blundering into the trap, is answered even before he protests. The inventory of identification between man and beast is, accordingly, as exhaustive as possible, the mass of evidence exposing man's animalism piled high in a last bid to provoke the urgency of the rational response. Man, distressingly, blatantly animal, must prove his rational component, and when he arrogantly assumes the high, unearned title of *animal rationale,* Swift scornfully uncovers his sordid secrets, exhibiting them, like Gulliver's excreta, to full public view. Jack's antinomian plunge into brutality, his ardent capitulation to the inescapable filth, recurs as Gulliver unprotestingly endorses the sickening catalogue of human depravity—rape, mugging, perversion, murder—as "all according to the due course of things," beyond complaint and correction. Gulliver's modest proposal is that man continue, without recrimination, the incurable Yahoo he is, if only he desert the one astounding offence for which he can be faulted: pride. Let him cherish his natural defects but renounce his unnatural one—a renunciation the more feasible for Gulliver in his bafflement at how such an animal acquired such a vice. The privilege of filth claimed by Jack is insultingly tossed by Gulliver to Yahoo man.

It is, of course, dangerous to assume that Swift underwrites this easy relegation of man to Yahoo, no more accountable for his misdeeds than for the movement of his bowels or the pressure on his bladder. But neither can we complacently assume that Swift is ridiculing a glaring category-confusion in Gulliver's failure to distinguish between reprehensible because corrigible immorality and the ineluctable facts of being human. The relationship between guilt and responsibility is as central to Swift as to Kafka—and as puzzling to determine; our answer should emerge from a grappling with the text, not a prior assumption as to what he *must* have meant. From the guilt of being human under an extreme Calvinist dispensation to the guilt of being Jewish in Hitler's Europe, men have often been schooled to feel the iniquity of an imposed fate, condemned for what they cannot control.

Swift certainly claimed to have consistently observed in his satire the distinction between what is and what is not corrigible—only conceited ugliness and strutting folly are legitimate targets:

> His Satire points at no Defect
> But what all Mortals may correct.

To justify this claim, the troublesome prominence of man's animalism in the *Travels* must be seen as serving a reformative purpose; the brute facts, so long kept locked away, are turned loose to roam the streets so that man will have to take refuge in the house of reason. The mystery of Judas is explained by De Quincey as a desperate bid to force Jesus' hand, the betrayed messiah compelled to manifest his power. In a similar mood of moral *jusqu'au boutisme,* of vexation at the long unfulfilled pledge, Swift delivers man to his animal drives so that his very survival depends upon an analogous manifestation of reason. In each case, the ostensible hostility, the act of betrayal (Bolingbroke's "bad design")—prove you are the Son of God, prove you are *animal rationale*—mask a desperate longing for the "adversary's" triumph. The partnership of *animal* and *rationale* has, for Swift, hitherto been distressingly uneven, with the substantive having all its own way; it is long overdue for the adjective to stop being a sleeping partner and assert instead its rights as the major shareholder.

Hence the strategic emphasis on animalism, the menace made so frightening that reason, with back to the wall, must conquer or perish. Swift's "realism" is very different from Machiavelli's. *The Prince* presents political man as he is and must be, with no hint of shaming him into going and sinning no more. Swift, by contrast, is an undercover man, a double agent whose real allegiance is to morality. The *Travels* presents animal man, noisomely offensive, all according to the due course of things, but with a challenge to change what is alleged to be incorrigible. We are meant to protest the portrait's partiality, to demand, in addition to the undeniable animal, the rational being, the complementary and redeeming truth of human nature. Swift, that prince of trappers, entices us to make this crucial protest and then invites us to make good our claim. It will not be allowed on the near-miraculous exploits of a sprinkling of moral supermen like the Glubbdubdrib sextumvirate—no more than Milton will Swift let men be saved by a deputy or scramble into heaven on the coattails of heroes and saints; freeloading is strictly forbidden. Nobody pretends that Shakespeare and Newton are representative of man's ability in poetry and mathematics; why do we cheat by claiming that More and Brutus represent us morally? The everyday deeds of ordinary men are the only admissible evidence for judgement. Swift, meanwhile, strenuously devil's-advocating, will continue to present man as "perfect Yahoo" (despite his impertinent snobbery towards his brother brutes), dismissing *animal rationale* as merely a parvenu's pretext for cutting embarrassing relatives.

Man's vaunted uniqueness totters as Swift invades certain privileged areas—love, marriage, parenthood—where human beings have long thought themselves securely separate from the animal world, with a demand for the impostor's extradition. The myth of superiority is challenged. That Lilliputian ideas of the parent-child relationship differ so radically from our own is a consequence of their honest resolve to rank man with his animal brethren. They reject the attempt to refine sex into romantic love, seeing behind the sublimation only biological categories. For them the conjunction of male and female is founded upon the great law of nature which ensures the propagation and continuation of the species—men and women, like other animals, are joined together by motives of concupiscence.

In tiny detail as in sustained assault Swift challenges highfalutin romanticism, unceasingly reminding man and his mate of their animal lineage. Glancing at the Laputans' crazy obsession with music and mathematics, Gulliver casually remarks that when they want to praise the beauty of a woman "or any other animal," they do so in terms taken from these subjects. The derogatory linking is the more insulting in its unemphatic, throwaway context; Gulliver's innocent aside masks his creator's provocative malice, the relish which places "other" and "animal" in venomous conjunction. In Brobdingnag the magnified flesh so meticulously exhibited gives the manikin a sense of claustrophobic nausea; the monstrous breast of the wetnurse, its hideous nipple so minutely observed, achieves an effect antipodal to the pornographer's art. The Brobdingnagian beauties turn Gulliver's stomach, not his head. Swift's campaign to maim the erotic impulse—what led Aldous Huxley to protest that a poem like "A Beautiful Young Nymph Going to Bed" is worse than pornography—springs from his belief that man is much more animal than he admits. Hence the harshness of his onslaught on romantic delusion. Romanticism—interpreted by Swift as a fatuous attempt to elevate unavoidable biological drives to a status higher than the rational, the flesh impudently presuming beyond its limits— is a major target in his work from youth onwards.

His first, false excursion along the road of eulogistic, exalted poetry (made, perhaps, with Temple's dislike of satire in mind) ends with a denunciation of the Duessa from whom he has broken free. The high poetic afflatus is brutally discarded as he turns to his true mate, verse satire, at once far more sensible and far less starstruck:

> There thy enchantment broke, and from this hour
> I here renounce thy visionary pow'r;
> And since thy essence on my breath depends,
> Thus with a puff the whole delusion ends.

Swift's decent muse, like a country virgin accosted by gallants or a young Houyhnhnm strayed among Yahoos, recoils disgusted from the "cattle she has got among" and departs as fast as she can. The delusion incorporates the fraud of romantic love as well as the phoney inspiration of romantic poetry. As trenchantly as Flaubert, Swift documents the disastrous consequences of romantic delusion, from the maidservant who causes the palace fire in Lilliput through dozing over a romance to the sordid heroine of "The Progress of Love," projecting herself as love's victim, as helpless as Racine's Phèdre: "*C'est Vénus toute entière à sa proie attachée.*" Phyllis justifies her shameful elopement with the butler on the eve of her wedding to another man, her family's choice, with the blasphemously threadbare appeal to love as heavenly dispensation:

> It was her Fate, must be forgiven,
> For Marriages are made in Heaven.

Swift prefers the Lilliputian view that marriages are of the earth, earthly, and comes, so contemptuous is he of Phyllis and her tribe, close to Iago's cynical reductionism—in her case, love *is* simply a lust of the blood and a permission of the will.

Swift's scornful intensity reflects his fear that so shameless an affront to self-restraint marks the fall into Yahoo bestiality, the point where the human definitively regresses into the zoological. Phyllis, rushing back to the zoo, is merely the sophisticated counterpart of the amorous she-Yahoo leaping upon the naked Gulliver, with the towering additional impudence that she dresses up her lust as the will of heaven. How much more decorous than this sordid imposture is the Houyhnhnm system of arranged marriage, how much superior eugenically in providing simultaneously for individual sex drives and the healthy perpetuation of the species, with no surrender to romantic folly. It would be misleading to say that in Houyhnhnmland eugenics prevails over love, for there is simply no contest. European women, by contrast, lamentably educated, woefully irrational, are "useless animals," good only for breeding—and for breeding badly. Love is, in Swift's lexicon, a capitulation to sexual abandon that guarantees the deterioration of the species in a flagrant disregard of elementary eugenics. Far from translating man, as its devotees claim, to a higher plane, it simply takes him down to the "Old Blue Boar" at Staines, to a cat-and-dog existence interspersed with prostitution, pimping and gonorrhea—such is Swift's ironical vision of the "progress" of love. The progress of love is the regress of man.

Parental love suffers a corresponding dislodgement. Human beings cannot point to tenderness for their young as signalling a superiority, since the impulse, in both human and animal, proceeds from the same strictly natural principle. Swift anticipates Kant's insistence that a love dictated by nature can neither claim nor accept moral credit. Why should a child, any more than a kitten or a piglet, feel grateful to its parents for the alleged gift of life? How can a pair of animals humped in concupiscence, with no thought of benefitting a third party, in a "love-encounter" of sheer self-gratification, be a suitable target for gratitude? The sad discrepancy between Houyhnhnm reason and human irrationalism is highlighted in the vocabulary of their differing sexual codes. The Houyhnhnms "meet together" in a programme of planned procreation aimed at one offspring of each sex; wherever the desired balance is not achieved, they obligingly swap around until every family has its correct quota, after which intercourse ceases— they only "meet again" where casualties have occurred and the depletion has to be made good.

The whole business of sex and procreation among the virtuous horses is a disciplined, rational synchronization of needs and resources, like the x-efficiency dream of modern economic theorists. The contrast with Lilliputian (and human) messiness is glaringly exposed in the expression "love-encounters," hinting at the haphazard and casual, at something unpremeditated and adventitious in the sexual act; children come as by-product, the credit of an impersonal nature, with procreation apparently as outwith human control as the laws of science. Where a Houyhnhnm might therefore legitimately feel grateful to his parents for deliberately deciding to conceive him, similar emotion would be absurdly misplaced in a Lilliputian or European. The sole obligation stipulated in Lilliput is that of fathers towards children, the duty to support one's offspring, however inadvertently conceived. When Gulliver leaves on his second voyage, he shows how well he has absorbed this lesson by scrupulously providing for his family. The money he makes from exhibiting and then selling the tiny cattle guarantees the Gullivers from cadging public charity—if irresponsible as progenitor, he is commendably responsible as provider.

As well as challenging man's unique status in these hitherto privileged areas of love and parenthood, violating sanctuaries where humanity has long thought itself safe from pursuit, Swift also mercilessly erodes other traditional distinctions that have reassuringly fenced off man from beast: to be an object of merchandise or financial exploitation, to be part of the food chain, to be kept for breeding purposes. Gulliver's tiny cattle persuade his rescuers that he is not a madman but it is not just his moral credit they save—back home he displays them for cash and then sells them for a high profit. An identical fate awaits Gulliver in Brobdingnag where he switches from exploiter to exploited, worked almost to death in daylong exhibitions by the greedy farmer before being knocked down to the Queen.

Gulliver has difficulty in deciding which he resents more: this cruel exploitation, "the ignominy of being carried about for a monster" and shown for cash—an indignity which the King of Great Britain, similarly circumstanced, would have likewise had to thole; or Glumdalclitch's tearful resentment at her father for deceiving her yet again, as he had with the pet lamb, promised to her but sold to the butcher as soon as it was fat. Better, of course, to be the girl's pet than her father's freak attraction, but the insult to human dignity is equally mortifying. Gulliver's cold farewell to the exploiting farmer reveals his resentment, though he himself felt no qualms over the Lilliputian cattle—naturally enough, assuming the axiomatic gulf between man and beast fixed in Eden when God made Adam lord of creation, with dominion over all creatures, to use as he thinks fit. Man's cherished distinction, by contrast, is that he is not, on pain of forfeiting his unique dignity, exploitable; he is an end in himself, not to be used, otherwise his special status is denied and he becomes just another beast with a market value.

Even in Lilliput, though without knowing it till later, Gulliver is a valuable commodity, a hot property. Brought to the metropolis, he is as big a box-office draw as King Kong and the secretaries of state make a killing in ticket sales.

But in Brobdingnag the humiliation comes from seeing, but being powerless to stop, his own exploitation. The amused delight he provokes there stems from his amazing simulation to a human being, a rational creature—he is for the giants a charming forgery, a marvellously ingenious imitation, which the mind knows as such even while the eye is pleasingly deluded. Any claim to human status is straightaway denied when his giant captor sets the newly-found creature on all fours as its natural mode of locomotion. Stand up though he may, all his efforts to be accepted as *homo erectus* misfire. The Houyhnhnm master is similarly perplexed at the gentle Yahoo's strange folly in going around on his rear legs—cannot he see the advantages that accrue from his brother brutes' sensible decision to stay foursquare on the earth? Why go perversely against nature and one's animal lineage for the sake of so futile an affectation? But whatever the direction of the attack, whether from giants who see him as an ingenious clockwork device or *lusus naturae,* or from horses puzzling over this curious Yahoo, it is always Gulliver's human status that is in question; big or small, commodity or freak, target of marvel or derision, Gulliver is throughout his travels stripped of dignity, reduced to the level of a Lilliputian sheep or a dancing bear or a Bedlamite in his cell with the day-trippers bent on diversion enjoying his antics.

The animal's vulnerability is most obvious in the ease with which it becomes some other creature's dinner, whether bred to that end by man himself or falling victim to a superior predator. Returning from Lilliput, Gulliver loses a sheep to the ship's rats and later finds its bones picked clean. The incongruity of a live sheep carried off and eaten by rats becomes nightmare in Brobdingnag when European man fights for his life against the giant rats and narrowly escapes, thanks to his sword, the fate of his tiny sheep. No more vivid illustration of man as animal—as extremely vulnerable animal—is conceivable than Gulliver desperately parrying the rat attack, the lord of creation a whisker away from being a rodent's lunch.

The terror of being eaten alive modulates into the shame of being kept as a stud animal. The gravest affront to Gulliver as human being, paralleling the more specific onslaught on his male dignity at the hands of the Brobdingnagian women, comes with the Giant King's direction that a female be found upon whom the manikin can breed and so perpetuate his species. Gulliver, on such a view, is significantly no different from the Lilliputian cattle he tries to encourage in England. On the assumption of his unique status as man, he takes this as the greatest of insults, but just as validly, his giant captors, on *their* assumptions, would reject his claim with derision. The giant rats see him as a meal, the giant people as a pet, to be treated kindly but never as an equal. Gulliver in Brobdingnag is handled with the same easy disdain as he himself has already shown towards inferior creatures—what he has done unto others is now done unto him until separate identity becomes blurred as man merges with beast.

There are two key moments in Brobdingnag which anticipate the final damning identification with the Yahoo. The first is when the monkey kidnaps Gulliver in the conviction that he is a young one of the species and tries to feed him, cramming its partly-digested filth into his mouth, and, with true paternal solicitude, "patting me when I would not eat." The monkey claiming Gulliver as child, the female Yahoo seeking her mate, are each offering, in these crucial areas of rearing and breeding, clues to the real identity beneath the pose. The second is when the Giant King delivers judgement on European man as little odious vermin crawling on the earth's surface (Epicurus's chosen home), and, recalling the giant lice rooting through the beggars' rags, we realize, appalled, that these are what he has in mind. Louse and Yahoo represent the nadir of Swift's meditations on man's bestiality, the lowest stages in the regression from human to zoological existence charted throughout the *Travels*. Man slides dismayingly down the life-chain, from human to animal to noisome pest, starting off as rational, ending as fit only for extermination.

The difference between animal and pest is the difference between *A Modest Proposal* and "A Voyage to the Houyhnhnms." Gulliver as animal anticipates the shock of the children of the Irish poor suddenly becoming items on a butcher's price list or courses on a menu. "A child just dropt from its dam" is indistinguishable from a newly littered piglet, save that in Ireland the piglet is better cared for—one of the proposal's merits is that its implementation may persuade Irish husbands to treat their pregnant wives at least as well as their livestock. What an advance it would be, what a breakthrough in solving the Irish question, if the Irish were somehow *raised* to animal level and managed to pass themselves off as two-footed cattle, beasts in all else save this strange habit of walking erect. That this is the destiny against which Gulliver in Brobdingnag rebels as the worst of degradations—to be tended and bred like an animal—simply proves that the Irish poor are far worse off than little Grildrig among the giants; and it is a measure of Ireland's plight that the only solution is a grateful surrender of human dignity.

A Modest Proposal presents the Irish as animals but not vermin, a useful addition to the food supply, comparable to the cows of Lilliput rather than the lice of Brobdingnag. Fit for human consumption: it is a kind of compliment and the extreme remedy of converting infants into meat to solve a population problem is no more inhumane and far more rational than reliance on starvation and infanticide. It is, after all, only this doomed surplus who end up in the kitchens; are cleavers any worse than the deaths to which we at present equably condemn them? A problem basically economic evokes a solution unchallengeably rational, given that the creatures in question do not differ significantly from other cattle. There are simply too many Irish for the needs of a healthy economy, so why not manage the Irish poor as we already manage Irish pigs—so many for stock, for breeding, for the slaughterhouse, as the market requires? The market rules and if we dislike the idea of people bred to its demands, we had better find a feasible alternative, for the surplus dies daily in any case. The frisson comes from hearing people discussed in terms of cattle control, units in a process that ignores all values but economic.

The Yahoo, by contrast, like the Jew under Hitler, is a problem in pest control, sanitary rather than economic, the cleansing of the world, not the regulation of the market. The Modest Proposer seeks the optimum number of Irish, not their extermination; but even *one* Jew or Yahoo left alive is an affront, a breeding pair a menace, to the sanitationists of Houyhnhnmland and the Reich—the aim *is* genocide. How to eliminate the Yahoo is the one debate in Houyhnhnmland and, ironically, the sole lesson his masters think worth learning from their gentle Yahoo is the castration technique that will extirpate his species forever without recourse to wholesale massacre. Did not the Emperor of Lilliput favour blinding and castration to summary execution as a gentler method of destroying the awkward giant? Imagine the unexceptionable zest with which the Nazi extermination apparatus would have been welcomed by the horses in solving *their* sanitation problem. The Irish are fit for food, the Yahoos only for extermination.

Swift's exasperation in Ireland is real enough. Every section of society is condemned for its lavish contribution to the nation's ruin: a drunken, improvident poor; a middle class sottishly selfish; a leadership venal and afraid. The note of bitter elation sounding through *A Modest Proposal* is sustained by a conviction that a guilty nation is getting its deserts. Ireland was made for Swift, catalyst for his pedagogic despair, confirming in him a wider application of the verdict he once passed on the people of Leicester: "a parcel of wretched fools." Even the basic sagacity and will to self-preservation of the animal seemed lacking among the Irish; the national totem was the Gadarene swine and Dublin was Swift's Ephesus, where, like St. Paul, he was conscious of fighting with beasts.

Nevertheless, we detect a contrary impulse in Swift that made him champion as well as chastiser of this people. Ireland's unforgivable failure to help herself notwithstanding—and Swift's own twelve-year campaign to promote reform from within shows how much could have been done—the system imposed upon her from abroad was unjust and vindictive. Foolish accomplices in their own ruin, the Irish are also victims, as hampered and misgoverned as the wretched citizens of Balnibarbi. London rule is at least partly responsible for Irish distress, whereas we have no ground for believing that the Houyhnhnm have made the Yahoos any worse than nature created them; on the contrary, but for the efficient policing of the horses, the Yahoos would run ungovernably wild, destroying themselves and everything else. Certainly, a major target of the proposal is the Irish themselves—Swift is furious at fools who connive at their own destruction; but equally undeniable, in however oblique and qualified a form, it is also a defence of an exploited people against rapacious predators. There is no such competing or balancing element in Swift's attitude to the Yahoo, no rage at the exploiter to temper contempt for the victim nor pity for the oppressed to mitigate anger at the fool. In contrast to the double face of the Irish—

villain and victim—the Yahoo appears as singly, irredeemably vermin; there can be nothing but relief and satisfaction at his suppression or even extermination, however achieved.

The events attending the expulsion from Houyhnhnmland make this vividly clear. Gulliver's leave-takings of the different countries he visits are dramatically appropriate, matching his role during residence. At the opening of the final chapter of Part One he finds "a real boat" and the Lilliputian adventure is over. Resuming real manhood, he ends the petty predicaments of Lilliput by simply leaving them—the Man-Mountain deciding to go, where is the power to stop him? He is, contrastingly, carried out of Brobdingnag by the giant bird, as helplessly subject to superior force as throughout a sojourn in which things are forever being done *to* him, whether by monkeys or maids-of-honour. He is taken leisurely to Japan, like the tourist he is throughout the third voyage, in a ship assigned him by the King of Luggnagg, but his vital involvement in the action of Part Four is reflected in the climactic expulsion that ironically echoes the leaving of Lilliput— ironically, because the surface similarity of single-handedly preparing his own departures from Lilliput and Houyhnhnmland masks crucial differences.

Outward preparation is similar but inward disposition is transformed. That he leaves Lilliput with relief, Houyhnhnmland with dread, dramatises the transition from lover of mankind to misanthrope, and the metamorphosis is visible in his preparations for departure. In Lilliput he greases the boat, which so opportunely floats his way, with the tallow of three hundred tiny cows. We accept this unblinkingly as being, among other things, what cows are for—to be used by men as men see fit, in accordance with God's promise in the Garden. But the attitude of the Houyhnhnm and their disciple Gulliver towards the Yahoo intentionally causes the reader discomfort. The easy brutality, the untroubled assumption that no treatment is too bad for them, that vermin have no rights and scruples are absurd, are all part of the book's provocation.

Before the catastrophe, Gulliver unexcitedly relates how he did his shoe repairs with the skins of Yahoos dried in the sun and collected birds' feathers with springes made of Yahoo hair; sentenced to expulsion, he casually describes how he built his canoe, covered with Yahoo skins, its chinks sealed with their tallow to keep out the sea. One last twist is given with the information that, the older animals being unsuitable, he made the sail from the skins of the youngest Yahoos. Old scores are settled, old insults wiped out, as Gulliver, with vengeful relish, perhaps reflects that the boy who soiled, the girl who attacked him, have ended up in his sail.

The casual callousness is underscored by the tearful farewell to the revered Houyhnhnm and the last solicitous exhortations of the sorrel nag. It is the same strange amalgam of tears and extermination, emotion and brutality, sentiment and atrocity, as appears in many of those who manned the death camps and the key in both cases is identical—pity is absurd when exterminating vermin.

But, as Swift well knows, this is no longer a matter of Lilliputian cows and he manipulates a significant shift in our response, a vague unease, a half-stifled disapproval trembling towards articulation. Old, reassuring distinctions between man and beast are now so darkened that the ground gives beneath us and we are left stateless in a realm where brute and human promiscuously merge—Orwell is never more Swift's pupil than at the end of *Animal Farm*. Discomfort is intensified by Houyhnhnm attitudes: that the Yahoos cannot help what they are does not make the horses more tolerant and their one recurring debate is merely procedural—a massacre of the pests in one genocidal swoop or the milder policy of male castration and gradual extinction. The reader's unease (deepened by a recollection of the Emperor of Lilliput's similar interpretation of mildness) testifies to the deadly accuracy of Swift's aim in Part Four; driven throughout towards unwilling alliance with the Yahoos, we are now much too close for comfort. While the cows of Lilliput left us totally untroubled, the Yahoos of Houyhnhnmland, lacking only our clothes and the jabber we call language, are our kinsmen, however unwelcome, and we are meant to feel a twinge of fearful resentment at their treatment—blood *is* thicker than water, more precious than tallow. Their fate and Houyhnhnm callousness alike disturb us and there is no need for Redriff to see how thoroughly Gulliver detests his own kind—the material sealing his canoe is proof enough. The question of sadism does not arise; rather, Gulliver's attitude anticipates and intensifies that of the Modest Proposer towards the Irish: an untroubled assumption that the creatures in question are either animal or vermin. Even in *A Modest Proposal* the door is not closed on *Endlösung;* it needs only one more step from man as animal to man as pest in "A Voyage to the Houyhnhnm."

Chronology

1667	Born in Dublin to English parents; father dies.
1674–82	Studies at Kilkenny School.
1682–88	Trinity College, Dublin; B.A. *speciali gratia* 1684; work toward M.A. interrupted by Glorious Revolution.
1689–94	Secretary to Sir William Temple, Moor Park; meets Stella; first outbreak of Ménière's Disease probably in 1690.
1694	Takes Anglican deacon's orders.
1695	Ordained priest in the Church of Ireland; moves to Kilroot parish, where he probably writes *A Tale of a Tub* (1697–98?).
1699–1710	Appointments and livings in the Church of Ireland. As domestic chaplain to the Earl of Berkeley, Lord Justice of Ireland, Swift begins his career as defender of the rights of the Church of Ireland, working with the Whigs.
1704	*A Tale of a Tub* published.
1707	Meets Vanessa.
1708–9	*The Bickerstaff Papers*.
1709	With Steele, founds the *Tatler*.
1710	Goes over to the Tories.
1713	Appointed Dean of St. Patrick's Cathedral, Dublin; from this time forward lives mostly in Ireland.
1724–25	*Drapier's Letters*.
1726	*Gulliver's Travels* published.
1742	Declared insane.
1745	Dies; buried in St. Patrick's Cathedral.

Contributors

HAROLD BLOOM, Sterling Professor of the Humanities at Yale University, is the author of *The Anxiety of Influence, Poetry and Repression,* and many other volumes of literary criticism. His forthcoming study, *Freud: Transference and Authority,* attempts a full-scale reading of all Freud's major writings. A MacArthur Prize Fellow, he is general editor of five series of literary criticism published by Chelsea House.

T. O. WEDEL was Canon and Warden Emeritus of Washington Cathedral, and previously a Professor of English at Carleton College and at Yale University. His writings include *The Pulpit Rediscovers Theology.*

PHYLLIS GREENACRE, M.D., is the author of numerous works in psychology, as well as *Swift and Carroll: A Psychoanalytic Study of Two Lives* and *The Quest for the Father: A Study of the Darwin-Butler Controversy, as a Contribution to the Understanding of the Creative Individual.*

KATHLEEN WILLIAMS is Professor of English at the University of California at Riverside; she has written extensively on Swift.

MARTIN PRICE is Sterling Professor of English Literature at Yale University and the author of *Swift's Rhetorical Art: A Study in Structure and Meaning, To the Palace of Wisdom: Studies in Order and Energy from Dryden to Blake, Forms of Life: Character and Moral Imagination in the Novel,* and other works.

PAUL FUSSELL teaches in the Department of English at the University of Pennsylvania. Some of his books are *Abroad: British Literary Traveling Between the Wars, The Great War and Modern Memory, Poetic Meter and Poetic Form, Theory of Prosody in Eighteenth-Century England, The Rhetorical World of Augustan Humanism: Ethics and Imagery from Swift to Burke,* and *Samuel Johnson and the Life of Writing.*

RONALD PAULSON is Professor of English at The Johns Hopkins University.

Among his works are *The Fictions of Satire, Satire and the Novel in Eighteenth-Century England, Theme and Structure in Swift's Tale of a Tub, The Art of Hogarth, Emblem and Expression: Meaning in English Art of the Eighteenth Century,* and *Literary Landscape: Turner and Constable.*

GRANT HOLLY is Associate Professor of English and Comparative Literature at Hobart and William Smith Colleges, Geneva, New York.

PATRICK REILLY is the author of *Jonathan Swift: The Brave Desponder.*

Bibliography

Battestin, Martin C. *The Providence of Wit: Aspects of Form in Augustan Literature and the Arts.* Oxford: Oxford University Press, 1974.

Bentman, Raymond. "Satiric Structure and Tone in the Conclusion of *Gulliver's Travels.*" *Studies in English Literature 1500–1900* 11 (1971): 535–48.

Bogel, Fredric V. "Irony, Inference, and Critical Uncertainty." *The Yale Review* 69, no. 4 (1980): 503–19.

Champion, Larry S. "Gulliver's Voyages: The Framing Events as a Guide to Interpretation." *Texas Studies in Literature and Language* 10 (1969): 529–36.

———, ed. *Quick Springs of Sense.* Athens: University of Georgia Press, 1974.

Clifford, Gay. *The Transformations of Allegory.* London and Boston: Routledge & Kegan Paul, 1974.

Fussell, Paul. *The Rhetorical World of Augustan Humanism.* Oxford: Oxford University Press, 1965.

Gill, James E. "Beast Over Man: Theriophilic Paradox in Gulliver's 'Voyage to the Country of the Houyhnhnms.' " *Studies in Philology* 67 (1970): 532–49.

Greenacre, Phyllis. *Swift and Carroll: A Psychoanalytic Study of Two Lives.* New York: International Universities Press, 1955.

Gubar, Susan. "The Female Monster in Augustan Satire." *Signs: Journal of Women in Culture and Society* 3, no. 2 (1977): 380–94.

Hilson, J. C., et al., eds. *Augustan Worlds: New Essays on Eighteenth-Century Literature.* Leicester: Leicester University Press, 1978.

Jeffares, A. Norman, ed. *Swift: Modern Judgements.* London: Macmillan, 1969.

McManmon, John J. "The Problem of a Religious Interpretation of Gulliver's Fourth Voyage." *Journal of the History of Ideas* 27 (1966): 59–72.

Mezciems, Jenny. "The Unity of Swift's 'Voyage to Laputa': Structure as Meaning in Utopian Fiction." *Modern Language Review* 72 (1977): 1–21.

Murry, John Middleton. *Jonathan Swift: A Critical Biography.* New York: Noonday Press, 1955.

Orwell, George. "Politics vs. Literature: An Examination of *Gulliver's Travels.*" In *The Collected Essays, Journalism and Letters of George Orwell.* London: Secker & Warburg, 1968.

Paulson, Ronald. *The Fictions of Satire.* Baltimore: The Johns Hopkins Press, 1967.

Pollak, Ellen. "Comment on Susan Gubar's 'The Female Monster in Augustan Satire' (vol. 3, no. 2)." *Signs: Journal of Women in Culture and Society* 3, no. 3 (1978): 729–32.

Price, Martin. *To the Palace of Wisdom: Studies in Order and Energy from Dryden to Blake*. Carbondale: Southern Illinois University Press, 1964.

Probyn, Clive T., ed. *The Art of Jonathan Swift*. New York: Barnes & Noble; London: Vision Press, 1978.

———, ed. *Jonathan Swift: The Contemporary Background*. Manchester: Manchester University Press, 1978.

Quilligan, Maureen. *The Language of Allegory*. Ithaca: Cornell University Press, 1979.

Quinlan, Maurice. "Swift's Use of Literalization as a Rhetorical Device." *PMLA* 82 (1967): 516–21.

Quintana, Ricardo. *The Mind and Art of Jonathan Swift*. New York and London: Oxford University Press, 1936.

Rawson, Claude, ed. *The Character of Swift's Satire: A Revised Focus*. Newark: University of Delaware Press, 1983.

Reed, Gail S. "Dr. Greenacre and Captain Gulliver: Notes on Conventions of Interpretation and Reading." *Literature and Psychology* 26 (1976): 185–90.

Reilly, Patrick. *Jonathan Swift: The Brave Desponder*. Carbondale: Southern Illinois University Press, 1982.

Steele, Peter. *Jonathan Swift: Preacher and Jester*. Oxford: Oxford University Press, 1978.

Williams, Kathleen. *Jonathan Swift and the Age of Compromise*. Lawrence: University of Kansas Press, 1958.

Acknowledgments

"On the Philosophical Background of *Gulliver's Travels*" by T. O. Wedel from *Swift: Gulliver's Travels: A Casebook,* edited by Richard Gravil, © 1974 by Richard Gravil. Reprinted by permission of the University of North Carolina Press, Chapel Hill and Macmillan Publishers Ltd. An earlier version of this essay appeared in *Studies in Philology* 23 (1926).

"Gulliver and Swift" by Phyllis Greenacre from *Swift and Carroll: A Psychoanalytic Study of Two Lives* by Phyllis Greenacre, © 1955 by International Universities Press, Inc. Reprinted by permission.

"*Animal Rationis Capax*" by Kathleen Williams from *Jonathan Swift and the Age of Compromise* by Kathleen Williams, © 1958 by the University of Kansas Press. Reprinted by permission.

"Order and Obligation: *Gulliver's Travels*" by Martin Price from *To the Palace of Wisdom: Studies in Order and Energy from Dryden to Blake* by Martin Price, © 1964 by Martin Price. Reprinted by permission of the author.

"The Paradox of Man" by Paul Fussell from *The Rhetorical World of Augustan Humanism* by Paul Fussell, © 1965 by the Oxford University Press. Reprinted by permission.

"The Role of the Horses in 'A Voyage to the Houyhnhnms' " by Conrad Suits from *University of Toronto Quarterly* 34, no. 2 (January 1965), © 1965 by University of Toronto Press. Reprinted by permission.

"Swiftean Picaresque: *Gulliver's Travels*" by Ronald Paulson from *The Fictions of Satire* by Ronald Paulson, © 1967 by The Johns Hopkins University Press. Reprinted by permission.

"Travel and Translation: Textuality in *Gulliver's Travels*" by Grant Holly from *Criticism* 21, no. 2 (Spring 1979), © 1979 by Wayne State University Press. Reprinted by permission of the Wayne State University Press.

"The Displaced Person" by Patrick Reilly from *Jonathan Swift: The Brave Desponder* by Patrick Reilly, © 1982 by Patrick Reilly. Reprinted by permission of Manchester University Press.

Index